George L Craik

A manuel of english literature and language

George L Craik

A manuel of english literature and language

ISBN/EAN: 9783742825292

Manufactured in Europe, USA, Canada, Australia, Japa

Cover: Foto ©Andreas Hilbeck / pixelio.de

Manufactured and distributed by brebook publishing software (www.brebook.com)

George L Craik

A manuel of english literature and language

EACH VOLUME SOLD SEPARATELY.

COLLECTION
OF
BRITISH AUTHORS

TAUCHNITZ EDITION.

VOL. 1449.

A MANUAL OF ENGLISH LITERATURE & LANGUAGE
BY
GEORGE L. CRAIK, LL.D.

IN TWO VOLUMES. — VOL. 2.

LEIPZIG: BERNHARD TAUCHNITZ.

PARIS: C. REINWALD, 15, RUE DES SAINTS PÈRES.

A MANUAL

OF

ENGLISH LITERATURE,

AND OF THE HISTORY OF

THE ENGLISH LANGUAGE,

FROM

THE NORMAN CONQUEST;

WITH NUMEROUS SPECIMENS.

BY

GEORGE L. CRAIK, LL.D.

PROFESSOR OF HISTORY AND OF ENGLISH LITERATURE IN QUEEN'S COLLEGE, BELFAST.

IN TWO VOLUMES. – VOL. II.

LEIPZIG

BERNHARD TAUCHNITZ

1874.

CONTENTS

OF VOLUME II.

	Page
MIDDLE AND LATTER PART OF THE SEVENTEENTH CENTURY	
Shirley, and end of the Old Drama	9
Giles Fletcher; Phineas Fletcher	10
Other Religious Poets:—Quarles; Herbert; Herrick; Crashaw .	12
Cartwright; Randolph; Corbet	13
Poets of the French School:—Carew; Lovelace; Suckling . .	15
Denham	17
Cleveland	20
Wither	21
William Browne	22
Prose Writers:—Charles I.	29
Milton's Prose Works	30
Hales; Chillingworth	32
Jeremy Taylor	35
Fuller	36
Sir Thomas Browne	37
Sir James Harrington	40
Newspapers	43
Retrospect of the Commonwealth Literature	44
Poetry of Milton	46
Cowley	48
Butler	60
Waller	61
Marvel	62
Other Minor Poets	65
Dryden	66
Dramatists	68
Prose Writers:—Clarendon	72
Hobbes	74
Henry Neville	75
Other Prose Writers:—Cudworth; More; Barrow; Bunyan; &c.	78
	79

CONTENTS OF VOLUME II.

	Page
THE CENTURY BETWEEN THE ENGLISH REVOLUTION AND THE FRENCH REVOLUTION	84
First Effects of the Revolution on our Literature	84
Surviving Writers of the preceding Period	85
Bishop Burnet	89
Thomas Burnet	91
Other Theological Writers:—Tillotson; South	91
Locke	93
Swift	94
Pope	100
Addison and Steele	105
Shaftesbury; Mandeville	107
Gay; Arbuthnot; Atterbury	110
Prior; Parnell	112
Bolingbroke	114
Garth; Blackmore	115
Defoe	116
Dramatic Writers	119
Minor Poets	122
Collins; Shenstone; Gray	129
Young; Thomson	130
Armstrong; Akenside; Wilkie; Glover	132
Scottish Poetry	133
The Novelists Richardson; Fielding; Smollett	137
Sterne	143
Goldsmith	144
Churchill	150
Falconer; Beattie; Mason	151
The Wartons; Percy; Chatterton; Macpherson	152
Dramatic Writers	154
Female Writers	155
Periodical Essayists	157
Political Writing:—Wilkes; Junius	160
Johnson	164
Burke	170
Metaphysical and Ethical Writers	184
Historical Writers:—Hume; Robertson; Gibbon	186
Political Economy; Theology; Criticism and Belles Lettres	190
THE LATTER PART OF THE EIGHTEENTH CENTURY	192
Cowper	192
Darwin	204
Burns	207
THE NINETEENTH CENTURY	225
Last Age of the Georges.—Wordsworth	228
Coleridge	244
Southey	252
Scott	253
Crabbe; Campbell; Moore	259
Byron	269

SPECIMENS TO VOLUME II.

	Page
Shelley	270
Keats	274
Hunt	273
Other Poetical Writers of the earlier part of the Nineteenth Century	282
Prose Literature	284
LITERATURE OF THE PRESENT DAY	286
Mrs. Browning	287
Tennyson	293
Browning	299
Hood	304
INDEX	306

SPECIMENS

TO VOLUME II.

Cleveland:—Epitaph on Ben Jonson	22
„ Eulogy on Jonson	22
Wither:—Amygdala Britannica; Prophecy	25
„ Songs and Hymns; Thanksgiving for Seasonable Weather	27
„ „ „ Thanksgiving for Victory	28
Fuller;—Worthies; Shakespeare and Ben Jonson	36
„ „ Philemon Holland	39
Milton:—College Exercise; His Native Language	49
Waller;—His Last Verses	63
Marvel:—The Picture of T. C.	65
Mandeville:—Fable of the Bees; Anticipation of Adam Smith	109
Burke:—Speech on Nabob of Arcot; Devastation of the Carnatic	177
„ Reflections on French Revolution; Hereditary Principle	179
„ Letter to Mr. Elliot; True Reform	180
„ Letters on a Regicide Peace; Right Way of making War	182
Cowper:—Table Talk; National Vice	198
„ Truth; Voltaire	199
„ Conversation; Meeting on the Road to Emmaus	200
„ Lines on his Mother's Picture	201

SPECIMENS TO VOLUME II.

	Page
Darwin:—Botanic Garden; "Flowers of the Sky"	206
" " " The Compass	207
Burns:—To a Mouse	209
" To a Mountain Daisy	212
" Epistle to a Young Friend	214
" The Vision (part)	217
" Highland Mary	221
" Verses from various Songs	222
Wordsworth:—The Fountain, a Conversation	234
" The Affliction of Margaret	235
" "Her Eyes are wild"	237
" Laodamia	239
Coleridge:—"Maid of my Love"	246
" Time, Real and Imaginary	247
" Work without Hope	248
" Youth and Age	249
" "Yes, yes! that boon!"	250
" Love, Hope, and Patience, in Education	251
Scott:—Marmion; The Battle (part)	256
Campbell:—Adelgitha	263
" Theodric; Letter of Constance	263
Crabbe:—Tales of the Hall; Story of the Elder Brother (part)	265
Moore:—Lalla Rookh; Calm after Storm	267
Shelley:—Ode to a Skylark	272
Keats:—Ode to a Nightingale	276
Hunt:—The Sultan Mahmoud	278
" The Fancy Concert	280
Mrs. Browning:—A Child's Grave at Florence	288
" Aurora Leigh; Pictures of England	291
" " " Paris	293
" " " Her Mother's Picture	294
Tennyson:—The Lord of Burleigh	296
" Wellington	298
R. Browning:—The Pied Piper of Hamelin (part)	300
Hood:—The Death-bed	305

MANUAL OF THE HISTORY
OF
ENGLISH LITERATURE.

MIDDLE AND LATTER PART OF THE SEVENTEENTH CENTURY.

EXCLUDING from our view the productions of the last fifty or sixty years, as not yet ripe for the verdict of history, we may affirm that our national literature, properly so called, that is, whatever of our literature by right of its poetic shape or spirit is to be held as peculiarly belonging to the language and the country, had its noonday in the period comprehending the last quarter of the sixteenth and the first of the seventeenth century. But a splendid afternoon flush succeeded this meridian blaze, which may be said to have lasted for another half century, or longer. Down almost to the Revolution, or at least to the middle of the reign of Charles II., our higher literature continued to glow with more or less of the coloured light and the heart of fire which it had acquired in the age of Elizabeth and James. Some of the greatest of it indeed—as the verse of Milton and the prose poetry of Jeremy Taylor—was not given to the world till towards the close of the space we have just indicated. But Milton, and Taylor, and Sir Thomas Browne, and Cudworth, and Henry More, and Cowley, the most eminent of our English writers in the interval from the Restoration to the Revolution (if we except Dryden, the founder of a new school, and Barrow, whose writings, full as they are of thought, have not much of the poetical or untranslatable) were all of them, it is worthy of observation, born before the close of the reign of James I. Nor would the stormy time that followed be without its nurture for such minds. A boyhood or youth passed in the days of Shakespeare and Bacon, and a manhood in those of the Great Rebellion, was a training which could not fail to rear high powers to their highest capabilities.

SHIRLEY, AND THE END OF THE OLD DRAMA.

The chief glory of our Elizabethan literature, however, belongs almost exclusively to the time we have already gone over. The only other name that remains to be mentioned to complete our sketch of the great age of the Drama, is that of James Shirley, who was born about the year 1594, and whose first play, the comedy of The Wedding, was published in 1629. He is the author of about forty dramatic pieces which have come down to us. "Shirley," observes Lamb, "claims a place among the worthies of this period, not so much for any transcendent genius in himself, as that he was the last of a great race, all of whom spoke nearly the same language, and had a set of moral feelings and notions in common. A new language and quite a new turn of tragic and comic interest came in with the Restoration."* Of this writer, who survived till 1666, the merits and defects have been well stated, in a few comprehensive words, by Mr. Hallam:—"Shirley has no originality, no force in conceiving or delineating character, little of pathos, and less, perhaps, of wit; his dramas produce no deep impression in reading, and of course can leave none in the memory. But his mind was poetical: his better characters, especially females, express pure thoughts in pure language; he is never tumid or affected, and seldom obscure; the incidents succeed rapidly; the personages are numerous, and there is

* Specimens, II. 119.

a general animation in the scenes, which causes us to read him with some pleasure."*

A preface by Shirley is prefixed to the first collection of part of the plays of Beaumont and Fletcher, which, as already mentioned, appeared in 1647. "Now, reader," he says, "in this tragical age, where the theatre hath been so much outacted, congratulate thy own happiness that, in this silence of the stage, thou hast a liberty to read these inimitable plays,—to dwell and converse in these immortal groves, —which were only showed our fathers in a conjuring-glass, as suddenly removed as represented." At this time all theatrical amusements were prohibited; and the publication of these and of other dramatic productions which were their property, or rather the sale of them to the booksellers, was resorted to by the players as a way of making a little money when thus cut off from the regular gains of their profession; the eagerness of the public to possess the said works in print being of course also sharpened by the same cause.

The permanent suppression of theatrical entertainments was the act of the Long Parliament. An ordinance of the Lords and Commons passed on the 2nd of September, 1642,—after setting forth that "public sports do not well agree with public calamities, nor public stage-plays with the seasons of humiliation, this being an exercise of sad and pious solemnity, and the other being spectacles of pleasure, too commonly expressing lascivious mirth and levity,"—ordained, "that, while these sad causes and set times of humiliation do continue, public stage-plays shall cease and be forborne." It has been plausibly conjectured that this measure originated, "not merely in a spirit of religious dislike to dramatic performances, but in a politic caution, lest play-writers and players should avail themselves of their power over the minds of the people to instil notions and opinions hostile to the authority of a puritanical parliament."** This ordinance

---
* Lit. of Eur. III. 345.
** Collier, Hist. Dram. Poet. II. 106.

certainly put an end at once to the regular performance of plays; although it is known to have been occasionally infringed.

GILES FLETCHER; PHINEAS FLETCHER.

Nor is the poetical produce other than dramatic of the quarter of a century that elapsed from the death of James to the establishment of the Commonwealth, of very considerable amount. Giles and Phineas Fletcher were brothers, cousins of the dramatist, and both clergymen. Giles, who died in 1623, is the author of a poem entitled Christ's Victory and Triumph in Heaven and Earth over and after Death, which was published in a quarto volume in 1610. It is divided into four parts, and is written in stanzas somewhat like those of Spenser, only containing eight lines each instead of nine: both the Fletchers, indeed, were professed disciples and imitators of the great author of the Fairy Queen. Phineas, who survived till 1650, published in 1633, along with a small collection of Piscatory Eclogues and other Poetical Miscellanies, a long allegorical poem, entitled The Purple Island, in twelve Books or Cantos, written in a stanza of seven lines. The idea upon which this performance is founded is one of the most singular that ever took possession of the brain even of an allegorist: the *purple island* is nothing else than the human body, and the poem is, in fact, for the greater part, a system of anatomy, nearly as minute in its details as if it were a scientific treatise, but wrapping up everything in a fantastic guise of double meaning, so as to produce a languid sing-song of laborious riddles, which are mostly unintelligible without the very knowledge they make a pretence of conveying. After he has finished his anatomical course, the author takes up the subject of psychology, which he treats in the same luminous and interesting manner. Such a work as this has no claim to be considered a poem even of the same sort with the Fairy

Queen. In Spenser, the allegory, whether historical or moral, is little more than formal: the poem, taken in its natural and obvious import, as a tale of "knights' and ladies' gentle deeds"—a song of their "fierce wars and faithful loves"—has meaning and interest enough, without the allegory at all, which, indeed, except in a very few passages, is so completely concealed behind the direct narrative, that we may well suppose it to have been nearly as much lost sight of and forgotten by the poet himself as it is by his readers: here, the allegory is the soul of every stanza and of every line—that which gives to the whole work whatever meaning, and consequently whatever poetry, it possesses—with which, indeed, it is sometimes hard enough to be understood, but without which it would be absolute inanity and nonsense. The Purple Island is rather a production of the same species with Dr. Darwin's Botanic Garden; but, forced and false enough as Darwin's style is in many respects, it would be doing an injustice to his poem to compare it with Phineas Fletcher's either in regard to the degree in which nature and propriety are violated in the principle and manner of the composition, or in regard to the spirit and general success of the execution. Of course, there is a good deal of ingenuity shown in Fletcher's poem; and it is not unimpregnated by poetic feeling, nor without some passages of considerable merit. But in many other parts it is quite grotesque; and, on the whole, it is fantastic, puerile, and wearisome.

OTHER RELIGIOUS POETS:—QUARLES; HERBERT; HERRICK; CRASHAW.

The growth of the religious spirit in the early part of the seventeenth century is shown in much more of the poetry of the time as well as in that of the two Fletchers. Others of the most notable names of his age are Quarles, Herrick, Herbert, and Crashaw. Francis Quarles, who died in 1644, was one of the most popular as well as voluminous writers of the day, and is still generally known by his volume of Emblems. His verses are characterized by ingenuity rather than fancy, but, although often absurd, he is seldom dull or languid. There is a good deal of spirit and coarse vigour in some of his pieces, as for instance in his well-known Song of Anarchus, portions of which have been printed both by Ellis and Campbell, and which may perhaps have suggested to Cowper, the great religious poet of a later day, his lines called The Modern Patriot. Quarles, however, though he appears to have been a person of considerable literary acquirement, must in his poetical capacity be regarded as mainly a writer for the populace. George Herbert, a younger brother of the celebrated Edward Lord Herbert of Cherbury, was a clergyman. His volume, entitled The Temple, was first published soon after his death in 1633, and was at least six or seven times reprinted in the course of the next quarter of a century. His biographer, Izaak Walton, tells us that when he wrote, in the reign of Charles II., twenty thousand copies of it had been sold. Herbert was an intimate friend of Donne, and no doubt a great admirer of his poetry; but his own has been to a great extent preserved from the imitation of Donne's peculiar style, into which it might in other circumstances have fallen, in all probability by its having been composed with little effort or elaboration, and chiefly to relieve and amuse his own mind by the melodious expression of his favourite fancies and contemplations. His quaintness lies in his thoughts rather than in their expression, which is in general sufficiently simple and luminous. Robert Herrick, who was also a clergyman, is the author of a thick octavo volume of verse, published in 1648, under the title of Hesperides. It consists, like the poetry of Donne, partly of love verses, partly of pieces of a devotional character, or, as the two sorts are styled in the title-page, Works Human and Divine. The same singular licence which even the most reverend persons, and the purest and most religious minds, in that age allowed themselves to take in light and amatory poetry is found in Herrick as well as in

Donne, a good deal of whose singular manner, and fondness for conceits both of sound and sense, Herrick has also caught. Yet some both of his hymns and of his anacreontics —for of such strange intermixture does his poetry consist— are beautifully simple and natural, and full of grace as well as fancy. Richard Crashaw was another clergyman, who late in life became a Roman Catholic, and died a canon of Loretto in 1650. He is perhaps, after Donne, the greatest of these religious poets of the early part of the seventeenth century. He belongs in manner to the same school with Donne and Herrick, and in his lighter pieces he has much of their lyrical sweetness and delicacy; but there is often a force and even occasionally what may be called a grandeur of imagination in his more solemn poetry which Herrick never either reaches or aspires to.

CARTWRIGHT; RANDOLPH; CORBET.

All the poetical clergymen of this time, however, had not such pious muses. The Rev. William Cartwright, who died at an early age in 1643, is said by Anthony Wood to have been "a most florid and seraphic preacher;" but his poetry, which is mostly amatory, is not remarkable for its brilliancy. He is the author of several plays, and he was one of the young writers who were honoured with the title of his sons by Ben Jonson, who said of him, "My son Cartwright writes all like a man." Another of Ben's poetical sons was Thomas Randolph, who was likewise a clergyman, and is also the author of several plays, mostly in verse, as well as of a quantity of other poetry. Randolph has a good deal of fancy, and his verse flows very melodiously; but his poetry has in general a bookish and borrowed air. Much of it is on subjects of love and gallantry; but the love is chiefly of the head, or, at most, of the senses—the gallantry, it is easy to see, that merely of a fellow of a college and a reader of Ovid. Randolph died under thirty in 1634, and his poems were first collected after his death by his brother. The volume, which also contains his Plays, was frequently reprinted in the course of the next thirty or forty years; the edition before us, dated 1668, is called the fifth.

One of the most remarkable among the clerical poets of this earlier half of the seventeenth century was Dr. Richard Corbet, successively Bishop of Oxford and of Norwich. Corbet, who was born in 1582, became famous both as a poet and as a wit early in the reign of James; but very little, if any, of his poetry was published till after his death, which took place in 1635. It is related, that after Corbet was a doctor of divinity he once sang ballads at the Cross at Abingdon: "On a market day," Aubrey writes, "he and some of his comrades were at the tavern by the Cross (which, by the way, was then the finest in England; I remember it when I was a freshman; it was admirable curious Gothic architecture, and fine figures in the niches; 'twas one of those built by King .... for his Queen). The ballad-singer complained he had no custom—he could not put off his ballads. The jolly doctor puts off his gown, and puts on the ballad-singer's leathern jacket, and, being a handsome man, and a rare full voice, he presently vended a great many, and had a great audience." Aubrey had heard, however, that as a bishop "he had an admirable grave and venerable aspect." Corbet's poetry, too, is a mixture or alternation of gravity and drollery. But it is the subject or occasion, rather than the style or manner, that makes the difference; he never rises to anything higher than wit; and he is as witty in his elegies as in his ballads. As that ingredient, however, is not so suitable for the former as for the latter, his graver performances are worth very little. Nor is his merriment of a high order; when it is most elaborate it is strained and fantastic, and when more natural it is apt to run into buffoonery. But much of his verse, indeed, is merely prose in rhyme, and very indifferent rhyme for the most part. His happiest effusions are the two that are best known, his Journey into France and his ballad of

The Fairies' Farewell. His longest and most curious poem is his Iter Boreale, describing a journey which he took in company with other three university men, probably about 1620, from Oxford as far north as Newark and back again.

POETS OF THE FRENCH SCHOOL:—CAREW; LOVELACE; SUCKLING.

Both our poetry and our prose eloquence continued to be generally infected by the spirit of quaintness and conceit, or over-refinement and subtlety of thought, for nearly a century after the first introduction among us of that fashion of writing. Even some of the highest minds did not entirely escape the contagion. If nothing of it is to be found in Spenser or Milton, neither Shakespeare nor Bacon is altogether free from it. Of our writers of an inferior order, it took captive not only the greater number, but some of the greatest, who lived and wrote from the middle of the reign of Elizabeth to nearly the middle of that of Charles II.—from Bishop Andrews, whom we have already mentioned, in prose, and Donne both in prose and verse, to Cowley inclusive. The style in question appears to have been borrowed from Italy: it came in, at least, with the study and imitation of the Italian poetry, being caught apparently from the school of Petrarch, or rather of his later followers, about the same time that a higher inspiration was drawn from Tasso and Ariosto. It is observable that the species or departments of our poetry which it chiefly invaded were those which have always been more or less influenced by foreign models: it made comparatively little impression upon our dramatic poetry, the most truly native portion of our literature; but our lyrical and elegiac, our didactic and satirical verse, was overrun and materially modified by it, as we have said, for nearly a whole century. The return to a more natural manner, however, was begun to be made long before the expiration of that term. And, as we had received the malady from one foreign literature, so we were indebted for the cure to another. It is commonly assumed that our modern English poetry first evinced a disposition to imitate that of France after the Restoration. But the truth is that the influence of French literature had begun to be felt by our own at a considerably earlier date. The court of Charles I. was far from being so thoroughly French as that of Charles II.; but the connexion established between the two kingdoms through Queen Henrietta could not fail to produce a partial imitation of French models both in writing and in other things. The distinguishing characteristic of French poetry (and indeed of French art generally), neatness in the dressing of the thought, had already been carried to considerable height by Malherbe, Racan, Malleville, and others; and these writers are doubtless to be accounted the true fathers of our own Waller, Carew, Lovelace, and Suckling, who all began to write about this time, and whose verses may be said to have first exemplified in our lighter poetry what may be done by correct and natural expression, smoothness of flow, and all that lies in the *ars celare artem*—the art of making art itself seem nature. Of the four, Waller was perhaps first in the field; but he survived almost till the Revolution, and did not rise to his greatest celebrity till after the Restoration, so that he will more fitly fall to be noticed in a subsequent page. The other three all belong exclusively to the times of Charles I. and of the Commonwealth.

Thomas Carew, styled on the title-page "One of the Gentlemen of the Privy Chamber, and Sewer in Ordinary to His Majesty," is the author of a small volume of poetry first printed in 1640, the year after his death. In polish and evenness of movement, combined with a diction elevated indeed in its tone, as it must needs be by the very necessities of verse, above that of mere good conversation, but yet in ease, lucidity, and directness rivalling the language of ordinary life, Carew's poetry is not inferior to Waller's; and, while his expression is as correct and natural, and his numbers as harmonious, the music of his verse is richer, and his imagination is warmer and more florid. But the texture of his composition is in general extremely slight, the substance of most of his pieces consisting merely of the elaboration of some single idea; and, if he has more tenderness than Waller, he is far from having so much dignity, variety, or power of sustained effort.

The poems of Colonel Richard Lovelace are contained in two small volumes, one entitled Lucasta, published in 1649; the other entitled Posthume Poems, published by his brother in 1659, the year after the author's death. They consist principally of songs and other short pieces. Lovelace's songs, which are mostly amatory, are many of them carelessly enough written, and there are very few of them not defaced by some harshness or deformity; but a few of his best pieces are as sweetly versified as Carew's, with perhaps greater variety of fancy as well as more of vital force; and a tone of chivalrous gentleness and honour gives to some of them a pathos beyond the reach of any mere poetic art.

Lovelace's days, darkened in their close by the loss of everything except honour, were cut short at the age of forty; his contemporary, Sir John Suckling, who moved gaily and thoughtlessly through his short life as through a dance or a merry game, died, in 1641, at that of thirty-two. Suckling, who is the author of a small collection of poems, as well as of four plays, has none of the pathos of Lovelace or Carew, but he equals them in fluency and natural grace of manner, and he has besides a sprightliness and buoyancy which is all his own. His poetry has a more impulsive air than theirs; and, while, in reference to the greater part of what he has produced, he must be classed along with them and Waller as an adherent to the French school of propriety and precision, some of the happiest of his effusions are remarkable for a cordiality and impetuosity of manner which has nothing foreign about it, but is altogether English, although there is not much resembling it in any of his predecessors any more than of his contemporaries, unless perhaps in some of Skelton's pieces. His famous ballad of The Wedding is the very perfection of gaiety and archness in verse; and his Session of the Poets, in which he scatters about his wit and humour in a more careless style, may be considered as constituting him the founder of a species of satire which Cleveland and Marvel and other subsequent writers carried into new applications, and which only expired among us with Swift.

DENHAM.

To this date belongs a remarkable poem, the Cooper's Hill of Sir John Denham, first published in 1642. It immediately drew universal attention. Denham, however, had the year before made himself known as a poet by his tragedy of The Sophy, on the appearance of which Waller remarked that he had broken out like the Irish rebellion, threescore thousand strong, when nobody was aware or in the least suspected it. Cooper's Hill may be considered as belonging in point of composition to the same school with Sir John Davies's Nosce Teipsum; and, if it has not all the concentration of that poem, it is equally pointed, correct, and stately, with, partly owing to the subject, a warmer tone of imagination and feeling, and a fuller swell of verse. The spirit of the same classical style pervades both; and they are the two greatest poems in that style which had been produced down to the date at which we are now arrived. Denham is the author of a number of other compositions in verse, and especially of some songs and other shorter pieces, several of which are very spirited; but the fame of his principal poem has thrown everything else he has written into the shade. It is remarkable that many biographical notices of this poet make him to have survived nearly till the Revolution, and relate various stories of the miseries of his protracted old age; when the fact is, that he died in 1668, at the age of fifty-three.

CLEVELAND.

But, of all the cavalier poets, the one who did his cause the heartiest and stoutest service, and who, notwithstanding much carelessness or ruggedness of execution, possessed perhaps, even considered simply as a poet, the richest and most various faculty, was John Cleveland, the most popular verse-writer of his own day, the most neglected of all his contemporaries ever since. Cleveland was the eldest son of the Rev. Thomas Cleveland, vicar of Hinckley and rector of Stoke, in Leicestershire, and he was born at Loughborough in that county in 1613. Down to the breaking out of the civil war, he resided at St. John's College, Cambridge, of which he was a Fellow, and seems to have distinguished himself principally by his Latin poetry. But, when every man took his side, with whatever weapons he could wield, for king or parliament, Anthony Wood tells us that Cleveland was the first writer who came forth as a champion of the royal cause in English verse. To that cause he adhered till its ruin; at last in 1655, after having led for some years a fugitive life, he was caught and thrown into prison at Yarmouth; but, after a detention of a few months, Cromwell, on his petition, allowed him to go at large. The transaction was honourable to both parties.

Cleveland is commonly regarded as a mere dealer in satire and invective, and as having no higher qualities than a somewhat rude force and vehemence. His prevailing fault is a straining after vigour and concentration of expression; and few of his pieces are free from a good deal of obscurity, harshness, or other disfigurement, occasioned by this habit or tendency, working in association with an alert, ingenious, and fertile fancy, a neglect of and apparently a contempt for neatness of finish, and the turn for quaintness and quibbling characteristic of the school to which he belongs—for Cleveland must be considered as essentially one of the old wit poets. Most of his poems seem to have been thrown off in haste, and never to have been afterwards corrected or revised. There are, however, among them some that are not without vivacity and sprightliness; and others of his more solemn verses have considerable dignity.

The following epitaph on Ben Jonson is the shortest and best of several tributes to the memory of that poet, with whose masculine genius that of Cleveland seems to have strongly sympathised:—

> The Muses' fairest light in no dark time:
> The wonder of a learned age: the line
> Which none can pass: the most proportioned wit
> To nature; the best judge of what was fit;
> The deepest, plainest, highest, clearest pen:
> The voice most echoed by consenting men:
> The soul which answered best to all well said
> By others, and which most requital made:
> Tuned to the highest key of ancient Rome,
> Returning all her music with his own:
> In whom with Nature Study claimed a part,
> Yet who unto himself owed all his art:
> Here lies Ben Jonson: every age will look
> With sorrow here, with wonder on his book.

Elsewhere he thus expresses his preference for Jonson, as a dramatist, over the greatest of his contemporaries:—

> Shakespeare may make griefs, merry Beaumont's style
> Ravish and melt anger into a smile;
> In winter nights or after meals they be,
> I must confess, very good company;
> But thou exact'st our best hours' industry:
> We may read them, we ought to study thee;
> Thy scenes are precepts: every verse doth give
> Counsel, and teach us, not to laugh, but live.

WITHER.

These last-mentioned writers—Carew, Lovelace, Suckling, Denham, and Cleveland—were all, as we have seen, cavaliers; but the cause of puritanism and the parliament had also its poets as well as that of love and loyalty. Of these the two most eminent were Marvel and Wither. Marvel's era, however, is rather after the Restoration. George Wither, who was born in 1588, covers nearly seventy years of the seventeenth century with his life, and not very far from sixty with his works: his first publication, his volume of satires entitled Abuses Stript and Whipt, having appeared in 1611, and some of his last pieces only a short time before his death in 1667. The entire number of his separate works, as they have been reckoned up by modern bibliographers, exceeds a hundred.

One excellence for which all Wither's writings are eminent, his prose as well as his verse, is their genuine English. His unaffected diction, even now, has scarcely a stain of age upon it,—but flows on, ever fresh and transparent, like a pebbled rill.

Down to the breaking out of the war between the king and the parliament, Wither, although his pious poetry made him a favourite with the puritans, had always professed himself a strong church and state man; even at so late a date as in 1639, when he was above fifty, he served as a captain of horse in the expedition against the Scotch Covenanters; and when two or three years after he took arms on the other side, he had yet his new principles in a great measure to seek or make. It appears not to have been till a considerable time after this that his old admiration of the monarchy and the hierarchy became suddenly converted into the conviction that both one and other were, and had been all along, only public nuisances—the fountains of all the misrule and misery of the nation. What mainly instigated him to throw himself into the commencing contest with such eagerness seems to have been simply the notion, which possessed and tormented him all his life, that he was born with a peculiar genius for public affairs, and that things had very little chance of going right unless he were employed. With his head full of this conceit, it mattered comparatively little on which side he took his stand to begin with: he would speedily make all even and right; the one thing needful in the first instance was, that his services should be taken advantage of. Of course, Wither's opinions, like those of other men, were influenced by his position, and he was no doubt perfectly sincere in the most extreme of the new principles which he was ultimately led to profess. The defect of men of his temper is not insincerity. But they are nevertheless apt to be almost as unstable as if they had no strong convictions at all. Their convictions, in truth, however strong, do not rest so much upon reason or principle, as upon mere passion. They see everything through so thick and deeply coloured an atmosphere of self, that its real shape goes for very little in their conception of it; change only the hue of the haze, or the halo, with which it is thus invested, and you altogether change to them the thing itself—making the white appear black, the bright dim, the round square, or the reverse. Wither, with all his ardour and real honesty, appears never in fact to have acquired any credit for reliability, or steadiness in the opinions he held, either from friends or opponents. He very naïvely lets out this himself in a prose pamphlet which he published in 1624, entitled The Scholar's Purgatory, being a vindication of himself addressed to the Bishops, in which, after stating that he had been offered more money and better entertainment if he would have employed himself in setting forth heretical fancies than he had any chance of ever obtaining by the profession of the truth, he adds, "Yea, sometimes I have been wooed to the profession of their wild and ill-grounded opinions by the sectaries of so many several separations, that, had I liked, or rather had not God been the more merciful to me, I might have been Lieutenant, if not Captain, of some new band of such volunteers long ere this time." Overtures of this kind are, of course, only made to persons who are believed to be open to them. It is plain from his own account that Wither was thus early notorious as a speculator or trader in such securities—as one ready, not precisely to sell himself, his opinions, and his conscience, to the highest bidder, but yet to be gained over if the offer were only made large enough to convert as well as purchase him. There is a great deal of very passable wearing and working honesty of this kind in the world.

The history of Wither's numerous publications has been elaborately investigated by the late Mr. Park in the first and second volumes of the British Bibliographer; many of his poems have been reprinted by Sir Egerton Brydges, and others of his admirers; and an ample account of his life and writings, drawn up with a large and intimate knowledge, as well as affectionate zeal and painstaking, which make it supersede whatever had been previously written on the subject, forms the principal article (extending over more than 130 pages) of Mr. Wilmott's Lives of Sacred Poets (8vo. Lon. 1834). Much injustice, however, has been done to Wither by the hasty judgment that has commonly been passed, even by his greatest admirers, upon his later political poetry, as if it consisted of mere party invective and fury, and all that he had written of any enduring value or interest was to be found in the productions of the early part of his life. Some at least of his political pieces are very remarkable for their vigour and terseness. As a specimen we will give a portion of a poem which he published without his name in 1647, under the title of "Amygdala Britannica; Almonds for Parrots; A Dish of Stone-fruit, partly shelled and partly unshelled; which, if cracked, picked, and well digested, may be wholesome against those epidemic distempers of the brain now predominant, and prevent some malignant diseases likely to ensue: Composed heretofore by a well-known modern author, and now published according to a copy found written with his own hand. *Qui bene latuit bene vixit.*" This fantastic title-page (with the manufacture of which the bookseller may have had more to do than Wither himself) was suited to the popular taste of the day, but would little lead a modern reader to expect the nervous concentration and passionate earnestness of such verses as the following:—

> The time draws near, and hasteth on,
> In which strange works shall be begun:
> And prosecutions, whereon shall
> Depend much future bliss or bale.

If to the left hand you decline,
Assured destruction they divine;
But, if the right-hand course ye take,
This island it will happy make.

A time draws nigh in which you may
As you shall please the chess-men play:
Remove, confine, check, leave, or take,
Dispose, depose, undo, or make,
Pawn, rook, knight, bishop, queen, or king,
And act your wills in every thing:
But, if that time let slip you shall,
For yesterday in vain you call.

A time draws nigh in which the sun
Will give more light than he hath done;
Then also you shall see the moon
Shine brighter than the sun at noon;
And many stars now seeming dull
Give shadows like the moon at full.
Yet then shall some, who think they see,
Wrapt in Egyptian darkness be.

A time draws nigh when with your blood
You shall preserve the viper's brood,
And starve your own; yet fancy than [1]
That you have played the pelican;
But, when you think the frozen snakes
Have changed their natures for your sakes,
They, in requital, will contrive
Your mischief who did them revive.

A time will come when they that wake
Shall dream; and sleepers undertake
The grand affairs; yet,[2] few men know
Which are the dreamers of these two;
And fewer care by which of these
They guided be, so they have ease:
But an alarum shall advance
Your drowsy spirits from that trance.

A time shall come ere long in which
Mere beggars shall grow soonest rich;
The rich with wants be pinched more
Than such as go from door to door;
The honourable by the base
Shall be despited to their face;
The truth defamed be with lies;
The fool preferred before the wise;
And he that fighteth to be free,
By conquering enslaved shall be.

. . . .

A time will come when see you shall
Toads fly aloft and eagles crawl;
Wolves walk abroad in human shapes;
Men turn to asses, hogs, and apes:

[1] Then.   [2] As yet.

> But, when that cursed time is come,
> Well's he that is both deaf and dumb;
> That nothing speaketh, nothing hears,
> And neither hopes, desires, nor fears.
>
> . . . . .
>
> When men shall generally confess
> Their folly and their wickedness;
> Yet act as if there neither were
> Among them conscience, wit, or fear:
> When they shall talk as if they had
> Some brains, yet do as they were mad;
> And nor by reason, nor by noise,
> By human or by heavenly voice,
> By being praised or reproved,
> By judgments or by mercies, moved:
> Then look for so much sword and fire
> As such a temper doth require.
>
> . . . . .
>
> Ere God his wrath on Balaam wreaks,
> First by his ass to him he speaks;
> Then shows him in an angel's hand
> A sword, his courses to withstand:
> But, seeing still he forward went,
> Quite through his heart a sword he sent,
> And God will thus, if thus they do,
> Still deal with kings, and subjects too:
> That, where his grace despised is grown,
> He by his judgments may be known.

Neither Churchhill nor Cowper ever wrote anything in the same style better than this. The modern air, too, of the whole, with the exception of a few words, is wonderful. But this, as we have said, is the character of all Wither's poetry —of his earliest as well as of his latest. It is nowhere more conspicuous than in his early religious verses, especially in his collection entitled Songs and Hymns of the Church, first published in 1624. There is nothing of the kind in the language more perfectly beautiful than some of these. We subjoin two of them:—

Thanksgiving for Seasonable Weather. Song 85.

> Lord, should the sun, the clouds, the wind,
>   The air, and seasons be
> To us so froward and unkind
>   As we are false to thee;
> All fruits would quite away be burned,
>   Or lie in water drowned,
> Or blasted be or overturned,
>   Or chilled on the ground.

But from our duty though we swerve,
 Thou still dost mercy show,
And deign thy creatures to preserve,
 That men might thankful grow;
Yea, though from day to day we sin,
 And thy displeasure gain,
No sooner we to cry begin
 But pity we obtain.

The weather now thou changed hast
 That put us late to fear,
And when our hopes were almost past
 Then comfort did appear.
The heaven the earth's complaints hath heard;
 They reconciled be;
And thou such weather hast prepared
 As we desired of thee.

For which, with lifted hands and eyes,
 To thee we do repay
The due and willing sacrifice
 Of giving thanks to-day
Because such offerings we should not
 To render thee be slow,
Nor let that mercy be forgot
 Which thou art pleased to show.

Thanksgiving for Victory. Song 88.

We love thee, Lord, we praise thy name,
 Who, by thy great almighty arm,
Hast kept us from the spoil and shame
 Of those that sought our causeless harm;
That art our life, our triumph-song,
 The joy and comfort of our heart;
To thee all praises do belong,
 And thou the God of Armies art.

We must confess it is thy power
 That made us masters of the field;
Thou art our bulwark and our tower,
 Our rock of refuge and our shield;
Thou taught'st our hands and arms to fight;
 With vigour thou didst gird us round;
Thou mad'st our foes to take their flight,
 And thou didst beat them to the ground.

With fury came our armed foes,
 To blood and slaughter fiercely bent;
And perils round did us inclose,
 By whatsoever way we went;
That, hadst not thou our Captain been,
 To lead us on, and off again,
We on the place had dead been seen,
 Or masked in blood and wounds had lain.

> This song we therefore sing to thee,
> And pray that thou for evermore
> Would'st our Protector deign to be,
> As at this time and heretofore;
> That thy continual favour shown
> May cause us more to thee incline,
> And make it through the world be known
> That such as are our foes are thine.

BROWNE.

Along with Wither ought to be mentioned a contemporary poet of a genius, or at least of a manner, in some respects kindred to his, and whose fate it has been to experience the same long neglect, William Browne, the author of Britannia's Pastorals, of which the first part was published in 1613, the second in 1616, and of The Shepherd's Pipe in Seven Eclogues, which appeared in 1614. Browne was a native of Tavistock in Devonshire, where he was born in 1590, and he is supposed to have died in 1645. It is remarkable that, if he lived to so late a date, he should not have written more than he appears to have done: the two parts of his Britannia's Pastorals were reprinted together in 1625; and a piece called The Inner Temple Masque, and a few short poems, were published for the first time in an edition of his works brought out, under the care of Dr. Farmer, in 1772; but the last thirty years of his life would seem, in so far as regards original production, to have been a blank. Yet a remarkable characteristic of his style, as well as of Wither's, is its ease and fluency; and it would appear, from what he says in one of the songs of his Pastorals, that he had written part of that work before he was twenty. His poetry certainly does not read as if its fountain would be apt soon to run dry. His facility of rhyming and command of harmonious expression are very great; and, within their proper sphere, his invention and fancy are also extremely active and fertile. His strength, however, lies chiefly in description, not the thing for which poetry or language is best fitted, and a species of writing which cannot be carried on long without becoming tiresome; he is also an elegant didactic declaimer; but of passion, or indeed of any breath of actual living humanity, his poetry has almost none. This, no doubt, was the cause of the neglect into which after a short time it was allowed to drop; and this limited quality of his genius may also very probably have been the reason why he so soon ceased to write and publish. From the time when religious and political contention began to wax high, in the latter years of King James, such poetry as Browne's had little chance of acceptance: from about that date Wither, as we have seen, who also had previously written his Shepherd's Hunting, and other similar pieces, took up a new strain; and Browne, if he was to continue to be listened to, must have done the same, which he either would not or could not. Yet, although without the versatility of Wither, and also with less vitality than Wither even in the kind of poetry which is common to the two, Browne rivals that writer both in the abundance of his poetic vein and the sweetness of his verse; and the English of the one has nearly all the purity, perspicuity, and unfading freshness of style which is so remarkable in the other.

PROSE WRITERS:—CHARLES I.

Most of the prose that was written and published in England in the middle portion of the seventeenth century, or the twenty years preceding the Restoration, was political and theological, but very little of it has any claim to be considered as belonging to the national literature. A torrent of pamphlets and ephemeral polemics supplied the ravenous public appetite with a mental sustenance which answered the wants of the moment, much as the bakers' ovens did with daily bread for the body. It was all devoured, and meant to be devoured, as fast as it was produced—devoured in the sense of being quite used up and consumed, so far as any good was to be got out of it. It was in no respect intended for posterity, any more than the linen and broadcloth then manufactured were intended for posterity. Still even this busy and excited time produced some literary performances which still retain more or less of interest.

The writings attributed to Charles I. were first collected and published at the Hague soon after his death, in a folio volume without date, under the title of Reliquiæ Sacræ Carolinæ, and twice afterwards in England, namely in 1660 and 1687, with the title of ΒΑΣΙΛΙΚΑ: The Works of King Charles the Martyr. If we except a number of speeches to the parliament, letters, despatches, and other political papers, the contents of this collection are all theological, consisting of prayers, arguments, and disquisitions on the controversy about church government, and the famous Eikon Basiliké, or, The Portraiture of his Sacred Majesty in his Solitude and Sufferings; which, having been printed under the care of Dr. Gauden (after the Restoration successively bishop of Exeter and Worcester), had been first published by itself immediately after the king's execution. It is now generally admitted that the Eikon was really written by Gauden, who, after the Restoration, openly claimed it as his own. Mr. Hallam, however, although he has no doubt of Gauden being the author, admits that it is, nevertheless, superior to his acknowledged writings. "A strain of majestic melancholy," he observes, "is well kept up; but the personated sovereign is rather too theatrical for real nature; the language is too rhetorical and amplified, the periods too artificially elaborated. None but scholars and practised writers employ such a style as this."[*] It is not improbable that the work may have been submitted to Charles's revisal, and that it may have received both his approval and his corrections. Charles, indeed, was more in the habit of correcting what had been written by others than of writing anything himself. "Though he was of as slow a pen as of speech," says Sir Philip Warwick, "yet both were very

[*] Lit. of Eur. III. 376.

significant; and he had that modest esteem of his own parts, that he would usually say, he would willingly make his own despatches, but that he found it better to be a cobbler than a shoemaker. I have been in company with very learned men, when I have brought them their own papers back from him with his alterations, who ever confessed his amendments to have been very material. And I once, by his commandment, brought him a paper of my own to read, to see whether it was suitable to his directions, and he disallowed it slightingly: I desired him I might call Dr. Sanderson to aid me, and that the doctor might understand his own meaning from himself; and, with his majesty's leave, I brought him whilst he was walking and taking the air; whereupon we two went back; but pleased him as little when we returned it: for, smilingly, he said, a man might have as good ware out of a chandler's shop; but afterwards he set it down with his own pen very plainly, and suitably to his own intentions." The most important of the literary productions which are admitted to be wholly Charles's own, are his papers in the controversy which he carried on at Newcastle in June and July, 1646, with Alexander Henderson, the Scotch clergyman, on the question between episcopacy and presbytery, and those on the same subject in his controversy with the parliamentary divines at Newport in October, 1648. These papers show considerable clearness of thinking and logical or argumentative talent; but it cannot be said that they are written with any force or elegance.

Milton's Prose Works.

We have already mentioned Bishop Hall, both as a poet and as a writer of prose. A part which Hall took in his old age in the grand controversy of the time brought him into collision with one with whose name in after ages the world was to resound. John Milton, then in his thirty-third year, and recently returned from his travels in France and Italy, had already, in 1641, lent the aid of his pen to the war of the Puritans against the established church by the publication of his treatise entitled Of Reformation, in Two Books. The same year Hall published his Humble Remonstrance in favour of Episcopacy; which immediately called forth an Answer by Smectymnuus,—a word formed from the initial letters of the names of five Puritan ministers by whom the tract was written—Stephen Marshall, Edmund Calamy, Thomas Young, Matthew Newcomen, and William (or, as he was on this occasion reduced to designate himself, Uuilliam) Spurstow. The Answer produced a Confutation by Archbishop Usher; and to this Milton replied in a treatise entitled Of Prelatical Episcopacy. Hall then published a Defence of the Humble Remonstrance; and Milton wrote Animadversions upon that. About the same time he also brought out a performance of much greater pretension, under the title of The Reason of Church Government urged against Prelaty, in Two Books. This is the work containing the magnificent passage in which he makes the announcement of his intention to attempt something in one of the highest kinds of poetry "in the mother-tongue," long afterwards accomplished in his great epic. Meanwhile a Confutation of the Animadversions having been published by Bishop Hall, or his son, Milton replied, in 1642, in an Apology for Smectymnuus, which was the last of his publications in this particular controversy. But, nearly all his other prose writings were given to the world within the period with which we are now engaged:—namely, his Tractate of Education, addressed to his friend Hartlib, and his noble Areopagitica, a Speech for the Liberty of Unlicensed Printing, in 1644: his Doctrine and Discipline of Divorce, and his Judgment of Martin Bucer concerning Divorce, the same year; his Tetrachordon, and Colasterion (both on the same subject) in 1645; his Tenure of Kings and Magistrates, his Eikonoclastes, in answer to the Eikon Basilike, and one or two other tracts of more temporary interest, all after the execution of the king, in 1649; his Defence for the People of England, in answer to Salmasius (in Latin), in 1651; his Second Defence (also in Latin), in reply to a work by Peter du Moulin, in 1654; two additional Latin tracts in reply to rejoinders of Du Moulin, in 1655; his treatises on Civil Power in Ecclesiastical Cases, and on The Means of Removing Hirelings out of the Church, in 1659; his Letter concerning the Ruptures of the Commonwealth, and Brief Delineation of a Free Commonwealth, the same year; and, finally, his Ready and Easy Way to establish a Free Commonwealth, and his Brief Notes upon a Sermon preached by Dr. Griffith, called The Fear of God and the King, in the spring of 1660, immediately before the king's return. Passages of great poetic splendour occur in some of these productions, and a fervid and fiery spirit breathes in all of them, though the animation is as apt to take the tone of mere coarse objurgation and abuse as of lofty and dignified scorn or of vigorous argument; but, upon the whole, it cannot be said that Milton's English prose is a good style. It is in the first place, not perhaps in vocabulary, but certainly in genius and construction, the most Latinized of English styles; but it does not merit the commendation bestowed by Pope on another style which he conceived to be formed after the model of the Roman eloquence, of being "so Latin, yet so English all the while," It is both soul and body Latin, only in an English dress. Owing partly to this principle of composition upon which he deliberately proceeded, or to the adoption of which his education and tastes or habits led him, partly to the character of his mind, fervid, gorgeous, and soaring, but having little involuntary impulsiveness or self-abandonment, rich as his style often is, it never moves with any degree of rapidity or easy grace even in passages where such qualities are most required, but has at all times something of a stiff, cumbrous, oppressive air, as if every thought, the lightest, and most evanescent as well as the gravest and stateliest, were attired in brocade and whalebone. There is too little relief from constant straining and striving; too little repose

and variety; in short, too little nature. Many things, no
doubt, are happily said; there is much strong and also some
brilliant expression; but even such imbedded gems do not
occur so often as might be looked for from so poetical a
mind. In fine, we must admit the truth of what he has himself confessed—that he was not naturally disposed to "this
manner of writing;" "wherein," he adds, "knowing myself
inferior to myself, led by the genial power of nature to another task, I have the use, as I may account it, but of my
left hand."* With all his quick susceptibility for whatever
was beautiful and bright, Milton seems to have needed the
soothing influences of the regularity and music of verse fully
to bring out his poetry, or to sublimate his imagination to
the true poetical state. This passion which is an enlivening
flame in his verse half suffocates him with its smoke in his
prose.

Hales; Chillingworth.

Two other eminent names of theological controversialists
belonging to this troubled age of the English church may
be mentioned together—those of John Hales and William
Chillingworth. Hales, who was born in 1584, and died in
1656, the same year with Hall and Usher, published in his
lifetime a few short tracts, of which the most important is a
Discourse on Schism, which was printed in 1642, and is considered to have been one of the works that led the way in
that bold revolt against the authority of the fathers, so
much cried up by the preceding school of Andrews and
Land, upon which has since been founded what many hold
to be the strongest defence of the Church of England
against that of Rome. All Hales's writings were collected
and published after his death, in 1659, in a quarto volume,
bearing the title of Golden Remains of the Ever-Memorable
Mr. John Hales,—a designation which has stuck to his name.

* Reason of Church Government, Book II.

The main idea of his treatise on Schism had, however, been much more elaborately worked out by his friend Chillingworth—the Immortal Chillingworth, as he is styled by his admirers—in his famous work entitled The Religion of Protestants a Safe Way to Salvation, published in 1637. This is one of the most closely and keenly argued polemical treatises ever written: the style in which Chillingworth presses his reasoning home is like a charge with the bayonet. He was still only in his early manhood when he produced this remarkably able work; and he died in 1644 at the age of forty-two.

Jeremy Taylor.

But the greatest name by far among the English divines of the middle of the seventeenth century is that of Jeremy Taylor. He was born in 1613, and died bishop of Down and Connor in 1667; but most of his works were written, and many of them were also published, before the Restoration. In abundance of thought; in ingenuity of argument; in opulence of imagination; in a soul made alike for the feeling of the sublime, of the beautiful, and of the picturesque; and in a style, answering in its compass, flexibility, and sweetness to the demands of all these powers, Taylor is unrivalled among the masters of English eloquence. He is the Spenser of our prose writers; and his prose is sometimes almost as musical as Spenser's verse. His Sermons, his Golden Grove, his Holy Living, and, still more, his Holy Dying, all contain many passages, the beauty and splendour of which are hardly to be matched in any other English prose writer. Another of his most remarkable works Theologica Eclectica, a Discourse of the Liberty of Prophesying, first published in 1647, may by placed beside Milton's Areopagitica, published three years before, as doing for liberty of conscience the same service which that did for the liberty of the press. Both remain the most eloquent and comprehensive defences we yet possess of these two great rights.

FULLER.

The last of the theological writers of this era that we shall notice is Fuller. Dr. Thomas Fuller was born in 1604, and died in 1661; and in the course of his not very extended life produced a considerable number of literary works, of which his Church History of Britain from the Birth of Jesus Christ until the Year 1648, which appeared in 1656, and his History of the Worthies of England, which was not published till the year after his death, are the most important. He is a most singular writer, full of verbal quibbling and quaintness of all kinds, but by far the most amusing and engaging of all the rhetoricians of this school, inasmuch as his conceits are rarely mere elaborate feats of ingenuity, but are usually informed either by a strong spirit of very peculiar humour and drollery, or sometimes even by a warmth and depth of feeling, of which too, strange as it may appear, the oddity of his phraseology is often a not ineffective exponent. He was certainly one of the greatest and truest wits that ever lived: he is witty not by any sort of effort at all, but as it were in spite of himself, or because he cannot help it. But wit, or the faculty of looking at and presenting things in their less obvious relations, is accompanied in him, not only by humour and heart, but by a considerable endowment of the irradiating power of fancy. Accordingly, what he writes is always lively and interesting, and sometimes even eloquent and poetical, though the eccentricities of his characteristic manner are not favourable, it must be confessed, to dignity or solemnity of style when attempted to be long sustained. Fuller, and it is no wonder, was one of the most popular writers, if not the most popular, of his own day: he observes himself, in the opening chapter of his Worthies, that hitherto no stationer (or publisher) had lost by him; and what happened in regard to one of his works, his *Holy State*, is perhaps without example in the history of book-publishing:—it appeared originally in a folio volume in 1642, and is believed to have been four times reprinted before the Restoration; but the publisher continued to describe the two last impressions on the title-page as still only the *third* edition, as if the demand had been so great that he felt (for whatever reason) unwilling that its extent should be known. It is conjectured that his motive probably was "a desire to lull suspicion, and not to invite prohibition from the ruling powers."*

Hardly anything can be found in Fuller that is dull or wearisome. The following interesting passage, often referred to, makes part of the account of Warwickshire in the Worthies:—

William Shakespeare was born at Stratford on Avon in this county; in whom three eminent poets may seem in some sort to be compounded: 1. Martial, in the warlike sound of his surname (whence some may conjecture him of a military extraction), Hastivibrans, or Shakespeare. 2. Ovid, the most natural and witty of all poets; and hence it was that Queen Elizabeth, coming into a grammar-school, made this extemporary verse,

"Persius a Crabstaff, Bawdy Martial, Ovid a fine wag."

3. Plautus, who was an exact comedian, yet never any scholar; as our Shakespeare, if alive, would confess himself. Add to all these, that, though his genius generally was jocular, and inclining him to festivity, yet he could, when so disposed, be solemn and serious, as appears by his tragedies; so that Heraclitus himself (I mean if secret and unseen) might afford to smile at his comedies, they were so merry; and Democritus scarce forbear to sigh at his tragedies, they were so mournful.

He was an eminent instance of the truth of that rule, *Poeta non fit, sed nascitur;* one is not made, but born a poet. Indeed his learning was very little, so that, as Cornish diamonds are not polished by any lapidary, but are pointed, and smoothed even, as they are taken out of the earth, so nature itself was all the art which was used upon him.

Many were the wit combats betwixt him and Ben Jonson. Which two I behold like a Spanish great galleon and an English man-of-war. Master Jonson, like the former, was built far higher in learning; solid, but slow, in his performances. Shakespeare, with the English man-of-war, lesser in bulk, but lighter in sailing, could turn with all tides, tack about, and take advantage of all winds, by the quickness of his wit and invention. He died anno Domini 16 . ., and was buried at Stratford upon Avon, the town of his nativity.

We may add another Warwickshire worthy, of a different order:—

* Preface by the Editor, Mr. James Nichols, to The Holy State. 8vo. Lon. 1841.

ENGLISH LITERATURE AND LANGUAGE. 39

Philemon Holland, where born is to me unknown, was bred in Trinity College in Cambridge a Doctor in Physic, and fixed himself in Coventry. He was the translator general in his age, so that those books alone of his turning into English will make a country gentleman a competent library for historians; in so much that one saith,

"Holland with his translations doth so fill us,
He will not let *Suetonius* be *Tranquillus*."

Indeed, some decry all translators as interlopers, spoiling the trade of learning, which should be driven amongst scholars alone. Such also allege that the best translations are works rather of industry than judgment, and, in easy authors, of faithfulness rather than industry; that many be but hunglers, forcing the meaning of the authors they translate, "forcing the lock when they cannot open it."

But their opinion resents too much of envy, that such gentlemen who cannot repair to the fountain should be debarred access to the stream. Besides, it is unjust to charge all with the faults of some; and a distinction must be made amongst translators betwixt cobblers and workmen, and our Holland had the true *knack* of translating.

Many of these his books he wrote with one pen, whereon he himself thus pleasantly versified:—

"With one sole pen I writ this book,
Made of a grey goose quill;
A pen it was when it I took,
And a pen I leave it still."

This monumental pen he solemnly kept, and showed to my reverend tutor, Doctor Samuel Ward. It seems he leaned very lightly on the neb thereof, though weightily enough in another sense, performing not slightly but solidly what he undertook.

But what commendeth him most to the praise of posterity is his translating Camden's Britannia, a translation more than a translation, with many excellent additions not found in the Latin, done fifty years since in Master Camden's lifetime, not only with his knowledge and consent, but also, no doubt, by his desire and help. Yet such additions (discoverable in the former part with asterisks in the margent) with some antiquaries obtain not equal authenticalness with the rest. This eminent translator was translated to a better life anno Domini 16 . . .

The translation of the translator took place in fact in 1636, when he had reached the venerable age of eighty-five, so that translating would seem to be not an unhealthy occupation. The above sketch is Fuller all over, in heart as well as in head and hand—the last touch especially, which, jest though it be, and upon a solemn subject, falls as gently and kindly as a tear on good old Philemon and his labours. The effect is as if we were told that even so gently fell the touch of death itself upon the ripe old man—even so easy, natural, and smiling, his labours over, was his leave-taking and exchange of this earth of many languages, the confusion or discord of which he had done his best to reduce, for that better world, where there is only one tongue, and translation is not needed or known. And Fuller's wit and jesting are always of this character; they have not in them a particle either of bitterness or of irreverence. No man ever (in writing at least) made so many jokes, good, bad, and indifferent; be the subject what it may, it does not matter; in season and out of season he is equally facetious; he cannot let slip an occasion of saying a good thing any more than a man who is tripped can keep himself from falling; the habit is as irresistible with him as the habit of breathing; and yet there is probably neither an ill-natured nor a profane witticism to be found in all that he has written. It is the sweetest-blooded wit that was ever infused into man or book. And how strong and weighty, as well as how gentle and beautiful, much of his writing is! The work perhaps in which he is oftenest eloquent and pathetic is that entitled The Holy State and the Profane State, the former great popularity of which we have already noticed. Almost no writer whatever tells a story so well as Fuller—with so much life and point and gusto.

Sir Thomas Browne.

Another of the most original and peculiar writers of the middle portion of the seventeenth century is Sir Thomas Browne, the celebrated author of the Religio Medici, published in 1642; the Pseudodoxia Epidemica, or Inquiries into Vulgar and Common Errors, in 1646; and the Hydriotaphia, Urn Burial, or a Discourse on the Sepulchral Urns found in Norfolk; and The Garden of Cyrus, or the Quincuncial Lozenge, or Network Plantations of the Ancients, Artificially, Naturally, Mystically Considered, which appeared together in 1658. Browne died in 1682, at the age of seventy-seven; but he published nothing after the Restoration, though some additional tracts found among his papers were given to the world after his death. The writer of a well-known review of Browne's literary productions, and of the characteristics of his singular genius, has sketched the history of his successive acts of authorship in a lively and striking passage:—"He had no sympathy with the great business of men. In that awful year when Charles I. went in person to seize five members of the Commons' House,—when the streets resounded with shouts of 'Privilege of Parliament,' and the king's coach was assailed by the prophetic cry, 'To your tents, O Israel,'—in that year, in fact, when the civil war first broke out, and when most men of literary power were drawn by the excitement of the crisis into patriotic controversy on either side,—appeared the calm and meditative reveries of the Religio Medici. The war raged on. It was a struggle between all the elements of government. England was torn by convulsion and red with blood. But Browne was tranquilly preparing his Pseudodoxia Epidemica; as if errors about basilisks and griffins were the paramount and fatal epidemic of the time; and it was published in due order in that year when the cause which the author advocated, as far as he could advocate anything political, lay at its last gasp. The king dies on the scaffold. The Protectorate succeeds. Men are again fighting on paper the solemn cause already decided in the field. Drawn from visions more sublime,—forsaking studies more intricate and vast than those of the poetical Sage of Norwich,—diverging from a career bounded by the most splendid goal,—foremost in the ranks shines the flaming sword of Milton: Sir Thomas Browne is lost in the quincunx of the ancient gardens; and the year 1658 beheld the death of Oliver Cromwell, and the publication of the Hydriotaphia." * The writings of Sir Thomas Browne, to be relished or rightly appreciated. must of course be read in the spirit suited to the species of literature to which they belong. If we look for matter of-fact in-

* Article in Edinburgh Review for October, 1836; No. 129, p. 34. (Understood to be by Sir Edward Bulwer Lytton.)

formation in a poem, we are likely to be disappointed; and
so are we likewise, if we go for the passionate or pictured
style of poetry to an encyclopædia. Browne's works, with
all their varied learning, contain very little positive information that can now be accounted of much value; very little
even of direct moral or economical counsel by which any
person could greatly profit; very little, in short, of anything
that will either put money in a man's pocket, or actual
knowledge in his head. Assuredly the interest with which
they were perused, and the charm that was found to belong
to them, could not at any time have been due, except in
very small part indeed, to the estimation in which their
readers held such pieces of intelligence as that the phœnix
is but a fable of the poets, and that the griffin exists only
in the zoology of the heralds. It would fare ill with Browne
if the worth of his books were to be tried by the amount of
what they contain of this kind of information, or, indeed, of
any other kind of what is commonly called useful knowledge;
for, in truth, he has done his best to diffuse a good many
vulgar errors as monstrous as any he had corrected. For
that matter, if his readers were to continue to believe with
him in astrology and witchcraft, we shall all agree that it was
of very little consequence what faith they may hold touching
the phœnix and the griffin. Mr. Hallam, we think, has, in
a manner which is not usual with him, fallen somewhat into
this error of applying a false test in the judgment he has
passed upon Browne. It is, no doubt, quite true that the
Inquiry into Vulgar Errors "scarcely raises a high notion of
Browne himself as a philosopher, or of the state of physical
knowledge in England;"* that the Religio Medici shows its
author to have been "far removed from real philosophy, both
by his turn of mind and by the nature of his erudition;"
and likewise that "he seldom reasons," that "his thoughts
are desultory," that "sometimes he appears sceptical or
paradoxical," but that "credulity and deference to authority

---

* Lit. of Eur. III. 461.

prevail" in his habits of thinking.* Understanding *philo-sophy* in the sense in which the term is here used, that is to say, as meaning the sifting and separation of fact from fiction, it may be admitted that there is not much of that in Sir Thomas Browne; his works are all rather marked by a very curious and piquant intermixture of the two. Of course, such being the case, what he writes is not to be considered solely or even principally with reference to its absolute truth or falsehood, but rather with reference to its relative truth and significance as an expression of some feeling or notion or other idiosyncracy of the very singular and interesting mind from which it has proceeded. Read in this spirit, the works of Sir Thomas Browne, more especially his Religio Medici, and his Urn Burial, will he found among the richest in our literature—full of uncommon thoughts, and trains of meditation leading far away into the dimmest inner chambers of life and death—and also of an eloquence, sometimes fantastic, but always striking, not seldom pathetic, and in its greatest passages gorgeous with the emblazonry of a warm imagination. Out of such a writer the rightly attuned and sympathizing mind will draw many things more precious than any mere facts.

Sir James Harrington.

We can merely mention Sir James Harrington's political romance entitled Oceana, which was published in 1656. Harrington's leading principles are, that the natural element of power in states is property; and that, of all kinds of property, that in land is the most important, possessing, indeed, certain characteristics which distinguish it, in its natural and political action, from all other property. "In general," observes Mr. Hallam, "it may be said of Harrington that he is prolix, dull, pedantic, yet seldom profound; but sometimes redeems himself by just observations."** This is true in so

* Lit. of Eur. III. 153.   ** Id. IV. 200.

far as respects the style of the Oceana; but it hardly does justice to the ingenuity, the truth, and the importance of certain of Harrington's views and deductions in the philosophy of politics. If he has not the merit of absolute originality in his main propositions, they had at least never been so clearly expounded and demonstrated by any preceding writer.

Newspapers.

It has now been satisfactorily shown that the three newspapers, entitled The English Mercurie, Nos. 50, 51, and 54, preserved among Dr. Birch's historical collections in the British Museum, professing to be "published by authority, for the contradiction of false reports," at the time of the attack of the Spanish Armada, on the credit of which the invention of newspapers used to be attributed to Lord Burleigh, are modern forgeries,—*jeux d'esprit*, in fact, of the reverend Doctor.[*] Occasional pamphlets, containing foreign news, began to be published in England towards the close of the reign of James I. The earliest that has been met with is entitled News out of Holland, dated 1619; and other similar papers of news from different foreign countries are extant which appeared in 1620, 1621, and 1622. The first of these news-pamphlets which came out at regular intervals appears to have been that entitled The News of the Present Week, edited by Nathaniel Butler, which was started in 1622, in the early days of the Thirty Years' War, and was continued, in conformity with its title, as a weekly publication. But the proper era of English newspapers, at least of those containing domestic intelligence, commences with the Long Parliament. The earliest that has been discovered is a quarto pamphlet of a few leaves, entitled The Diurnal Occurrences, or Daily Proceedings of Both Houses,

[*] See A Letter to Antonio Panizzi, Esq. By Thomas Watts, of the British Museum. 8vo. Lond. 1839.

in this great and happy parliament, from the 3rd of November, 1640, to the 3rd of November, 1641; London, printed for William Cooke, and are to be sold at his shop at Furnival's Inn Gate, in Holborn, 1641.* More than a hundred newspapers, with different titles, appear to have been published between this date and the death of the king, and upwards of eighty others between that event and the Restoration.** "When hostilities commenced," says the writer from whom we derive this information, "every event, during a most eventful period, had its own historian, who communicated *News* from *Hull*, *Truths* from *York*, *Warranted Tidings* from *Ireland*, and *Special Passages* from *several places*. These were all occasional papers. Impatient, however, as a distracted people were for information, the news were never distributed daily. The various newspapers were published weekly at first; but in the progress of events, and the ardour of curiosity, they were distributed twice or thrice in every week.† Such were the French Intelligencer, the Dutch Spy, the Irish Mercury, and the Scots Dove, the Parliament Kite, and the Secret Owl. *Mercurius Acheronticus* brought them hebdomadal *News from Hell*; *Mercurius Democritus* communicated wonderful news from the World in the Moon; the *Laughing Mercury* gave perfect news from the Antipodes; and *Mercurius Mastix* faithfully lashed all Scouts, Mercuries, Posts, Spies, and other Intelligencers." †† Besides the newspapers, also, the great political and religious questions of the time were debated, as already mentioned, in a prodigious multitude of separate pamphlets, which appear to have been read quite as universally and as eagerly. Of such pamphlets printed in the twenty years from the meeting of the Long Parliament to the Restora-

* See Chronological List of Newspapers from the Epoch of the Civil Wars, in Chalmers's Life of Ruddiman, pp. 404—448.
** See Chalmers's Life of Ruddiman, p. 114.
† In December, 1642, however, Spalding, the Aberdeen annalist, in a passage which Mr. Chalmers has quoted, tells us that "now printed papers *daily* came from London, called *Diurnal Occurrences*, declaring what is done in parliament."—Vol. 1 p. 336.
†† Chalmers, p. 116.

tion there are still preserved in the British Museum, forming the collection called the King's Pamphlets, no fewer than thirty thousand, which would give a rate of four or five new ones every day.

Where our modern newspapers begin, the series of our old chroniclers closes with Sir Richard Baker's Chronicle of the Kings of England, written while its author was confined for debt in the Fleet Prison, where he died in 1645, and first published in a folio volume in 1641. It was several times reprinted, and was a great favourite with our ancestors for two or three succeeding generations; but it has now lost all interest, except for a few passages relating to the author's own time. Baker, however, himself declares it to be compiled "with so great care and diligence, that, if all others were lost, this only will be sufficient to inform posterity of all passages memorable or worthy to be known." Sir Richard and his Chronicle are now popularly remembered principally as the trusted historical guides and authorities of Addison's incomparable Sir Roger de Coverley.*

Retrospect of the Commonwealth Literature.

It thus appears that the age of the Civil War and the Commonwealth does not present an absolute blank in the history of our highest literature; but, unless we are to except the Areopagitica of Milton, the Liberty of Prophesying, and a few other controversial or theological treatises of Jeremy Taylor, some publications by Fuller, and the successive apocalypses of the imperturbable dreamer of Norwich, no work of genius of the first class appeared in England in the twenty years from the meeting of the Long Parliament to the Restoration; and the literary productions having any enduring life in them at all, that are to be assigned to that space, make but a very scanty sprinkling. It was a time when men wrote and thought, as they acted,

* See Spectator, No. 329.

merely for the passing moment. The unprinted plays of Beaumont and Fletcher, indeed, were now sent to the press, as well as other dramatic works written in the last age; the theatres, by which they used to be published in another way, being shut up—a significant intimation, rather than anything else, that the great age of the drama was at an end. A new play continued to drop occasionally from the commonplace pen of Shirley—almost the solitary successor of the Shakespeares, the Fletchers, the Jonsons, the Massingers, the Fords, and the rest of that bright throng. All other poetry, as well as dramatic poetry, was nearly silent—hushed partly by the din of arms and of theological and political strife, more by the frown of triumphant puritanism, boasting to itself that it had put down all the other fine arts as well as poetry, never again to lift their heads in England. It is observable that even the confusion of the contest that lasted till after the king's death did not so completely banish the Muses, or drown their voice, as did the grim tranquillity under the sway of the parliament that followed. The time of the war, besides the treatises just alluded to of Milton, Taylor, Fuller, and Browne, produced the Cooper's Hill, and some other poetical pieces, by Denham, and the republication of the Comus and other early poems of Milton; the collection of the plays of Beaumont and Fletcher, and Cowley's volume entitled The Mistress, appeared in 1647, in the short interval of doubtful quiet between the first and the second war; the volume of Herrick's poetry was published the next year, while the second war was still raging, or immediately after its close; Lovelace's first volume, in 1649, probably before the execution of the king. Hobbes's Leviathan, and one or two other treatises of his, all written some time before, were printed at London in 1650 and 1651, while the author was resident in Paris. For some years from this date the blank is nearly absolute. Then, when the more liberal despotism of Cromwell had displaced the Presbyterian moroseness of the parliament, we have Fuller's Church History printed in 1655; Harrington's Oceana, and the collection of Cowley's poetry, in 1656; Browne's Hydriotaphia and Garden of Cyrus, in 1658; Lovelace's second volume, and Hales's Remains, in 1659; together with two or three philosophical publications by Hobbes, and a few short pieces in verse by Waller, of which the most famous is his Panegyric on Oliver Cromwell, written after the Protector's death, an occasion which also afforded its first considerable theme to the ripening genius of Dryden. It is to be noted, moreover, that, with one illustrious exception, none of the writers that have been named belonged to the prevailing faction. If Waller and Dryden took that side in their verses for a moment, it must be admitted that they both amply made up for their brief conformity; Denham, Browne, Taylor, Herrick, Lovelace, Fuller, Hales, Hobbes, Cowley, were all consistent, most of them ardent, royalists; Harrington was a theoretical republican, but even he was a royalist by personal attachments; Milton alone was in life and heart a Commonwealth-man and a Cromwellian.

POETRY OF MILTON.

From the appearance of his minor poems, in 1645, Milton had published no poetry, with the exception of a sonnet to Henry Lawes, the musician, prefixed to a collection of Psalm tunes by that composer in 1648, till he gave to the world his Paradise Lost, in Ten Books, in 1667. In 1671 appeared his Paradise Regained and Samson Agonistes; in 1673 a new edition of his minor poems, with nine new sonnets and other additions; and in 1674, what is properly the second edition of the Paradise Lost, now distributed (by the bisection of the seventh and tenth) into twelve books. He died on Sunday the 8th of November, in that year, when within about a month of completing the sixty-sixth year of his age. His prose writings have been already noticed. Verse, however, was the form in which his genius had earliest expressed itself, and also that in which he had first come forth as an author. Passing over his paraphrases of one or two Psalms, done at a still earlier age, we have abundant promise of the future great poet in his lines On the Death of a Fair Infant, beginning,

> O fairest flower, no sooner blown but blasted,

written in his seventeenth year; and still more in the College Exercise, written in his nineteenth year. A portion of this latter is almost as prophetic as it is beautiful; and, as the verses have not been much noticed,* we will here give a few of them:—

> Hail, native Language, that by sinews weak
> Didst move my first endeavouring tongue to speak,
> And mad'st imperfect words with childish trips,
> Half-unpronounced, slide through my infant lips:
> . . . . . .
> I have some naked thoughts that rove about,
> And loudly knock to have their passage out;
> And, weary of their place, do only stay
> Till thou hast deck'd them in their best array.
> . . . . . .
> Yet I had rather, if I were to choose,
> Thy service in some graver subject use,
> Such as may make thee search thy coffers round,
> Before thou clothe my fancy in fit sound;
> Such where the deep transported mind may soar
> Above the wheeling poles, and at heaven's door
> Look in, and see each blissful deity
> How he before the thunderous throne doth lie,
> Listening to what unshorn Apollo sings
> To the touch of golden wires, while Hebe brings
> Immortal nectar to her kingly sire:
> Then, passing through the spheres of watchful fire,
> And misty regions of wide air next under,
> And hills of snow, and lofts of piled thunder,
> May tell at length how green-eyed Neptune raves,
> In heaven's defiance mustering all his waves;
> Then sing of secret things that came to pass
> When beldame Nature in her cradle was;
> And last of kings, and queens, and heroes old,
> Such as the wise Demodocus once told
> In solemn songs at King Alcinous' feast,
> While sad Ulysses' soul and all the rest
> Are held with his melodious harmony
> In willing chains and sweet captivity.

---

* Mr. Hallam, in his work on the Literature of Europe (III. 269) inadvertently assumes that we have no English verse of Milton's written before his twenty-second year.

This was written in 1627. Fourteen years later, after his return from Italy, where some of his juvenile Latin compositions, and some others in the same language, which as he tells us, he "had shifted in scarcity of books and conveniences to patch up amongst them, were received with written encomiums, which the Italian is not forward to bestow on men of this side the Alps;" and when assenting in so far to these commendations, and not less to an inward prompting which now grew daily upon him, he has ventured to indulge the hope that, by labour and study—"which I take," he nobly says, "to be my portion in this life"—joined with the strong propensity of nature, he "might perhaps. leave something so written in after-times as they should not willingly let it die"—he continued still inclined to fix all the industry and art he could unite to the adorning of his native tongue—or, as he goes on to say, "to be an interpreter and relater of the best and sagest things among mine own citizens, throughout this island, in the motherdialect;—that what the greatest and choicest wits of Athens, Rome, or modern Italy, and those Hebrews of old, did for their country, I, in my proportion, with this over and above of being a Christian, might do for mine; not caring to be once named abroad, though perhaps I could attain to that, but content with these British islands as my world;" and he again, more distinctly than before, though still only in general expressions, announced the great design, "of highest hope and hardest attempting," which he proposed to himself one day to accomplish—whether in the epic form, as exemplified by Homer, Virgil, and Tasso, or after the dramatic, "wherein Sophocles and Euripides reign"—or in the style of "those magnific odes and hymns" of Pindarus and Callimachus; not forgetting that of all these kinds of writing the highest models are to be found in the Holy Scriptures —in the Book of Job, in the Song of Solomon and the Apocalypse of St. John, in the frequent songs interspersed throughout the Law and the Prophets. "The thing which I had to say," concluded this remarkable announcement, "and those intentions which have lived within me ever since I could conceive myself anything worth to my country, I return to crave excuse that urgent reason hath plucked from me by an abortive and foredated discovery. And the accomplishment of them lies not but in a power above man's to promise; but that none hath by more studious ways endeavoured, and with more unwearied spirit that none shall, that I dare almost aver of myself, as far as life and free leisure will extend; and that the land had once enfranchised herself from this impertinent yoke of prelaty, under whose inquisitorious and tyrannical duncery no free and splendid wit can flourish. Neither do I think it shame to covenant with any knowing reader, that for some few years yet I may go on trust with him toward the payment of what I am now indebted; as being a work not to be raised from the heat of youth or the vapours of wine, like that which flows at waste from the pen of some vulgar amourist, or the trencher fury of a rhyming parasite; nor to be obtained by the invocation of dame Memory and her Siren daughters; but by devout prayer to that eternal Spirit, who can enrich with all utterance and knowledge, and sends out his seraphim, with the hallowed fire of his altar, to touch and purify the lips of whom he pleases. To this must be added industrious and select reading, steady observation, insight into all seemly and generous arts and affairs. Till which in some measure be accomplished, at mine own peril and cost I refuse not to sustain this expectation from as many as are not loth to hazard as much credulity upon the best pledges that I can give them."*

Before this, there had appeared in print of Milton's poetry only his Comus and Lycidas; the former in 1637, the latter with some other Cambridge verses on the same occasion, the loss at sea of his friend Edward King, in 1638; but, besides some of his sonnets and other minor pieces, he had also written the fragment entitled Arcades, and the two

* The Reason of Church Government urged against Prelaty (published in 1641).

companion poems the L'Allegro and the Il Penseroso. These productions already attested the worthy successor of the greatest writers of English verse in the preceding age— recalling the fancy and the melody of the minor poems of Spenser and Shakespeare, and of the Faithful Shepherdess of Fletcher. The Comus, indeed, might be considered as an avowed imitation of the last-mentioned production. The resemblance in poetical character between the two sylvan dramas of Fletcher and Milton is very close; and they may be said to stand apart from all else in our literature—for Ben Jonson's Sad Shepherd is not for a moment to be compared with either, and in the Midsummer Night's Dream, Shakespeare, ever creative, passionate, and dramatic beyond all other writers, has soared so high above both, whether we look to the supernatural part of his fable or to its scenes of human interest, that we are little reminded of his peopled woodlands, his fairies, his lovers, or his glorious "rude mechanicals," either by the Faithful Shepherdess or the Comus. Of these two compositions, Milton's must be admitted to have the higher moral inspiration, and it is also the more elaborate and exact as a piece of writing; but in all that goes to make up dramatic effect, in the involvement and conduct of the story, and in the eloquence of natural feeling, Fletcher's is decidedly superior. It has been remarked that even in Shakespeare's early narrative poems— his Venus and Adonis, and his Tarquin and Lucrece—we may discern the future great dramatist by the full and unwithholding abandonment with which he there projects himself into whatever character he brings forward, and the power of vivid conception with which he realizes the visionary scene, and brings it around him almost in the distinctness of broad daylight, as shown by a peculiar directness and life of expression evidently coming everywhere unsought, and escaping from his pen, one might almost say without his own consciousness,—without apparently any feeling, at least, of either art exercised or feat achieved.*

* See this illustrated in Coleridge's Biographia Literaria, vol. II.

In the case of Milton, on the contrary, his first published poem and earliest poetical attempt of any considerable extent, although in the dramatic form, affords abundant evidence that his genius was not dramatic. Comus is an exquisitely beautiful poem, but nearly destitute of everything we more especially look for in a drama—of passion, of character, of story, of action or movement of any kind. It flows on in a continued stream of eloquence, fancy, and most melodious versification; but there is no dialogue, properly so called, no replication of diverse emotions or natures; it is Milton alone who sings or declaims all the while,—sometimes of course on one side of the argument, sometimes on the other, and not, it may be, without changing his attitude and the tone of his voice, but still speaking only from one head, from one heart, from one ever-present and ever-dominant constitution of being. And from this imprisonment within himself Milton never escapes, either in his dramatic or in his other poetry; it is the characteristic which distinguishes him not only from our great dramatists, but also from other great epic and narrative poets. His poetry has been sometimes described as to an unusual degree wanting in the expression of his own personal feelings; and, notwithstanding some remarkable instances of exception, not only in his minor pieces, but in his great epic, the remark is true in a certain sense. He is no habitual brooder over his own emotions, no self-dissector, no systematic resorter for inspiration to the accidents of his own personal history. His subject in some degree forbade this; his proud and lofty nature still more withheld him from it. But, although disdaining thus to picture himself at full length either for our pity or admiration, he has yet impressed the stamp of his own individuality—of his own character, moral as well as intellectual—as deep on all he has written as if his theme had been ever so directly himself. Compare him in this respect with Homer. We scarcely conceive of the old Greek poet as having a sentient existence at all, any more than we do of the sea or the breezes of heaven, whose music his continuous, undulating verse, ever various, ever the same, resembles. Who in the delineation of the wrath of Achilles finds a trace of the temper or character of the delineator? Who in Milton's Satan does not recognize much of Milton himself? But, although the spirit of his poetry is thus essentially egotistic, the range of his poetic power is not thereby confined within narrow limits. He had not the "myriad-minded" nature of Shakespeare—the all-penetrating sympathy by which the greatest of dramatists could transform himself for the time into any one of the other existences around him, no matter how high, no matter how low: conceive the haughty genius of Milton employed in the task of developing such a character as Justice Shallow, or Bottom the weaver, or a score of others to be found in the long, various, brilliant procession headed by Falstaff and ending with Dogberry! Anything of this kind he could scarcely have performed much better than the most ordinarily gifted of the sons of men; he had no more the wit or humour requisite for it than he had the power of intense and universal sympathy. But his proper region was still a vast one; and there, his vision, though always tinged with the colour of his own passions and opinions, was, notwithstanding, both as far reaching and as searching as any poet's ever was. In its style or form his poetry may be considered to belong rudimentally to the same Italian school with that of the greatest of his predecessors—of Spenser and of Shakespeare, if not also of Chaucer. But, as of these others, so it is true of him, that the inspiration of his Italian models is most perceptible in his earlier and minor verses, and that in his more mature and higher efforts he enriched this original basis of his poetic manner with so much of a different character, partly derived from other foreign sources, partly peculiar to himself, that the mode of conception and expression which he ultimately thus worked out is most correctly described by calling it his own. Conversant as he was with the language and literature of Italy, his poetry probably acquired what it has of Italian in its character principally through the medium of the elder poets of his own country; and it is, accordingly, still more English than Italian. Much of its inner spirit, and something also of its outward fashion, is of Hebrew derivation: it may be affirmed that from the fountain of no other foreign literature did Milton drink with so much eagerness as from this, and that by no other was his genius so much nourished and strengthened. Not a little, also, one so accomplished in the lore of classic antiquity must needs have acquired from that source; the tones of the poetry of Greece and Rome are heard more or less audibly everywhere in that of the great epic poet of England. But do we go too far in holding that in what he has actually achieved in his proper domain, the modern writer rises high "above all Greek, above all Roman fame?" Where in the poetry of the ancient world shall we find anything which approaches the richness and beauty, still less the sublimity, of the most triumphant passages in Paradise Lost? The First Book of that poem is probably the most splendid and perfect of human compositions—the one, that is to say, which unites these two qualities in the highest degree; and the Fourth is as unsurpassed for grace and luxuriance as that is for magnificence of imagination. And, though these are perhaps the two greatest books in the poem, taken each as a whole, there are passages in every one of the other books equal or almost equal to the finest in these. And worthy of the thoughts that breathe are the words that burn. A tide of gorgeous eloquence rolls on from beginning to end, like a river of molten gold; outblazing, we may surely say, everything of the kind in any other poetry. Finally, Milton's blank verse, both for its rich and varied music and its exquisite adaptation, would in itself almost deserve to be styled poetry, without the words; alone of all our poets, before or since, he has brought out the full capabilities of the language in that form of composition. Indeed, out of the drama, he is still our only great blank verse writer. Compared to his, the blank verse of no other of our narrative or didactic poets, unless we are to except a few of the happiest attempts at the direct imitation of his pauses and cadences, reads like anything else than a sort of muffled rhyme—rhyme spoilt by the ends being blunted or broken off. Who remembers, who can repeat, any narrative blank verse but his? In whose ear does any other linger? What other has the true organ tone which makes the music of this form of verse—either the grandeur or the sweetness?

It is natural, in comparing, or contrasting, Milton's Paradise Lost with his Paradise Regained, to think of the two great Homeric epics; the Iliad commonly believed by antiquity to have proceeded from the inspired poet in the vigour and glow of his manhood or middle age, the Odyssey to reflect the milder radiance of his imagination in the afternoon or evening of his life. It has been common accordingly to apply to the case of the English poet also the famous similitude of Longinus, and to say that in the Paradise Regained we have the sun on his descent, the same indeed as ever in majesty ($\tau\grave{o}$ $\mu\acute{\epsilon}\gamma\epsilon\vartheta o\varsigma$), but deprived of his overpowering ardour ($\delta\acute{\iota}\chi\alpha$ $\tau\widetilde{\eta}\varsigma$ $\sigma\varphi o\delta\varrho\acute{o}\tau\eta\tau o\varsigma$). Some have gone farther, not claiming for the Paradise Regained the honour of being sunshine at all, but only holding it worthy of being applauded in the spirit and after the fashion in which Pope has eulogized the gracious though not dazzling qualities of his friend Martha Blount:—

> So, when the sun's broad beam has tired the sight,
> All mild ascends the moon's more sober light;
> Serene in virgin modesty she shines,
> And unobserved the glaring orb declines.

An ingenious theory has been put forth by one of the editors of the Paradise Regained, Mr. Charles Dunster; he conceives that Milton designed this poem for an example of what he has himself in the remarkable passage of his Reason of Church Government, to which we have already had occasion to refer, spoken of as the *brief epic*, and distinguished from the *great and diffuse epic*, such as those of Homer and of Virgil, and his own Paradise Lost. Milton's words in full are:—"Time serves not now, and, perhaps, I might seem too profuse, to give any certain account of what the mind at home, in the spacious circuits of her musing, hath liberty to propose to herself, though of highest hope and hardest attempting; whether that epic form, whereof the two poems of Homer, and those other two of Virgil and Tasso, are a diffuse, and the book of Job a brief, model." Dunster accordingly thinks that we may suppose the model which Milton set before him in his Paradise Regained to have been in a great measure the book of Job.*

But surely the comparison which the companionship or sequence of the two Miltonic epics most forcibly suggests to a true feeling of both their resemblance and their difference, and of the prevailing spirit that animates each, is that of the Old and the New Testament. The one is distinctively Hebrew, the other as distinctively Christian. With much in common, they have also, like the two religions, and the two collections of sacred books, much in which they are unlike, and in a certain sense opposed to one another, both in manner and in sentiment. The poetry of the Paradise Lost, all life and movement, is to that of the Paradise Regained what a conflagration is to a sunlit landscape. In the one we have the grandeur of the old worship, in the other the simplicity of the new. The one addresses itself more to the sense, the other to the understanding. In respect either of force or of variety, either of intense and burning passion or of imaginative power mingling and blending all the wonders of brightness and gloom, there can be no comparison between them. There is the same poetic art, it is true, in both poems; they are more unmistakeably products of the same mind, perhaps, than are the Iliad and the Odyssey; and yet the difference between them in tone and character is greater than that between the two Greek epics. It is in some respects like the difference between an oil-painting and a painting in water-colours. The mere brevity of the one as

---

* Paradise Regained; with notes. By Charles Dunster, M.A. 4to. Lond. 1795. p. 2.

compared with the other would stamp it as a work of inferior pretension, and it is still more limited in subject or scope than it is in dimensions. The Paradise Regained must be considered, in fact, as only an appendage to the Paradise Lost. Yet, comparatively short as it is, the thread of the narrative is felt to be spun out and over-much attenuated. It contains some highly finished and exquisite passages; but perhaps the only poetical quality in which it can be held to match, if it does not sometimes even surpass, the Paradise Lost, is picturesqueness. In that it more resembles the L'Allegro and the Il Penseroso than it does its companion epic. Even the argumentative eloquence, of which it is chiefly made up, brilliant as it is, is far from being equal to the best of that in the Paradise Lost. It has the same ingenuity and logic, with as much, or perhaps even more, concentration in the expression; but, unavoidably, it may be, from the circumstances of the case, it has not either the same glow and splendour or even the same tone of real feeling. The fallen spirits thronging Pandemonium, or stretched on the burning lake before that gorgeous pile "rose like an exhalation," consult and debate, in their misery and anxious perplexity, with an accent of human earnestness which it was impossible to give either to the conscious sophistry of their chief in that other scene or to the wisdom more than human by which he is refuted and repelled.

It is commonly said that Milton himself professed to prefer the Paradise Regained to the Paradise Lost. The probability is that, if he asserted the former to be the better poem of the two, it was only in a qualified sense, or with reference to something else than its poetical merits, and in the same feeling with which he explained the general prevalence of the opposite opinion by attributing it to most people having a much stronger feeling of regret for the loss of Paradise than desire for the recovery of it, or at least inclination for the only way in which it was to be recovered. It was very characteristic of him, however, to be best pleased with what he had last produced, as well as to be only confirmed in his partiality by having the general voice against him and by his contempt for what of extravagance and injustice there was in the popular depreciation of the new poem. He was in all things by temper and mental constitution essentially a partisan; seeing clearly, indeed, all that was to be said on both sides of any question, but never for all that remaining in suspense between them, or hesitating to make up his mind and to take his place distinctly on one side. This is shown by the whole course of his life. Nor is it less expressively proclaimed not only by the whole tone and manner of his poetry, everywhere so ardent, impetuous, and dogmatical, and so free from the faintest breath either of suspicion or of any kind of self-distrust, but even in that argumentative eloquence which is one of its most remarkable characteristics. For one of the chief necessary conditions of the existence of oratorical or debating power, and, indeed, of every kind of fighting ability, is that it should, at one and the same time, both feel passionately in favour of its own side of the question and discern clearly the strength of the adverse position. Whatever may be the fact as to his alleged preference of the Paradise Regained to the Paradise Lost, Milton has, at any rate, pronounced judgment in a sufficiently decisive and uncompromising way upon another point in regard to which both these works stand contrasted with much of his earlier poetry. We refer to his vehement denunciation, in a notice prefixed to the Paradise Lost,* of rhyme as being, in all circumstances, for he makes no exception, "a thing of itself, to all judicious ears, trivial and of no true musical delight," and as having no claim to be regarded as anything else than the barbarous invention of a barbarous age, and a mere jingle and life-repressing bondage. We certainly rejoice that the Paradise Lost is not written in rhyme; but we are very glad that these

---

* This notice, commonly headed *The Verse* in modern editions of the poem, is found in three of the five various forms of the first edition (1667, 1668, and 1669), and there bears the superscription *The Printer to the Reader;* but there can be no doubt that it is Milton's own.

strong views were not taken up by the great poet till after he had produced his L'Allegro and Il Penseroso, his Lycidas and his Sonnets.

Cowley.

The poetry of Milton, though principally produced after the Restoration, belongs in everything but in date to the preceding age; and this is also nearly as true of that of Cowley. Abraham Cowley, born in London in 1618, published his first volume of verse, under the title of Poetic Blossoms, in 1633, when he was yet only a boy of fifteen: one piece contained in this publication, indeed—The Tragical History of Pyramus and Thisbe—was written when he was only in his tenth year. The four books of his unfinished epic entitled Davideis were mostly written while he was a student at Trinity College, Cambridge. His pastoral drama of Love's Riddle, and his Latin comedy called Naufragium Joculare, were both published in 1638. In 1647 appeared his collection of amatory poems entitled The Mistress, and in 1653 his comedy of The Guardian, afterwards altered, and republished as The Cutter of Coleman Street. After the Restoration he collected such of his pieces as he thought worth preserving, and republished them, together with some additional productions, of which the most important were his Davideis, and his Pindarique Odes.

Few poets have been more popular, or more praised, in their own time than Cowley. Milton is said to have declared that the three greatest English poets were Spenser, Shakespeare, and Cowley; though it does not follow that he held all three to be equally great. Sir John Denham, in some verses on Cowley's Death and Burial on the 3rd of August, 1667, in Westminster Abbey, sets him above all the English poets that had gone before him, and prophesies that posterity will hold him to have been equalled by Virgil alone among those of antiquity. For a long time, too, his works appear to have been more generally read than those of any other English poet, if a judgment may be formed from the frequency with which they were reprinted, and the numerous copies of them in various forms that still exist.* This popular favour they seem to have shared with those of Donne, whose legitimate successor Cowley was considered to be; or rather, when the poetry of Donne became obsolete or unfashionable, that of Cowley took its place in the reading and admiration of the poetical part of the public. Cowley, indeed, is in the main a mere modernization and dilution of Donne. With the same general characteristics of manner he is somewhat less forced and fantastical, a good deal less daring in every way, but unfortunately also infinitely less poetical. Everything about him, in short, is less deep, strong, and genuine. His imagination is tinsel, or mere surface gilding, compared to Donne's solid gold; his wit little better than word-catching, to the profound meditative quaintness of the elder poet; and of passion, with which all Donne's finest lines are tremulous, Cowley has none. Considerable grace and dignity occasionally distinguish his Pindaric Odes (which, however, are Pindaric only in name); and he has shown much elegant playfulness of style and fancy in his translations from and imitations of Anacreon, and in some other verses written in the same manner. As for what he intends for love verses, some of them are pretty enough frost-work; but the only sort of love there is in them is the love of point and sparkle.

BUTLER.

This manner of writing is more fitly applied by another celebrated poet of the same date, Samuel Butler, the immortal author of Hudibras. Butler (b. 1612, d. 1680) is said to have written most of his great poem during the inter-

* A twelfth edition of the collection formed by Cowley himself was published by Tonson in 1721.

regnum; but the first part of it was not published till 1663. The poetry of Butler has been very happily designated as merely the comedy of that style of composition which Donne and Cowley practised in its more serious form—the difference between the two modes of writing being much the same with that which is presented by a countenance of a peculiar cast of features when solemnized by deep reflection, and the same countenance when lighted up by cheerfulness or distorted by mirth.* And it may be added, that the gayer and more animated expression is here, upon the whole, the more natural. The quantity of explosive matter of all kinds which Butler has contrived to pack up in his verses is amazing; it is crack upon crack, flash upon flash, from the first line of his long poem to the last. Much of this incessant bedazzlement is, of course, merely verbal, or otherwise of the humblest species of wit; but an infinite number of the happiest things are also thrown out. And Hudibras is far from being all mere broad farce. Butler's power of arguing in verse, in his own way, may almost be put on a par with Dryden's in his; and, perseveringly as he devotes himself upon system to the exhibition of the ludicrous and grotesque, he sometimes surprises us with a sudden gleam of the truest beauty of thought and expression breaking out from the midst of the usual rattling fire of smartnesses and conundrums—as when in one place he exclaims of a thin cloud drawn over the moon—

> Mysterious veil; of brightness made,
> At once her lustre and her shade!

He must also be allowed to tell his story and to draw his characters well, independently of his criticisms.

WALLER.

The most celebrated among the minor poets of the period between the Restoration and the Revolution was

* Scott, in Life of Dryden.

Waller. Edmund Waller, born in 1605, had, in point of fact, announced himself as a writer of verse before the close of the reign of James I., by his lines on the escape of Prince Charles at the port of San Andero, in the Bay of Biscay, on his return from Spain, in September, 1623; and he continued to write till after the accession of James II., in whose reign he died, in the year 1687. His last production was the little poem concluding with one of his happiest, one of his most characteristic, and one of his best-known passages:—

> The soul's dark cottage, battered and decayed,
> Lets in new light through chinks that time has made;
> Stronger by weakness, wiser men become
> As they draw near to their eternal home:
> Leaving the old, both worlds at once they view,
> That stand upon the threshold of the new.

Fenton, his editor, tells us that a number of poems on religious subjects, to which these verses refer, were mostly written when he was about [above?] eighty years old; and he has himself intimated that his bodily faculties were now almost gone:—

> When we for age could neither read nor write,
> The subject made us able to indite.

Waller, therefore, as well as Milton, Cowley, and Butler, may be considered to have formed his manner in the last age; but his poetry does not belong to the old English school even so much as that of either Butler or Cowley. The contemporaries of the earlier portion of his long career were Carew and Lovelace; and with them he is properly to be classed in respect of poetical style and manner. Both Lovelace and Carew, however, as has been already intimated, have more passion than Waller, who, with all his taste and elegance, was incapable of either expressing or feeling anything very lofty or generous—being, in truth, poet as he was, a very mean-souled description of person, as his despicable political course sufficiently evinced. His poetry accordingly is beyond the reach of critical animadversion on the score of such extravagance as is sometimes prompted by strong emotion. Waller is always perfectly master of himself, and idolizes his mistress with quite as much coolness and self-possession as he flatters his prince. But, although cold and unaffecting at all times, he occasionally rises to much dignity of thought and manner. His panegyric on Cromwell, the offering of his gratitude to the Protector for the permission granted to him of returning to England after ten years' exile, is one of the most graceful pieces of adulation ever offered by poetry to power: and the poet is here probably more sincere than in most of his effusions, for the occasion was one on which he was likely to be moved to more than usual earnestness of feeling. A few years after he welcomed Charles II. on his restoration to the throne of his ancestors in another poem, which has been generally considered a much less spirited composition: Fenton accounts for the falling off by the author's advance in the meanwhile from his forty-ninth to his fifty-fifth year —"from which time," he observes, "his genius began to decline apace from its meridian;" but the poet himself assigned another reason:—when Charles frankly told him that he thought his own panegyric much inferior to Cromwell's, "Sir," replied Waller, "we poets never succeed so well in writing truth as in fiction." Perhaps the true reason, after all, might be that his majesty's return to England was not quite so exciting a subject to Mr. Waller's muse as his own return had been. One thing must be admitted in regard to Waller's poetry; it is free from all mere verbiage and empty sound; if he rarely or never strikes a very powerful note, there is at least always something for the fancy or the understanding, as well as for the ear, in what he writes. He abounds also in ingenious thoughts, which he dresses to the best advantage, and exhibits with great transparency of style. Eminent, however, as he is in his class, he must be reckoned in that subordinate class of poets who think and express themselves chiefly in similitudes, not among those who conceive and write passionately and metaphorically.

He had a decorative and illuminating, but not a transforming imagination.

MARVEL.

The chief writer of verse on the popular side after the Restoration was Andrew Marvel, the noble-minded member for Hull, the friend of Milton, and, in that age of brilliant profligacy, renowned alike as the first of patriots and of wits. Marvel, the son of the Rev. Andrew Marvel, master of the grammar-school of Hull, was born there in 1620, and died in 1678. His poetical genius has scarcely had justice done to it. He is the author of a number of satires in verse, in which a rich vein of vigorous, though often coarse, humour runs through a careless, extemporaneous style, and which did prodigious execution in the party warfare of the day; but some of his other poetry, mostly perhaps written in the earlier part of his life, is eminent both for the delicate bloom of the sentiment and for grace of form. His Song of the Exiles, beginning "Where the remote Bermudas ride," is a gem of melody, picturesqueness, and sentiment, nearly without a flaw, and is familiar to every lover of poetry. The following verses, which are less known, are exquisitely elegant and tuneful. They are entitled The Picture of T. C. in a Prospect of Flowers:—

> See with what simplicity
> This nymph begins her golden days!
> In the green grass she loves to lie,
> And there with her fair aspect tames
> The wilder flowers, and gives them names:
> But only with the roses plays,
> And them does tell
> What colour best becomes them, and what smell.
>
> Who can foretell for what high cause
> This darling of the gods was born?
> See this is she whose chaster laws
> The wanton Love shall one day fear,
> And, under her command severe,
> See his bow broke and ensigns torn.
> Happy who can
> Appease this virtuous enemy of man!

Craik, Engl. Lit. II.

> O then let me in time compound,
> And parley with those conquering eyes;
> Ere they have tried their force to wound,
> Ere with their glancing wheels they drive
> In triumph over hearts that strive,
> And them that yield but more despise.
> Let me be laid
> Where I may see the glory from some shade.
>
> Meantime, whilst every verdant thing
> Itself does at thy beauty charm,[1]
> Reform the errors of the spring:
> Make that the tulips may have share
> Of sweetness, seeing they are fair;
> And roses of their thorns disarm:
> But most procure
> That violets may a longer age endure.
>
> But oh, young beauty of the woods,
> Whom nature courts with fruits and flowers,
> Gather the flowers, but spare the buds;
> Lest Flora, angry at thy crime
> To kill her infants in their prime,
> Should quickly make the example yours;
> And, ere we see,
> Nip in the blossom all our hopes in thee.

Certainly neither Carew, nor Waller, nor any other court poet of that day, has produced anything in the same style finer than these lines. But Marvel's more elaborate poetry is not confined to love songs and other such light exercises of an ingenious and elegant fancy. Witness his verses on Milton's Paradise Lost—"When I beheld the poet blind, yet bold"—which have throughout almost the dignity, and in parts more than the strength, of Waller.

Other Minor Poets.

Of the other minor poets of this date we shall only mention the names of a few of the most distinguished. Sir Charles Sedley is the Suckling of the time of Charles II., with less impulsiveness and more insinuation, but a kindred gaiety and sprightliness of fancy, and an answering liveliness and at the same time courtly ease and elegance of diction.

---

[1] *Charm itself*, that is, delight itself.

King Charles, a good judge of such matters, was accustomed to say that Sedley's style, either in writing or discourse, would be the standard of the English tongue; and his contemporary, the Duke of Buckingham (Villiers) used to call his exquisite art of expression *Sedley's witchcraft*. Sedley's genius early ripened and bore fruit: he was born only two or three years before the breaking out of the Civil War; and he was in high reputation as a poet and a wit within six or seven years after the Restoration. He survived both the Revolution and the century, dying in the year 1701. Sedley's fellow debauchee, the celebrated Earl of Rochester (Wilmot)—although the brutal grossness of the greater part of his verse has deservedly made it and its author infamous —was perhaps a still greater genius. There is immense strength and pregnancy of expression in some of the best of his compositions, careless and unfinished as they are. Rochester had not completed his thirty-third year when he died, in July 1680. Of the poetical productions of the other court wits of Charles's reign the principal are, the Duke of Buckingham's satirical comedy of the Rehearsal, which was very effective when first produced, and still enjoys a great reputation, though it would probably be thought but a heavy joke now by most readers not carried away by the prejudice in its favour; the Earl of Roscommon's very commonplace Essay on Translated Verse; and the Earl of Dorset's lively and well-known song, "To all you ladies now on land," written at sea the night before the engagement with the Dutch on the 3rd of June, 1665, or rather professing to have been then written, for the asserted poetic tranquillity of the noble author in expectation of the morrow's fight has been disputed. The Marquis of Halifax and Lord Godolphin were also writers of verse at this date; but neither of them has left anything worth remembering. Among the minor poets of the time, however, we ought not to forget Charles Cotton, best known for his humorous, though somewhat coarse, travesties of Virgil and Lucian, and for his continuation of Izaak Walton's Treatise on Angling, and his fine idiomatic translation of Montaigne's Essays, but also the author of some short original pieces in verse, of much fancy and liveliness. One entitled an Ode to Winter, in particular, has been highly praised by Wordsworth.

DRYDEN.

By far the most illustrious name among the English poets of the latter half of the seventeenth century—if we exclude Milton as belonging properly to the preceding age—is that of John Dryden. Born in 1632, Dryden produced his first known composition in verse in 1649, his lines on the death of Lord Hastings, a young nobleman of great promise, who was suddenly cut off by small-pox, on the eve of his intended marriage, in that year. This earliest of Dryden's poems is in the most ambitious style of the school of Donne and Cowley: Donne himself, indeed, has scarcely penned anything quite so extravagant as one passage, in which the fancy of the young poet runs riot among the phenomena of the loathsome disease to which Lord Hastings had fallen a victim:—

> So many spots, like naeves on Venus' soil,
> One jewel set off with so many a foil:
> Blisters with pride swell'd, which through 's flesh did sprout
> Like rose-buds stuck i' the lily skin about.
> Each little pimple had a tear in it,
> To wail the fault its rising did commit:—

and so forth. Almost the only feature of the future Dryden which this production discloses is his deficiency in sensibility or heart; exciting as the occasion was, it does not contain an affecting line. Perhaps, on comparing his imitation with Donne's own poetry, so instinct with tenderness and passion, Dryden may have seen or felt that his own wanted the very quality which was the light and life of that of his master; at any rate, wiser than Cowley, who had the same reason for shunning a competition with Donne, he abandoned this style with his first attempt, and, indeed, for anything that appears, gave up the writing of poetry for some years altogether. His next verses of any consequence are dated nine years later,—his Heroic Stanzas on the death of Oliver Cromwell,—and, destitute as they are of the vigorous conception and full and easy flow of versification which he afterwards attained, they are free from any trace of the elaborate and grotesque absurdity of the Elegy on Lord Hastings. His Astræa Redux, or poem on the return of the king, produced two years after, evinces a growing freedom and command of style. But it is in his Annus Mirabilis, written in 1666, that his genius breaks forth for the first time with any promise of that full effulgence, at which it ultimately arrived; here, in spite of the incumbrance of a stanza (the quatrain of alternately rhyming heroics) which he afterwards wisely exchanged for a more manageable kind of verse, we have much both of the nervous diction and the fervid fancy which characterize his latest and best works. From this date to the end of his days Dryden's life was one long literary labour; eight original poems of considerable length, many shorter pieces, twenty-eight dramas, and several volumes of poetical translation from Chaucer, Boccaccio, Ovid, Theocritus, Lucretius, Horace, Juvenal, Persius, and Virgil, together with numerous discourses in prose, some of them very long and elaborate, attest the industry as well as the fertility of a mind which so much toil and so many draughts upon its resources were so far from exhausting, that its powers continued not only to exert themselves with unimpaired elasticity, but to grow stronger and brighter, to the last. The genius of Dryden certainly did not, as that of Waller is said to have done, begin "to decline apace from its meridian" after he had reached his fifty-fifth year. His famous Alexander's Feast and his Fables, which are among his happiest performances, were the last he produced, and were published together in the year 1700, only a few months before his death, at the age of sixty-eight.

Dryden has commonly been considered to have founded a new school of English poetry; but perhaps it would be more strictly correct to regard him as having only carried to higher perfection—perhaps to the highest to which it has yet been brought—a style of poetry which had been cultivated long before his day. The satires of Hall and of Marston, and also the Nosce Teipsum of Sir John Davies, all published before the end of the sixteenth century, not to refer to other less eminent examples, may be classed as of the same school with his poetry. It is a school very distinguishable from that to which Milton and the greatest of our elder poets belong, deriving its spirit and character, as it does, chiefly from the ancient Roman classic poetry, whereas the other is mainly the offspring of the middle ages, of Gothic manners and feelings and the Romance or Provençal literature. The one therefore may be called, with sufficient propriety, the classic, the other the romantic school of poetry. But it seems to be a mistake to assume that the former first arose in England after the Restoration, under the influence of the imitation of the French, which then became fashionable; the most that can be said is, that the French taste which then became prevalent among us may have encouraged its revival; for undoubtedly what has been called the classic school of poetry had been cultivated by English writers at a much earlier date; nor is there any reason to suppose that the example of the modern poetry of France had had any share in originally turning our own into that channel. Marston and Hall, and Sackville in his Ferrex and Porrex, and Ben Jonson in his comedies and tragedies, and the other early writers of English poetry in the classic vein, appear not to have imitated any French poets, but to have gone to the fountain-head, and sought in the productions of the Roman poets themselves,—in the plays of Terence and Seneca, and the satires of Juvenal and Persius,—for examples and models. Nay, even Dryden, at a later period, probably formed himself almost exclusively upon the same originals and upon the works of these his predecessors among his own countrymen, and was little, if at all, indebted to or influenced by any French pattern. His poetry, unlike as it is to that of Milton or Spenser, has still a thoroughly English character—an English force and heartiness, and, with all its classicality, not a little even of the freedom and luxuriance of the more genuine English style. Smooth Waller, who preceded him, may have learned something from the modern French poets; and so may Pope, who came after him; but Dryden's fiery energy and "full-resounding line" have nothing in common with them in spirit or manner. Without either creative imagination or any power of pathos, he is in argument, in satire, and in declamatory magnificence, the greatest of our poets. His poetry, indeed, is not the highest kind of poetry, but in that kind he stands unrivalled and unapproached. Pope, his great disciple, who, in correctness, in neatness, and in the brilliancy of epigrammatic point, has outshone his master, has not come near him in easy flexible vigour, in indignant vehemence, in narrative rapidity, any more than he has in sweep and variety of versification. Dryden never writes coldly, or timidly, or drowsily. The movement of verse always sets him on fire, and whatever he produces is a coinage hot from the brain, not slowly scraped or pinched into shape, but struck out as from a die with a few stout blows or a single wrench of the screw. It is this fervour especially which gives to his personal sketches their wonderful life and force: his Absalom and Achitophel is the noblest portrait-gallery in poetry.

It is chiefly as a dramatic writer that Dryden can be charged with the imitation of French models. Of his plays, nearly thirty in number, the comedies for the most part in prose, the tragedies in rhyme, few have much merit considered as entire works, although there are brilliant passages and spirited scenes in most of them. Of the whole number, he has told us that his tragedy of All for Love, or the World well Lost (founded on the story of Antony and Cleopatra), was the only play he wrote for himself; the rest, he admits, were sacrifices to the vitiated taste of the age. His Almanzor, or the Conquest of Granada (in two parts), although extravagant, is also full of genius. Of his comedies, the Spanish Friar is perhaps the best; it has some most effective scenes.

DRAMATISTS.

Many others of the poets of this age whose names have been already noticed were also dramatists. Milton's Comus was never acted publicly, nor his Samson Agonistes at all. Cowley's Love's Riddle and Cutter of Coleman Street were neither of them originally written for the stage; but the latter was brought out in one of the London theatres after the Restoration, and was also revived about the middle of the last century. Waller altered the fifth act of Beaumont and Fletcher's Maid's Tragedy, making his additions to the blank verse of the old dramatists in rhyme, as he states in a prologue:—

> In this old play what's new we have expressed
> In rhyming verse distinguish'd from the rest;
> That, as the Rhone its hasty way does make
> (Not mingling waters) through Geneva's lake,
> So, having here the different styles in view,
> You may compare the former with the new.

Villiers, Duke of Buckingham, besides his Rehearsal, wrote a farce entitled the Battle of Sedgmoor, and also altered Beaumont and Fletcher's comedy of The Chances. The tragedy of Valentinian of the same writers was altered by the Earl of Rochester. Sedley wrote three comedies, mostly in prose, and three tragedies, one in rhyme and two in blank verse. And Davenant is the author of twenty-five tragedies, comedies, and masques, produced between 1629 and his death in 1668. But the most eminent dramatic names of this era are those of Thomas Otway, Nathaniel Lee, John Crowne, Sir George Etherege, William Wycherley, and Thomas Southerne. Of six tragedies and four comedies written by Otway, his tragedies of the Orphan and Venice Preserved still sustain his fame and popularity as the most pathetic and tear-drawing of all our dramatists. Their licentiousness has necessarily banished his comedies from the stage, with most of those of his contemporaries. Lee has also great tenderness, with much more fire and imagination than Otway; of his pieces, eleven in number—all tragedies—his Theodosius, or the Force of Love, and his Rival Queens, or Alexander the Great, are the most celebrated. Crowne, though several of his plays were highly successful when first produced, was almost forgotten, till Mr. Lamb reprinted some of his scenes in his Dramatic Specimens, and showed that no dramatist of that age had written finer things. Of seventeen pieces produced by Crowne between 1671 and 1698, his tragedy of Thyestes and his comedy of Sir Courtley Nice are in particular of eminent merit the first for its poetry, the second for plot and character. Etherege is the author of only three comedies, the Comical Revenge (1664), She Would if She Could (1668), and the Man of Mode, or Sir Fopling Flutter (1676); all remarkable for the polish and fluency of the dialogue, and entitled to be regarded as having first set the example of that modern style of comedy which was afterwards cultivated by Wycherley, Farquhar, Vanbrugh, and Congreve. Wycherley who was born in 1640, and lived till 1715, produced his only four plays, Love in a Wood, The Gentleman Dancing Master, The Country Wife, and The Plain Dealer, all comedies, between the years 1672 and 1677. The two last of these pieces are written with more elaboration than anything of Etherege's, and both contain some bold delineation of character and strong satiric writing, reminding us at times of Ben Jonson; but, like him, too, Wycherley is deficient in ease and nature. Southerne, who was only born in the year of the Restoration, and lived till 1746, had produced no more than his two first plays before the Revolution of 1688,—his tragedy of The Loyal Brother in 1682, and his comedy of The Disappointment in 1684. Of ten dramatic pieces of which he is the author, five are comedies, and are of little value; but his tragedies of The Fatal Marriage (1692), Oroonoko (1696), and The Spartan Dame (1719), are interesting and affecting.

Prose Writers:—Clarendon.

Eminent as he is among the poets of his age, Dryden is also one of the greatest of its prose writers. In ease, flexibility, and variety, indeed, his English prose has scarcely ever been excelled. Cowley, too, is a charming writer of prose: the natural, pure, and flowing eloquence of his Essays is better than anything in his poetry. Waller, Suckling, and Sedley, also, wrote all well in prose and Marvel's literary reputation is founded more upon his prose than upon his verse. Of writers exclusively in prose belonging to the space between the Restoration and the Revolution, Clarendon may be first mentioned, although his great work, his History of the Rebellion and Civil Wars, was not published till the year 1702, nor his Life and Continuation of his History, before 1759. His style cannot be commended for its correctness; the manner in which he constructs his sentences, indeed, often sets at defiance all the rules of syntax; but yet he is never unintelligible or obscure— with such admirable expository skill is the matter arranged and spread out, even where the mere verbal sentence-making is the most negligent and entangled. The style, in fact, is that proper to speaking rather than to writing, and had, no doubt, been acquired by Clarendon, not so much from books as from his practice in speaking at the bar and in parliament; for, with great natural abilities, he does not seem to have had much acquaintance with literature, or much acquired knowledge of any kind resulting from study. But his writing possesses the quality that interests above all the graces or artifices of rhetoric—the impress of a mind informed by its subject, and having a complete mastery over it; while the broad full stream in which it flows makes the reader feel as if he were borne along on its tide. The abundance, in particular, with which he pours out his stores of language and illustration in his characters of the eminent persons engaged on both sides of the great contest seems inexhaustible. The historical value of his history, however, is not very considerable; it has not preserved very many facts which are not to be found elsewhere; and, whatever may be thought of its general bias, the inaccuracy of its details is so great throughout, as demonstrated by the authentic evidences of the time, that there is scarcely any other contemporary history which is so little trustworthy as an authority with regard to minute particulars. Clarendon, in truth, was far from being placed in the most favourable circumstances for giving a perfectly correct account of many of the events he has undertaken to record: he was not, except for a very short time, in the midst of the busy scene: looking to it, as he did, from a distance, while the mighty drama was still only in progress, he was exposed to some chances of misconception to which even those removed from it by a long interval of time are not liable; and, without imputing to him any further intention to deceive than is implied in the purpose which we may suppose he chiefly had in view in writing his work, the vindication of his own side of the question, his position as a partisan, intimately mixed up with the affairs and interests of one of the two contending factions, could not fail both to bias his own judgment, and even in some measure to distort or colour the reports made to him by others. On the whole, therefore, this celebrated work is rather a great literary performance than a very valuable historical monument.

HOBBES.

Another royalist history of the same times and events to which Clarendon's work is dedicated, the Behemoth of Thomas Hobbes of Malmesbury, introduces one of the most distinguished names both in English literature and in modern metaphysical, ethical, and political philosophy. Hobbes, born in 1588, commenced author in 1628, at the age of forty, by publishing his translation of Thucydides, but did not produce his first original work, his Latin treatise entitled De Cive, till 1642. This was followed by his treatises entitled Human Nature and De Corpore Politico, in 1650; his Leviathan, in 1651; his translations in verse of the Iliad and Odyssey, in 1675; and his Behemoth, or History of the Causes of the Civil Wars of England, and of the Counsels and Artifices by which they were carried on, from the year 1640 to the year 1660, a few months after his death, at the age of ninety-two, in 1679. Regarded merely as a writer of English, there can be little difference of opinion about the high rank to be assigned to Hobbes. He has been described as our first uniformly careful and correct writer;* and he may be admitted to have at least set the first conspicuous and influential example in what may be called our existing English (for Roger Ascham, Sir Thomas Elyot, and one or two other early writers, seem to have aimed at the same thing in a preceding stage of the language), of that regularity of style which has since his time been generally attended to. This, however, is his least merit. No writer has succeeded in making language a more perfect exponent of thought than it is as employed by Hobbes. His style is not poetical or glowingly eloquent, because his mind was not poetical, and the subjects about which he wrote would have rejected the exaggerations of imaginative or passionate expression if he had been capable of supplying such. But in the prime qualities of precision and perspicuity, and also in economy and succinctness, in force and in terseness, it is the very perfection of a merely expository style. Without any affectation of point, also, it often shapes itself easily and naturally into the happiest aphoristic and epigrammatic forms. Hobbes's clearness and aptness of expression, the effect of which is like that of reading a book with a good light, never forsake him—not even in that most singular performance, his version of Homer, where there is scarcely a trace of ability of any

* Hallam, Lit. of Eur. iv. 316.

other kind. It has been said that there are only two lines in that work in which he is positively poetical; those describing the infant Astyanax in the scene of the parting of Hector and Andromache, in the Sixth Book of the Iliad:—

> Now Hector met her with her little boy,
> That in the nurse's arms was carried;
> And like a star upon her bosom lay
> His beautiful and shining golden head.

But there are other passages in which by dint of mere directness and transparency of style he has rendered a line or two happily enough—as, for instance, in the description of the descent of Apollo at the prayer of Chryses, in the beginning of the poem:—

> His prayer was granted by the deity,
> Who, with his silver bow and arrows keen,
> Descended from Olympus silently,
> In likeness of the sable night unseen.

As if expressly to proclaim and demonstrate, however, that this momentary success was merely accidental, immediately upon the back of this stanza comes the following:—

> His bow and quiver both behind him hang,
> The arrows chink as often as he jogs,
> And as he shot the bow was heard to twang,
> And first his arrows flew at mules and dogs.

For the most part, indeed, Hobbes's Iliad and Odyssey are no better than travesties of Homer's, the more ludicrous as being undesigned and unconscious. Never was there a more signal revenge than that which Hobbes afforded to imagination and poetry over his own unbelieving and scoffing philosophism by the publication of this work. It was almost as if the man born blind, who had all his lifetime been attempting to prove that the sense which he himself wanted was no sense at all, and that that thing, colour, which it professed peculiarly to discern, was a mere delusion, should have himself at last taken the painter's brush and pallet in hand, and attempted, in confirmation of his theory, to produce a picture by the mere senses of touch, taste, smell, and hearing.*

* It is right, however, to state that Coleridge, in a note to the second (1819)

NEVILE.

The most remarkable treatise on political philosophy which appeared in the interval between the Restoration and the Revolution is Henry Nevile's Plato Redivivus, or a Dialogue concerning Government; which was first published in 1681, and went through at least a second edition the same year. Nevile, who was born in 1620, and survived till 1694, had in the earlier part of his life been closely connected with Harrington, the author of the Oceana, and also with the founders of the Commonwealth, and he is commonly reckoned a republican writer; but the present work professes to advocate a monarchical form of government. Its leading principle is the same as that on which Harrington's work is founded, the necessity of all stable government being based upon property; but, in a Preface, in the form of an Address from the Publisher to the Reader, pains are taken to show that the author's application of this principle is different from Harrington's. It is observed, in the first place, that the principle in question is not exclusively or originally Harrington's; it had been discoursed upon and maintained in very many treatises and pamphlets before ever the Oceana came out; in particular in A Letter from an Officer in Ireland to His Highness the Lord Protector, printed in 1653, "which was more than three years before Oceana was written." Besides, continues the writer, who is evidently Nevile himself, "Oceana was written (it being thought lawful so to do in those times) to evince out of these principles that England was not capable of any other government than a democracy. And this author, out of the same maxims or aphorisms of politics, endeavours to

edition of the Friend, *Introd. Essay* iv., admits that in the original edition of that work he had spoken too contemptuously of Hobbes's Odyssey, which when he so wrote of it he had not seen. "It is doubtless," he adds, "as much too ballad-like as the later versions are too epic; but still, on the whole, it leaves a much truer impression of the original."

prove that they may be applied, naturally and fitly, to the redressing and supporting one of the best monarchies in the world, which is that of England." The tenor of the work is throughout in conformity with this declaration.

OTHER PROSE WRITERS:—CUDWORTH, MORE; BARROW; BUNYAN; &c.

The most illustrious antagonist of metaphysical Hobbism, when first promulgated, was Dr. Ralph Cudworth, the First Part of whose True Intellectual System of the Universe, wherein all the Reason and Philosophy of Atheism is Confuted, was first published in 1678. As a vast storehouse of learning, and also as a display of wonderful powers of subtle and far-reaching speculation, this celebrated work is almost unrivalled in our literature; and it is also written in a style of elastic strength and compass which places its author in a high rank among our prose classics. Along with Cudworth may be mentioned his friend and brother Platonist, Dr. Henry More, the author of numerous theological and philosophical works, and remarkable for the union of some of the most mystic notions with the clearest style, and of the most singular credulity with powers of reasoning of the highest order. Other two great theological writers of this age were the voluminous Richard Baxter and the learned and eloquent Dr. Robert Leighton, Archbishop of Glasgow. "Baxter," says Bishop Burnet, "was a man of great piety; and, if he had not meddled in too many things, would have been esteemed one of the learned men of the age. He writ near two hundred books; of these three are large folios: he had a very moving and pathetical way of writing, and was his whole life long a man of great zeal and much simplicity; but was most unhappily subtle and metaphysical in everything."* Of Leighton, whom he knew intimately, the same writer has given a much more copious account, a few sen-

* Own Time, i. 180.

tences of which we will transcribe:—"His preaching had a sublimity both of thought and expression in it. The grace and gravity of his pronunciation was such that few heard him without a very sensible emotion.... It was so different from all others, and indeed from everything that one could hope to rise up to, that it gave a man an indignation at himself and all others.... His style was rather too fine; but there was a majesty and beauty in it that left so deep an impression that I cannot yet forget the sermons I heard him preach thirty years ago."* The writings of Archbishop Leighton that have come down to us have been held by some of the highest minds of our own day—Coleridge for one—to bear out Burnet's affectionate panegyric. But perhaps the greatest genius among the theological writers of this age was the famous Dr. Isaac Barrow, popularly known chiefly by his admirable Sermons, but renowned also in the history of modern science as, next to Newton himself, the greatest mathematician of his time. "As a writer," the late Professor Dugald Stewart has well said of Barrow, "he is equally distinguished by the redundancy of his matter and by the pregnant brevity of his expression; but what more peculiarly characterizes his manner is a certain air of powerful and of conscious facility in the execution of whatever he undertakes. Whether the subject be mathematical, metaphysical, or theological, he seems always to bring to it a mind which feels itself superior to the occasion, and which, in contending with the greatest difficulties, puts forth but half its strength. He has somewhere spoken of his Lectiones Mathematicæ (which it may, in passing, be remarked, display *metaphysical* talents of the highest order) as extemporaneous effusions of his pen; and I have no doubt that the same epithet is still more literally applicable to his pulpit discourses. It is, indeed, only thus that we can account for the variety and extent of his voluminous remains, when we recollect that the author died at the age of forty-six."**

* Own Time, 1. 135.
** Dissertation on the Progress of Philosophy, p. 45.

But the name that in popular celebrity transcends all others, among the theological writers of this age, is that of John Bunyan, the author of various religious works, and especially of the Pilgrim's Progress. One critic has in our time had the courage to confess in print, that to him this famous allegory appeared "mean, jejune, and wearisome." Our late brilliant essayist, Lord Macaulay, on the other hand, in a paper published in 1830, has written:—"We are not afraid to say, that, though there were many clever men in England during the latter half of the seventeenth century, there were only two minds which possessed the imaginative faculty in a very eminent degree. One of those minds produced the Paradise Lost, the other the Pilgrim's Progress." And, to the end of his life, we find him faithful to the same enthusiasm.* He conceives it to be the characteristic peculiarity of the Pilgrim's Progress "that it is the only work of its kind which possesses a strong human interest." The pilgrimage of the great Italian poet through Hell, Purgatory, and Paradise is of course regarded as not properly an allegory. But high poetry is treated somewhat unceremoniously throughout this paper. Of the Fairy Queen it is said:—"Of the persons who read the first canto, not one in ten reaches the end of the first book, and not one in a hundred perseveres to the end of the poem. Very few and very weary are those who are in at the death of the Blatant Beast. If the last six books, which are said to have been destroyed in Ireland, had been preserved, we doubt whether any heart less stout than that of a commentator would have held out to the end." It must be admitted that, as a story, the Pilgrim's Progress is a great deal more interesting than the Fairy Queen. And we suspect that, if we are to take the verdict of the most numerous class of readers, it will carry off the palm quite as decidedly from the Paradise Lost. Very few, comparatively, and very weary we apprehend, are the readers of that great poem, too, who have

* See the Review of Ranke's History of the Popes (1840); and again the lively, though slight, sketch of Bunyan's history in the Biographies.

made their way steadily through it from the beginning of the First Book to the end of the Twelfth. Still, although Bunyan had undoubtedly an ingenious, shaping, and vivid imagination, and his work, partly from its execution, partly from its subject, takes a strong hold, as Macaulay has well pointed out, of minds of very various kinds, commanding the admiration of the most fastidious critics, such, for instance, as Doctor Johnson, while it is loved by those who are too simple to admire it, we must make a great distinction between the power by which such general attraction as this is produced and what we have in the poetry of Milton and Spenser. The difference is something of the same kind with that which exists between any fine old popular ballad and a tragedy of Sophocles or of Shakespeare. Bunyan could rhyme too, when he chose; but he has plenty of poetry without that, and we cannot agree with the opinion expressed by good Adam Clarke, "that the Pilgrim's Progress would be more generally read, and more abundantly useful to a particular class of readers, were it turned into decent rhyme." We suspect the ingenious gentleman who, in the early part of the last century, published an edition of Paradise Lost turned into prose had a more correct notion of what would be most useful, and also most agreeable, to a pretty numerous class of readers.

What Lord Macaulay says of Bunyan's English, though his estimate is, perhaps, a little high-pitched, is worth quoting:—"The style of Bunyan is delightful to every reader, and invaluable as a study to every person who wishes to obtain a wide command over the English language. The vocabulary is the vocabulary of the common people. There is not an expression, if we except a few technical terms of theology, which would puzzle the rudest peasant. We have observed several pages which do not contain a single word of more than two syllables. Yet no writer has said more exactly what he meant to say. For magnificence, for pathos, for vehement exhortation, for subtle disquisition, for every purpose of the poet, the orator, and the divine, this homely dialect, the dialect of plain working men, was perfectly sufficient. There is no book in our literature on which we would so readily stake the fame of the old unpolluted English language, no book which shows so well how rich that language is in its own proper wealth, and how little it has been improved by all that it has borrowed."

To the names that have been mentioned may be added those of Izaak Walton, the mild-tempered angler and biographer; Sir William Temple, the lively, agreeable, and well-informed essayist and memoirist; and many others that might be enumerated if it were our object to compile a catalogue instead of noticing only the principal lights of our literature.

ENGLISH LITERATURE SINCE THE REVOLUTION OF 1688.

FIRST EFFECTS OF THE REVOLUTION ON OUR LITERATURE.

THE Revolution, brought on by some of the same causes that had given birth to the Commonwealth, and restoring something of the same spirit and condition of things, came like another nightfall upon our higher literature, putting out the light of poetry in the land still more effectually than had even that previous triumph of the popular principle. Up to this date English literature had grown and flourished chiefly in the sunshine of court protection and favour; the public appreciation and sympathy were not yet sufficiently extended to afford it the necessary warmth and shelter. Its spirit, consequently, and affections were in the main courtly; it drooped and withered when the encouragement of the court was withdrawn, from the deprivation both of its customary support and sustenance and of its chief inspiration. And, if the decay of this kind of light at the Revolution was, as we have said, still more complete than that which followed upon the setting up of the Commonwealth, the difference seems to have been mainly owing to there having been less of it to extinguish at the one epoch than at the other. At the Restoration the impulse given by the great poets of the age of Elizabeth and James was yet operating, without having been interrupted and weakened by any foreign influence, upon the language and the national mind. Doubtless, too, whatever may be thought of the literary tendencies of puritanism and republicanism when they had got into the ascendant, the nurture both for head and heart furnished by the ten years of high deeds, and higher hopes and speculations, that ushered in the Commonwealth, must have been of a far other kind than any that was to be got out of the thirty years, or thereby, of laxity, frivolity, denationalization, and insincerity of all sorts, down the comparatively smooth stream of which men slid, without effort and without thought, to the Revolution. No wonder that some powerful minds were trained by the former, and almost none by the latter.

SURVIVING WRITERS OF THE PRECEDING PERIOD.

With the exception of some two or three names, none of them of the highest class, to be presently mentioned, almost the only writers that shed any lustre on the first reign after the Revolution are those of a few of the survivors of the preceding era. Dryden, fallen on what to him were evil days and evil tongues, and forced in his old age to write for bread with less rest for his wearied head and hand than they had ever had before, now produced some of his most laborious and also some of his most happily executed works: his translation of Virgil, among others, his Fables, and his Alexander's Feast. Lee, the dramatic poet, discharged from Bedlam, finished two more tragedies, his Princess of Cleve and his Massacre of Paris, before, "returning one night from the Bear and Harrow, in Butcher-Row, through Clare Market, to his lodgings in Duke Street, overladen with wine, he fell down on the ground as some say, according to others on a bulk, and was killed or stifled in the snow," early in the year 1692. The comic Etherege also outlived the deposition of his patron James II., but is not known to have written anything after that event; he followed James to France, and is reported to have died characteristically at Ratisbon a year or two after: "having treated some company with a liberal entertainment at his house there, where he had taken his glass too freely, and, being, through his great complaisance, too forward in waiting on his guests at their departure, flushed as he was, he tumbled down stairs and broke his neck, and so fell a martyr to jollity and civility." Wycherley, who at the date of the Revolution was under fifty, lived to become a correspondent of Pope, and even saw out the reign of Anne; but he produced nothing in that of William, although he published a volume of poems in 1704, and left some other trifles behind him, which were printed long afterwards by Theobald. Southerne, indeed, who survived till 1746, continued to write and publish till within twenty years of his death; his two best dramas—his Fatal Marriage and his Oroonoko—were both produced in the reign of William. Southerne, though not without considerable pathetic power, was fortunate in a genius on the whole not above the appreciation of the unpoetical age he lived in: "Dryden once took occasion to ask him how much he got by one of his plays; to which he answered that he was really ashamed to inform him. But, Mr. Dryden being a little importunate to know, he plainly told him that by his last play he cleared seven hundred pounds, which appeared astonishing to Dryden, as he himself had never been able to acquire more than one hundred by his most successful pieces."* Southerne, who, whatever estimate may be formed of his poetry, was not, we may gather from this anecdote, without some conscience and modesty, had worse writers than himself to keep him in countenance by their preposterous prosperity, in this lucky time for mediocrity and dulness. Shadwell was King William's first poet laureate, and Nahum Tate his next. Tate, indeed, and his friend Dr. Nicholas Brady, were among the most flourishing authors and greatest public favourites of this reign: it was now that they perpetrated in concert their version, or perversion, of the Psalms, with which we are still afflicted. Brady also published a play, and, at a later date, some volumes of sermons and a translation of the

* Biog. Dram.

Æneid, which, fortunately, not having been imposed or recommended by authority, are all among the most forgotten of books. Elkanah Settle, too, was provided for as City poet.

Among writers of another class, perhaps the most eminent who, having been distinguished before the Revolution, survived and continued to write after that event, was Sir William Temple. His Miscellanies, by which he is principally known, though partly composed before, were not published till then. John Evelyn, who, however, although a very miscellaneous as well as voluminous writer, has hardly left any work that is held in esteem for either style or thought, or for anything save what it may contain of positive information or mere matter of fact, also published one or two books in the reign of William, which he saw to an end; for he died, at the age of eighty-five, in 1706. Bishop Stillingfleet, who had been known as an author since before the Restoration, for his Irenicum appeared in 1659, when he was only in his twenty-fourth year, and who had kept the press in employment by a rapid succession of publications during the next five-and-twenty years, resumed his pen after the Revolution, which raised him to the bench, to engage in a controversy with Locke about some of the principles of his famous essay; but, whether it was that years had abated his powers, or that he had a worse cause to defend, or merely that the public taste was changed, he gained much less applause for his dialectic skill on this than on most former occasions. Stillingfleet lived to the year 1699.

John Norris, also, one of the last of the school of English Platonists, which may be considered as having been founded in the latter part of the seventeenth century by Cudworth and Henry More, had, we believe, become known as a writer some years before the Revolution; but the greater number of his publications first appeared in the reign of William, and he may be reckoned one of the best writers properly or principally belonging to that reign. Yet he is not for a moment to be compared for learning, compass of thought, or power and skill of expression, to either Cudworth or More. Norris's principal work is his Essay on the Ideal World, published in two parts in 1701 and 1702. He is also the author of a volume of religious poetry, of rather a feeble character, which has been often reprinted. Bishop Sprat, though a clergyman, as well as a writer both of prose and verse, cannot be called a divine: he had in earlier life the reputation of being the finest writer of the day, but, although he lived till very nearly the end of the reign of Anne, he published nothing, we believe, after the Revolution, nor indeed for a good many years before it. His style, which was so much admired in his own age, is a Frenchified English, with an air of ease and occasionally of vivacity, but without any true grace or expressiveness.

Good old Richard Baxter, who had been filling the world with books for half a century, just lived to see the Revolution. He died, at the age of seventy-six, in the beginning of December, 1691. And in the end of the same month died, a considerably younger man, Robert Boyle, another of the most voluminous writers of the preceding period, and famous also for his services in the cause of religion, as well as of science. In the preceding May, at a still less advanced age, had died the most eminent Scotch writer of the period between the Restoration and the Revolution, Sir George Mackenzie, lord-advocate under both Charles II. and his successor; the author of the Institution of the Laws of Scotland, and many other professional, historical, and antiquarian works, but the master also of a flowing pen in moral speculation, the belles lettres, and even in the department of fancy and fiction—as may be gathered from the titles of his Aretina, or the Serious Romance, 1660; Religio Stoici, or the Virtuoso, 1663; Solitude preferred to Public Employment, 1665; Moral Gallantry, 1667. Mackenzie may be regarded as the first successor of his countryman Drummond of Hawthornden in the cultivation of an English style; he was the correspondent of Dryden and other distinguished English writers of his day; but he has no pretensions of his own to any high rank either for the graces of his expression or the value of his matter. Whatever may have been his professional learning, too, his historical disquisitions are as jejune and uncritical as his attempts at fine writing are, with all their elaboration, at once pedantic and clownish. He has nothing either of the poetry or the elegance of Drummond.

Bishop Burnet.

The most active and conspicuous undoubtedly of the prose writers who, having acquired distinction in the preceding period, continued to prosecute the business of authorship after the Revolution, was the celebrated Dr. Gilbert Burnet, now Bishop of Salisbury. Of 145 distinct publications (many of them, however, only single sermons and other short pamphlets), which are enumerated as having proceeded from his incessant pen between 1669 and his death, at the age of seventy-two, in 1715 (including, indeed, his History of his Own Time, and his Thoughts on Education, which did not appear till after his death), we find that 71, namely 21 historical works and 50 sermons and tracts, belong to the period before the Revolution; 36, namely 5 historical works and 31 sermons and tracts, to the reign of William; and the remaining 38, namely one historical work and 37 pamphlets, to a later date. Many of what we have called historical works, however, are mere pamphlets: in fact Burnet's literary performances of any considerable extent are only three in number:—his Memoirs of James and William, Dukes of Hamilton, published, in one volume folio, in 1676; his History of the Reformation of the Church of England, 3 volumes folio, 1679, 1681, and 1714; and his History of his Own Time, in two volumes folio, published after his death in 1723 and 1734. There is enough of literary labour, as well as of historical value, in these works to preserve to the author a very honourable name; each of them contains much matter now nowhere else to be found, and they must always continue to rank among the original

sources of our national history, both ecclesiastical and civil.
In regard to their execution, too, it must be admitted that
the style is at least straightforward and unaffected, and
generally as unambiguous as it is unambitious; the facts are
clearly enough arranged; and the story is told not only intelligibly, but for the most part in rather a lively and interesting way. On the other hand, to any high station as a
writer Burnet can make no claim; he is an industrious collector of intelligence, and a loquacious and moderately lively
gossip: but of eloquence, or grace, or refinement of any
sort, he is as destitute as he is (and that is altogether) of
imagination, and wit, and humour, and subtlety, and depth
and weight of thought, and whatever other qualities give
anything either of life or lustre to what a man utters out of
his own head or heart. We read him for the sake of his
facts only; he troubles us with but few reflections, but of
that no reader will complain. He does not see far into anything, nor indeed, properly speaking, into it at all; for that
matter he is little more, to adopt a modern term, than a
penny-a-liner on a large scale, and best performs his task
when he does not attempt to be anything else. Nor is he a
neat-handed workman even of that class; in his History of
his Own Time, in particular, his style, with no strength, or
flavour, or natural charm of any kind, to redeem its rudeness, is the most slovenly undress in which a writer ever
wrapt up what he had to communicate to the public. Its
only merit, as we have observed, is that it is without any air
of pretension, and that it is evidently as extemporaneous
and careless as it is unelevated, shapeless, and ungramma-
tical. Among the most important and best known of
Burnet's other works are, that entitled Some Passages of
the Life and Death of the Right Honourable John Wilmot,
Earl of Rochester, 1680; his Life of Bishop Bedel, 1685; his
Travels through France, Italy, Germany, and Switzerland,
1685; and his Exposition of the Thirty-Nine Articles, 1699.
The first mentioned of these is the best written of all his
works.

Thomas Burnet.

In the same year with Bishop Burnet, but at a more advanced age, died Dr. Thomas Burnet, the learned and eloquent author of the Telluris Sacra Theoria, first published in Latin in 1680, and afterwards translated into English by the author; of the Archæologia Philosophica, published in 1692; and of two or three other treatises, also in Latin, which did not appear till after his death. Burnet's system of geology has no scientific value whatever; indeed, it must be considered as a mere romance, although, from the earnestness of the author's manner and his constant citation of texts of Scripture in support of his positions, as well as from more than one answer which he afterwards published to the attacks made upon his book, it is evident that he by no means intended it to be so received. But, with his genius and imagination and consummate scholarship, he is a very different species of writer from his garrulous and mitred namesake: his English style is singularly flowing and harmonious, as well as perspicuous and animated, and rises on fit occasions to much majesty and even splendour.

Other Theological Writers:—Tillotson; South.

Another name that may be here mentioned is that of Archbishop Tillotson, who was a very popular preacher among the Presbyterians before the Restoration, and began publishing sermons so early as in the year 1661, while he still belonged to that sect. He died in 1694, in his sixty-fourth year. Tillotson's Sermons, still familiarly known by reputation, long continued to be the most generally esteemed collection of such compositions in the language; but are probably now very little read. They are substantial per-

formances, such as make the reader feel, when he has got through one of them, that he has accomplished something of a feat; and, being withal as free from pedantry and every other kind of eccentricity or extravagance as from flimsiness, and exceedingly sober in their strain of doctrine, with a certain blunt cordiality in the expression and manner, they were in all respects very happily addressed to the ordinary peculiarities of the national mind and character. But, having once fallen into neglect, Tillotson's writings have no qualities that will ever revive attention to them. There is much more of a true vitality in the sermons of Dr. Robert South, whose career of authorship commenced in the time of the Protectorate, though his life was extended till after the accession of George I. He died in 1716, at the age of eighty-three. South's sermons, the first of which dates even before the earliest of Tillotson's, and the last after Tillotson's latest, are very well characterised by Mr. Hallam:—
"They were," he observes, "much celebrated at the time, and retain a portion of their renown. This is by no means surprising. South had great qualifications for that popularity which attends the pulpit, and his manner was at that time original. Not diffuse, nor learned, nor formal in argument like Barrow, with a more natural structure of sentences, a more pointed though by no means a more fair and satisfactory turn of reasoning, with a style clear and English, free from all pedantry, but abounding with those colloquial novelties of idiom, which, though now become vulgar and offensive, the age of Charles II. affected, sparing no personal or temporary sarcasm, but, if he seems for a moment to tread on the verge of buffoonery, recovering himself by some stroke of vigorous sense and language: such was the witty Dr. South, whom the courtiers delighted to hear. His sermons want all that is called unction, and sometimes even earnestness; but there is a masculine spirit about them, which, combined with their peculiar characteristics, would naturally fill the churches where he might be heard."* Both

* Lit. of Europe, iv. 56.

South and Tillotson are considered to belong as divines to the Arminian, or, as it was then commonly called, the Latitudinarian school—as well as Cudworth More, and Stillingfleet.

LOCKE.

The only considerable literary name that belongs exclusively, or almost exclusively, to the first reign after the Revolution is that of Locke. John Locke, born in 1632, although his Adversariorum Methodus, or New Method of a Common-Place-Book, had appeared in French in Leclerc's Bibliothèque for 1686, and an abridgment of his celebrated Essay, and his first Letter on Toleration, both also in French, in the same publication for 1687 and 1688, had published nothing in English, or with his name, till he produced in 1690 the work which has ever since made him one of the best known of English writers, both in his own and in other countries, his Essay concerning Human Understanding. This was followed by his Second Letter on Toleration, and his two Treatises on Government, in the same year; his Considerations on Lowering the Interest of Money, in 1691; his Third Letter on Toleration, in 1692; his Thoughts concerning Education, in 1693; his Reasonableness of Christianity, in 1695; and various controversial tracts in reply to his assailants, Dr. Edwards and Bishop Stillingfleet, between that date and his death in 1704. After his death appeared his Conduct of the Understanding, and several theological treatises, the composition of which had been the employment of the last years of his industrious and productive old age. Locke's famous Essay was the first work, perhaps in any language, which professedly or systematically attempted to popularise metaphysical philosophy. It is the first comprehensive survey that had been attempted of the whole mind and its faculties; and the very conception of such a design argued an intellect of no common reach, originality, and boldness. It will remain also of very considerable value as an extensive register of facts, and a storehouse of acute and often suggestive observations on psychological phenomena, whatever may be the fate of the views propounded in it as aspiring to constitute a metaphysical system. Further, it is not to be denied that this work has exercised a powerful influence upon the course of philosophical inquiry and opinion ever since its appearance. At first, in particular, it did good service in putting finally to the rout some fantastic notions and methods that still lingered in the schools; it was the loudest and most comprehensive proclamation that had yet been made of the liberation of philosophy from the dominion of authority; but Locke's was a mind stronger and better furnished for the work of pulling down than of building up: he had enough of clearsightedness and independence of mental character for the one; whatever endowments of a different kind he possessed, he had too little imagination, or creative power, for the other. Besides, the very passionless character of his mind would have unfitted him for going far into the philosophy of our complex nature, in which the passions are the revealers and teachers of all the deepest truths, and alone afford us any intimation of many things which, even with the aid of their lurid light, we discern but as fearful and unfathomable mysteries. What would Shakespeare's understanding of the philosophy of human nature have been, if he had had no more imagination and passion in his own nature than Locke?

SWIFT.

His renowned Tale of a Tub and a tract entitled The Battle of the Books, published together in 1704, were the first announcement of the greatest master of satire at once comic and caustic that has yet appeared in our language. Swift, born in Dublin in 1667, had already, in the last years of the reign of King William, made himself known by two volumes of Letters selected from the papers of his friend Temple (who died in 1699), and also by a political pamphlet in favour of the ministry of the day, which attracted little notice, and gave as little promise of his future eminence as a writer. To politics and to satire, however, he adhered throughout his career—often blending the two, but producing scarcely anything, if we may not except some of his effusions in verse, that was not either satirical or political. His course of authorship as a political writer may be considered properly to begin with his Letter concerning the Sacramental Test, and another high Tory and high Church tract, which he published in 1708; in which same year he also came forward with his ironical Argument for the Abolition of Christianity, and, in his humorous Predictions, first assumed his *nom de guerre* of Isaac Bickerstaff, Esquire, subsequently made so famous by other *jeux d'esprit* in the same style, and by its adoption soon after by the wits of the Tatler. Of his other most notable performances, his Conduct of the Allies was published in 1712; his Public Spirit of the Whigs, in 1714; his Drapier's Letters, in 1724; his immortal Gulliver's Travels, in 1727; and his Polite Conversation, which, however, had been written many years before, in 1738. His poem of Cadenus and Vanessa, besides, had appeared, without his consent, in 1723, soon after the death of Miss Hester Vanhomrigh, its heroine. The History of the Four Last Years of Queen Anne (if his, which there can hardly be a doubt that it is), the Directions for Servants, many of his verses and other shorter pieces, and his Diary written to Stella (Miss Johnson, whom he eventually married), were none of them printed till after, some of them not till long after, his death, which took place in 1745.

"O thou!" exclaims his friend Pope,

—— "whatever title please thine ear,
Dean, Drapier, Bickerstaff, or Gulliver!
Whether thou choose Cervantes' serious air,
Or laugh and shake in Rabelais' easy chair,
Or praise the court, or magnify mankind,
Or thy grieved country's copper chains unbind,"

lines that describe comprehensively enough the celebrated dean's genius and writings—what he did and what he was. And the first remark to be made about Swift is, that into everything that came from his pen he put a strong infusion of himself; that in his writings we read the man—not merely his intellectual ability, but his moral nature, his passions, his principles, his prejudices, his humours, his whole temper and individuality. The common herd of writers have no individuality at all; those of the very highest class can assume at will any other individuality as perfectly as their own—they have no exclusiveness. Next under this highest class stand those whose individuality is at once their strength and their weakness;—their strength, inasmuch as it distinguishes them from and lifts them far above the multitude of writers of mere talent or expository skill; their weakness and bondage, in that it will not be thrown off, and that it withholds them from ever going out of themselves, and rising from the merely characteristic, striking, or picturesque, either to the dramatic or to the beautiful, of both of which equally the spirit is unegotistic and universal. To this class, which is not the highest but the next to it, Swift belongs. The class, however, like both that which is above and that which is below it, is one of wide comprehension, and includes many degrees of power, and even many diversities of gifts. Swift was neither a Cervantes nor a Rabelais; but yet, with something that was peculiar to himself, he combined considerable portions of both. He had more of Cervantes than Rabelais had, and more of Rabelais than was given to Cervantes. There cannot be claimed for him the refinement, the humanity, the pathos, the noble elevation of the Spaniard—all that irradiates and beautifies his satire and drollery as the blue sky does the earth it bends over; neither, with all his ingenuity and fertility, does our English wit and humourist anywhere display either the same inexhaustible abundance of grotesque invention, or the same gaiety and luxuriance of fancy, with the historian of the Doings and Sayings of the Giant Gargantua. Yet neither Cervantes nor Rabelais, nor both combined, could have written the Tale of a Tub. The torrent of triumphant merriment is broader and more rushing than anything of the same kind in either. When we look indeed to the perfection and exactness of the allegory at all points, to the biting sharpness and at the same time the hilarity and comic animation of the satire, to its strong and unpausing yet easy and natural flow, to the incessant blaze of the wit and humour, and to the style so clear, so vivid and expressive, so idiomatic, so English, so true and appropriate in all its varieties, narrative, didactic, rhetorical, colloquial, as we know no work of its class in our own language that as a whole approaches this, so we doubt if there be another quite equal to it in any language.

Swift was undoubtedly the most masculine intellect of his age, the most earnest thinker of a time in which there was less among us of earnest and deep thinking than in any other era of our literature. In its later and more matured form, his wit itself becomes earnest and passionate, and has a severity, a fierceness, a *sæva indignatio*, that are all his own, and that have never been blended in any other writer with so keen a perception of the ludicrous and so much general comic power. The breath of his rich, pungent, original jocularity is at the same time cutting as a sword and consuming as fire. Other masters of the same art are satisfied if they can only make their readers laugh; this is their main, often their sole aim: with Swift, to excite the emotion of the ludicrous is, in most of his writings, only a subordinate purpose,—a means employed for effecting quite another and a much higher end; if he labours to make anything ridiculous, it is because he hates it, and would have it trodden into the earth or extirpated. This, at least, became the settled temper of all the middle and latter portion of his life. No sneaking kindness for his victim is to be detected in his crucifying raillery; he is not a mere admirer of the comic picturesque, who will sometimes rack or gibbet an unhappy individual for the sake of the fantastic grimaces he may make, or the capers he may cut in the air; he has the true spirit of an executioner, and only loves his joke as sauce and seasoning to more serious work. Few men have been more perversely prejudiced and self-willed than Swift, and therefore of absolute truth his works may probably contain less than many others not so earnestly written; but of what was truth to the mind of the writer, of what he actually believed and desired, no works contain more. Here, again, as well as in the other respect already noticed, Swift is in the middle class of writers; far above those whose whole truth is truth of expression—that is, correspondence between the words and the thoughts (possibly without any between the thoughts and the writer's belief); but below those who both write what they think, and whose thoughts are preeminently valuable for their intrinsic beauty or profoundness. Yet in setting honestly and effectively before us even his own passions and prejudices a writer also tells us the truth—the truth, at least, respecting himself, if not respecting anything else. This much Swift does always; and this is his great distinction among the masters of wit and humour;—the merriest of his jests is an utterance of some real feeling of his heart at the moment, as much as the fiercest of his invectives. Alas! with all his jesting and merriment, he did not know what it was to have a mind at ease, or free from the burden and torment of dark, devouring passions, till, in his own words, the cruel indignation that tore continually at his heart was laid at rest in the grave. In truth, the insanity which ultimately fell down upon and laid prostrate his fine faculties had cast something of its black shadow athwart their vision from the first—as he himself probably felt or suspected when he determined to bequeath his fortune to build an hospital in his native country for persons afflicted with that calamity; and sad enough, we may be sure, he was at heart, when he gaily wrote that he did so merely

> To show, by one satiric touch,
> No nation wanted it so much.*

Yet the madness, or predisposition to madness, was also part and parcel of the man, and possibly an element of his genius—which might have had less earnestness and force, as well as less activity, productiveness, and originality, if it had not been excited and impelled by that perilous fervour. Nay, something of their power and peculiar character Swift's writings may owe to the exertions called forth in curbing and keeping down the demon which, like a proud steed under a stout rider, would have mastered him, if he had not mastered it, and, although support and strength to him so long as it was held in subjection, would, dominant over him, have rent him in pieces, as in the end it did. Few could have maintained the struggle so toughly and so long.

Swift would probably have enjoyed a higher reputation as a poet if he had not been so great a writer in prose. His productions in verse are considerable in point of quantity, and many of them admirable of their kind. But those of them that deserve to be so described belong to the humblest kind of poetry—to that kind which has scarcely any distinctively poetical quality or characteristic about it except the rhyme. He has made some attempts in a higher style, but with little success. His Pindaric Odes, written and published when he was a young man, drew from Dryden (who was his relation) the emphatic judgment, "Cousin Swift, you will never be a poet:" and, though Swift never forgave this frankness, he seems to have felt that the prognostication was a sound one, for he wrote no more Pindaric Odes. Nor indeed did he ever afterwards attempt anything considerable in the way of serious poetry, if we except his Cadenus and

---

* "I have often," says Lord Orrery, "heard him lament the state of childhood and idiotism to which some of the greatest men of this nation were reduced before their death. He mentioned, as examples within his own time, the Duke of Marlborough and Lord Somers; and, when he cited these melancholy instances, it was always with a heavy sigh, and with gestures that showed great uneasiness, as if he felt an impulse of what was to happen to him before he died."—Remarks, p. 188.

Vanessa (the story of Miss Vanhomrigh), his effusion entitled Poetry, a Rhapsody, and that on his own death—and even these are chiefly distinguished from his other productions by being longer and more elaborate, the most elevated portions of the first mentioned scarcely rising above narrative and reflection, and whatever there is of more dignified or solemn writing in the two others being largely intermixed with comedy and satire in his usual easy ambling style. With all his liveliness of fancy, he had no grandeur of imagination, as little feeling of the purely graceful or beautiful, no capacity of tender emotion, no sensibility to even the simplest forms of music. With these deficiencies it was impossible that he should produce anything that could be called poetical in a high sense. But of course he could put his wit and fancy into the form of verse—and so as to make the measured expression and the rhyme give additional point and piquancy to his strokes of satire and ludicrous narratives or descriptions. Some of his lighter verses are as good as anything of the kind in the language.

POPE.

Of Swift's contemporaries, by far the most memorable name is that of Alexander Pope. If Swift was at the head of the prose writers of the early part of the last century, Pope was as incontestably the first of the writers in verse of that day, with no other either equal or second to him. Born a few months before the Revolution, he came forth as a poet, by the publication of his Pastorals in Tonson's Miscellany, in 1709, when he was yet only in his twenty-first year; and they had been written five years before. Nor were they the earliest of his performances; his Ode on Solitude, his verses upon Silence, his translations of the First Book of the Thebais and of Ovid's Epistle from Sappho to Phaon, and his much more remarkable paraphrases of Chaucer's January and May and the Prologue to the Wife of Bath's Tale, all preceded the composition of the Pastorals. His Essay on Criticism (written in 1709) was published in 1711; the Messiah the same year (in the Spectator); the Rape of the Lock in 1712; the Temple of Fame (written two years before) the same year; his Windsor Forest (which he had commenced at sixteen) in 1713; the first four books of his translation of the Iliad in 1715; his Epistle from Eloisa to Abelard (written some years before) we believe in 1717, when he published a collected edition of his poems; the remaining portions of the Iliad at different times, the last in 1720; his translation of the Odyssey (in concert with Fenton and Broome) in 1725; the first three books of the Dunciad in 1728; his Essay on Man in 1733 and 1734; his Imitations of Horace, various other satirical pieces, the Prologue and Epilogue to the Satires, his four epistles styled Moral Essays and his modernised version of Donne's Satires between 1730 and 1740; and the fourth book of the Dunciad in 1742. Besides all this verse, collections of his Letters were published, first surreptitiously by Curl, and then by himself, in 1737; and, among other publications in prose, his clever *jeu d'esprit* entitled a Narrative of the Frenzy of John Dennis appeared in 1713; his Preface to Shakespeare, with his edition of the works of that poet, in 1721; his Treatise of the Bathos, or Art of Sinking in Poetry, and his Memoirs of P. P., Clerk of This Parish (in ridicule of Burnet's History of his Own Time), in 1727. He died in May, 1744, about a year and a half before his friend Swift, who, more than twenty years his senior, had naturally anticipated that he should be the first to depart, and that, as he cynically, and yet touchingly too, expressed it, while Arbuthnot grieved for him a day, and Gay a week, he should be lamented a whole month by "poor Pope,"—whom, of all those he best knew, he seems to have the most loved.

Pope, with talent enough for anything, might deserve to be ranked among the most distinguished prose writers of his time, if he were not its greatest poet; but it is in the latter character that he falls to be noticed in the history of our literature. And what a broad and bright region would be cut off from our poetry if he had never lived! If we even confine ourselves to his own works, without regarding the numerous subsequent writers who have formed themselves upon him as an example and model, and may be said to constitute the school of which he was the founder, how rich an inheritance of brilliant and melodious fancies do we not owe to him! For what would any of us resign the Rape of the Lock, or the Epistle of Eloisa, or the Essay on Man, or the Moral Essays, or the Satires, or the Epistle to Dr. Arbuthnot, or the Dunciad? That we have nothing in the same style in the language to be set beside or weighed against any one of these performances will probably be admitted by all; and, if we could say no more, this would be to assign to Pope a rank in our poetic literature which certainly not so many as half a dozen other names are entitled to share with his. Down to his own day at least, Chaucer, Spenser, Shakespeare, Milton, and Dryden alone had any pretentions to be placed before him or by his side. It is unnecessary to dilate upon what has been sufficiently pointed out by all the critics, and is too obvious to be overlooked, the general resemblance of his poetry, in both its form and spirit, to that of Dryden rather than to that of our elder great writers. A remarkable external peculiarity of it is, that he is probably the only one of our modern poets of eminence who has written nothing in blank verse; while even in rhyme he has nearly confined himself to that one decasyllabic line upon which it would almost seem to have been his purpose to impress a new shape and character. He belongs to the classical school as opposed to the romantic, to that in which a French rather than to that in which an Italian inspiration may be detected. Whether this is to be attributed principally to his constitutional temperament and the native character of his imagination, or to the influences of the age in which he lived and wrote, we shall not stop to inquire. It is enough that such is the fact. But, though he may be regarded as in the main the pupil and legitimate successor of Dryden, the amount of what he learned or borrowed from that master was by no means so considerable as to prevent his manner from having a great deal in it that is distinctive and original. If Dryden has more impetuosity and a freer flow, Pope has far more delicacy, and, on fit occasions, far more tenderness and true passion. Dryden has written nothing in the same style with the Rape of the Lock on the one hand, or with the Epistle to Abelard and the Elegy on the Death of an Unfortunate Lady on the other. Indeed, these two styles may be said to have been both, in so far as the English tongue is concerned, invented by Pope. In what preceding writer had he an example of either? Nay, did either the French or the Italian language furnish him with anything to copy from nearly so brilliant and felicitous as his own performances? In the sharper or more severe species of satire, again, while in some things he is inferior to Dryden, in others he excels him. It must be admitted that Dryden's is the nobler, the more generous scorn; it is passionate, while Pope's is frequently only peevish: the one is vehement, the other venomous. But, although Pope does not wield the ponderous, fervid scourge with which his predecessor tears and mangles the luckless object of his indignation or derision, he knows how, with a lighter touch, to inflict a torture quite as maddening at the moment, and perhaps more difficult to heal. Neither has anything of the easy elegance, the simple natural grace, the most exquisite artifice simulating the absence of all art, of Horace; but the care, and dexterity, and superior refinement of Pope, his neatness, and concentration, and point, supply a better substitute for these charms than the ruder strength, and more turbulent passion, of Dryden. If Dryden, too, has more natural fire and force, and rises in his greater passages to a stormy grandeur to which the other does not venture to commit himself, Pope in some degree compensates for that by a dignity, a quiet, sometimes pathetic, majesty, which we find nowhere in Dryden's poetry. Dryden has translated the Æneid, and Pope the Iliad; but the two tasks would apparently have been better distributed if Dryden had chanced to have taken up Homer, and left Virgil to Pope. Pope's Iliad, in truth, whatever may be its merits of another kind, is, in spirit and style, about the most unhomeric performance in the whole compass of our poetry, as Pope had, of all our great poets, the most unhomeric genius. He was emphatically the poet of the highly artificial age in which he lived; and his excellence lay in, or at least was fostered and perfected by, the accordance of all his tastes and talents, of his whole moral and intellectual constitution, with the spirit of that condition of things. Not touches of natural emotion, but the titillation of wit and fancy,—not tones of natural music, but the tone of good society,—make up the charm of his poetry; the polish, pungency, and brilliance of which, however, in its most happily executed passages leave nothing in that style to be desired. Pope, no doubt, wrote with a care and elaboration that were unknown to Dryden; against whom, indeed, it is a reproach made by his pupil, that, copious as he was, he

—— wanted or forgot
The last and greatest art—the art to blot.

And so perhaps, although the expression is a strong and a startling one, may the said art, not without some reason, be called in reference to the particular species of poetry which Dryden and Pope cultivated, dependent as that is for its success in pleasing us almost as much upon the absence of faults as upon the presence of beauties. Such partial obscuration or distortion of the imagery as we excuse, or even admire, in the expanded mirror of a lake reflecting the woods and hills and overhanging sky, when its waters are ruffled or swayed by the fitful breeze, would be intolerable in a looking glass, were it otherwise the most splendid article of the sort that upholstery ever furnished.

Addison and Steele.

Next to the prose of Swift and the poetry of Pope, perhaps the portion of the literature of the beginning of the last century that was both most influential at the time, and still lives most in the popular remembrance, is that connected with the names of Addison and Steele. These two writers were the chief boast of the Whig party, as Swift and Pope were of the Tories. Addison's poem, The Campaign, on the victory of Blenheim, his imposing but frigid tragedy of Cato, and some other dramatic productions, besides various other writings in prose, have given him a reputation in many departments of literature; and Steele also holds a respectable rank among our comic dramatists as the author of The Tender Husband and The Conscious Lovers; but it is as the first, and on the whole the best, of our English essayists, the principal authors (in every sense) of the Tatler, the Spectator, and the Guardian, that these two writers have sent down their names with most honour to posterity, and have especially earned the love and gratitude of their countrymen. Steele was in his thirty-ninth, and his friend Addison in his thirty-eighth year, when the Tatler was started by the former in April, 1709. The paper, published thrice a week, had gone on for about six weeks before Addison took any part in it; but from that time he became, next to Steele, the chief contributor to it, till it was dropped in January, 1711. "I have only one gentleman," says Steele in his preface to the collected papers, "who will be nameless, to thank for any frequent assistance to me, which indeed it would have been barbarous in him to have denied to one with whom he has lived in an intimacy from childhood, considering the great ease with which he is able to dispatch the most entertaining pieces of this nature." The person alluded to is Addison. "This good office," Steele generously adds, "he performed with such force of genius, humour, wit, and learning, that I fared like a distressed prince who calls in a powerful neighbour to his aid: I was undone by my auxiliary; when I had once called him in, I could not subsist without dependence on him." By far the greater part of the Tatler, however, is Steele's. Of 271 papers of which it consists, above 200 are attributed either entirely or in the greater part to him, while those believed to have been written by Addison are only about fifty. Among the other contributors Swift is the most frequent. The Spectator was begun within two months after the discontinuance of the Tatler, and was carried on at the rate of six papers a week till the 6th of December, 1712, on which day Number 555 was published. In these first seven volumes of the Spectator Addison's papers are probably more numerous than Steele's; and between them they wrote perhaps four-fifths of the whole work. The Guardian was commenced on the 12th of March, 1713, and, being also published six times a week, had extended to 175 numbers, when it was brought to a close on the 1st of October in the same year. There is only one paper by Addison in the first volume of the Guardian, but to the second he was rather a more frequent contributor than Steele. This was the last work in which the two friends joined; for Addison, we believe, wrote nothing in the Englishman, the fifty-seven numbers of which were published, at the rate of three a week, between the 6th of October, 1713, and the 15th of February following; nor Steele any of the papers, eighty in number, forming the eighth volume of the Spectator, of which the first was published on the 18th of June, 1714, the last on the 20th of December in the same year, the rate of publication being also three times a week. Of these additional Spectators twenty-four are attributed to Addison. The friendship of nearly half a century which had united these two admirable writers was rent asunder by political differences some years before the death of Addison, in 1719: Steele survived till 1729.

Invented or introduced among us as the periodical essay

may be said to have been by Steele and Addison, it is a species of writing, as already observed, in which perhaps they have never been surpassed, or on the whole equalled, by any one of their many followers. More elaboration and depth, and also more brilliancy, we may have had in some recent attempts of the same kind; but hardly so much genuine liveliness, ease, and cordiality, anything so thoroughly agreeable, so skilfully adapted to interest without demanding more attention than is naturally and spontaneously given to it. Perhaps so large an admixture of the speculative and didactic was never made so easy of apprehension and so entertaining, so like in the reading to the merely narrative. But, besides this constant atmosphere of the pleasurable arising simply from the lightness, variety, and urbanity of these delightful papers, the delicate imagination and exquisite humour of Addison, and the vivacity, warmheartedness, and altogether generous nature of Steele, give a charm to the best of them, which is to be enjoyed, not described. We not only admire the writers, but soon come to love them, and to regard both them and the several fictitious personages that move about in the other little world they have created for us as among our best and best-known friends.

SHAFTESBURY; MANDEVILLE.

Among the prose works of the early part of the last century which used to have the highest reputation for purity and elegance of style, is that by Lord Shaftesbury entitled Characteristics of Men, Manners, Opinions, and Things. Its author, Anthony Ashley Cooper, third Earl of Shaftesbury (grandson of the first Earl, the famous meteoric politician of the reign of Charles II.), was born in 1671 and died in 1713; and the Characteristics, which did not appear in its present form, or with that title, till after his death, consists of a collection of disquisitions on various questions in moral, metaphysical, and critical philosophy, most of which he had previously published separately.

But the most remarkable philosophical work of this time, at least in a literary point of view, is Mandeville's Fable of the Bees. Bernard de Mandeville was a native of Holland, in which country he was born about the year 1670, but after having studied medicine and taken his doctor's degree he came over to England about the end of that century, and he resided here till his death in 1733. His Fable of the Bees originally appeared in 1708, in the form of a poem of 400 lines in octosyllabic verse, entitled The Grumbling Hive, or Knaves turned Honest, and it was not till eight years afterwards that he added the prose notes which make the bulk of the first volume of the work as we now have it. The second volume, or part, which consists of a series of six dialogues, was not published till 1729. The leading idea of the book is indicated by its second title, Private Vices Public Benefits;—in other words, that what are called and what really are vices in themselves, and in the individual indulging in them, are nevertheless, in many respects serviceable to the community. Mandeville holds in fact, to quote the words in which he sums up his theory at the close of his first volume, "that neither the friendly qualities and kind affections that are natural to man, nor the real virtues he is capable of acquiring by reason and self-denial, are the foundation of society; but that what we call evil in this world, moral as well as natural, is the grand principle that makes us sociable creatures, the solid basis, the life and support, of all trades and employments without exception; that there we must look for the true origin of all arts and sciences; and that the moment evil ceases the society must be spoiled, if not totally destroyed." The doctrine had a startling appearance thus nakedly announced; and the book occasioned a great commotion; but it is now generally admitted that, whatever may be the worth, or worthlessness, of the philosophical system propounded in it, the author's object was not an immoral one. Independently altogether of its general principles and conclusions, the work is full both of curious matter and of vigorous writing.

Mandeville, certainly, is no flatterer of human nature; his book, indeed, is written throughout in a spirit not only satirical, but cynical. Every page, however, bears the stamp of independent thinking; and many of the remarks he throws out indicate that he had at least glimpses of views which were not generally perceived or suspected at that day. It would probably be found that the Fable of the Bees has been very serviceable in the way of suggestion to various subsequent writers who have not adopted the general principles of the work. The following paragraphs, for example, are remarkable as an anticipation of a famous passage in the Wealth of Nations:—

> If we trace the most flourishing nations in their origin, we shall find, that, in the remote beginnings of every society, the richest and most considerable men among them were a great while destitute of a great many comforts of life that are now enjoyed by the meanest and most humble wretches; so that many things which were once looked upon as the inventions of luxury are now allowed even to those that are so miserably poor as to become the objects of public charity, nay counted so necessary that we think no human creature ought to want them. . . . . A man would be laughed at that should discover luxury in the plain dress of a poor creature that walks along in a thick parish gown, and a coarse shirt underneath it; and yet what a number of people, how many different trades, and what a variety of skill and tools must be employed to have the most ordinary Yorkshire cloth! What depth of thought and ingenuity, what toil and labour, and what length of time must it have cost, before man could learn from a seed to raise and prepare so useful a product as linen!—Remark T, vol. i. pp. 182-183 (edit. of 1724).
>
> What a bustle is there to be made in several parts of the world before a fine scarlet or crimson cloth can be produced; what multiplicity of trades and artificers must be employed! Not only such as are obvious, as woolcombers, spinners, the weaver, the cloth-worker, the scourer, the dyer, the setter, the drawer, and the packer; but others that are more remote, and might seem foreign to it,—as the mill-wright, the pewterer, and the chemist, which yet are all necessary, as well as a great number of other handicrafts, to have the tools, utensils, and other implements belonging to the trades already named. But all these things are done at home, and may be performed without extraordinary fatigue or danger; the most frightful prospect is left behind, when we reflect on the toil and hazard that are to be undergone abroad, the vast seas we are to go over, the different climates we are to endure, and the several nations we must be obliged to for their assistance. Spain alone, it is true, might furnish us with wool to make the finest cloth; but what skill and pains, what experience and ingenuity, are required to dye it of those beautiful colours! How widely are the drugs and other ingredients dispersed through the universe that are to meet in one kettle! Alum, indeed, we have of our

own; argot we might have from the Rhine, and vitriol from Hungary: all this is in Europe. But then for saltpetre in quantity we are forced to go as far as the East Indies. Cochenil, unknown to the ancients, is not much nearer to us, though in a quite different part of the earth; we buy it, 'tis true, from the Spaniards: but, not being their product, they are forced to fetch it for us from the remotest corner of the new world in the West Indies. Whilst so many sailors are broiling in the sun and sweltered with heat in the East and West of us, another set of them are freezing in the North to fetch potashes from Russia.—Search into the Nature of Society (appended to the second edition), pp. 411-413.

In another place, indeed (Remark Q, pp. 213—216), Mandeville almost enunciates one of the great leading principles of Smith's work; after showing how a nation might be undone by too much money, he concludes, "Let the value of gold and silver either rise or fall, the enjoyment of all societies will ever depend upon the fruits of the earth and the *labour* of the people; both which joined together are a more certain, a more inexhaustible, and a more real treasure than the gold of Brazil or the silver of Potosi." It might be conjectured also from some of his other writings that Smith was a reader of Mandeville: the following sentence, for instance (Remark C, p. 55), may be said almost to contain the germ of the Theory of the Moral Sentiments: —"That we are often ashamed and blush for others ... is nothing else but that sometimes we make the case of others too nearly our own;—so people shriek out when they see others in danger:—whilst we are reflecting with too much earnest on the effect which such a blameable action, if it was ours, would produce in us, the spirits, and consequently the blood, are insensibly moved after the same manner as if the action was our own, and so the same symptoms must appear."

GAY; ARBUTHNOT; ATTERBURY.

Along with Pope, as we have seen, Swift numbers among those who would mourn his death, Gay and Arbuthnot. He survived them both, Gay having died, in his forty-fourth year, in 1732, and Arbuthnot at a much more advanced age in 1735.

John Gay, the author of a considerable quantity of verse and of above a dozen dramatic pieces, is now chiefly remembered for his Beggar's Opera, his Fables, his mock-heroic poem of Trivia, or the Art of Walking the Streets of London, and some of his ballads. He has no pretensions to any elevation of genius, but there is an agreeable ease, nature, and sprightliness in everything he has written; and the happiest of his performances are animated by an archness, and light but spirited raillery, in which he has not often been excelled. His celebrated English opera, as it was the first attempt of the kind, still remains the only one that has been eminently successful. Now, indeed, that much of the wit has lost its point and application to existing characters and circumstances, the dialogue of the play, apart from the music, may be admitted to owe its popularity in some degree to its traditionary fame: but still what is temporary in it is intermixed with a sufficiently diffused, though not very rich, vein of general satire, to allow the whole to retain considerable piquancy. Even at first the Beggar's Opera was probably indebted for the greater portion of its success to the music; and that is so happily selected that it continues still as fresh and as delightful as ever.

Dr. John Arbuthnot, a native of Scotland, besides various professional works of much ability, is generally regarded as the author of the Memoirs of Martinus Scriblerus, printed in the works of Pope and Swift, and said to have been intended as the commencement of a general satire on the abuses of learning, of which, however, nothing more was ever written except Pope's treatise already mentioned on the Bathos, and one or two shorter fragments. The celebrated political satire entitled The History of John Bull, which has been the model of various subsequent imitations, but of none in which the fiction is at once so apposite and so ludicrous, is also attributed to Arbuthnot. Pope's highly wrought and noble Prologue to his Satires, which is addressed to Arbuthnot, or rather in which the latter figures as the poet's interlocutor, will for ever preserve both the memory of their friendship, and also some traits of the character and manner of the learned, witty, and kind-hearted physician.

The commencement of the reign of the Whigs at the accession of the House of Hanover, which deprived Arbuthnot of his appointment of one of the Physicians Extraordinary—leaving him, however, in the poet's words,

<blockquote>social, cheerful, and serene,
And just as rich as when he served a queen—</blockquote>

was more fatal to the fortunes of another of Pope's Tory or Jacobite friends, Francis Atterbury, the celebrated Bishop of Rochester, believed to have been the principal author of the reply to Bentley's Dissertation on Phalaris. Atterbury also took a distinguished part in the professional controversies of his day, and his sermons and letters, and one or two short copies of verse by him, are well known; but his fervid character probably flashed out in conversation in a way of which we do not gather any notion from his writings. Atterbury was deprived and outlawed in 1722; and he died abroad in 1731, in his sixty-ninth year.

PRIOR; PARNELL.

Matthew Prior is another distinguished name in the band of the Tory writers of this age, and he was also an associate of Pope and Swift, although we hear less of him in their epistolary correspondence than of most of their other friends. Yet perhaps no one of the minor wits and poets of the time has continued to enjoy higher or more general favour with posterity. Much that he wrote, indeed, is now forgotten; but some of the best of his comic tales in verse will live as long as the language, which contains nothing that surpasses them in the union of ease and fluency with sprightliness and point, and in all that makes up the spirit of humorous and graceful narrative. They are our happiest examples of a style that has been cultivated with more frequent success by French writers than by our own. In one poem, his Alma, or The Progress of the Mind, extending to three cantos, he has even applied this light and airy manner of treatment with remarkable felicity to some of the most curious questions in mental philosophy. In another still longer work, again, entitled Solomon on the Vanity of the World, in three Books, leaving his characteristic archness and pleasantry, he emulates not unsuccessfully the dignity of Pope, not without some traces of natural eloquence and picturesqueness of expression which are all his own. Prior, who was born in 1664, commenced author before the Revolution, by the publication in 1688 of his City Mouse and Country Mouse, written in concert with Charles Montagu, afterwards Earl of Halifax, in ridicule of Dryden's Hind and Panther; and he continued a Whig nearly to the end of the reign of William; but he then joined the most extreme section of the Tories, and acted cordially with that party down to his death in 1721. Such also was the political course of Parnell, only that, being a younger man, he did not make his change of party till some years after Prior. The Rev. Dr. Thomas Parnell was born at Dublin in 1679, and left his original friends the Whigs at the same time with Swift, on the ejection of Lord Godolphin's ministry, in 1710. He died in 1718. Parnell is always an inoffensive and agreeable writer; and sometimes, as, for example, in his Nightpiece on Death, which probably suggested Gray's more celebrated Elegy, he rises to considerable impressiveness and solemn pathos. But, although his poetry is uniformly fluent and transparent, and its general spirit refined and delicate, it has little warmth or richness, and can only be called a sort of water-colour poetry. One of Parnell's pieces, we may remark,—his Fairy Tale of Edwin and Sir Topaz,—may have given some hints to Burns for his Tam o' Shanter.

BOLINGBROKE.

The mention of Prior naturally suggests that of his friend and patron, and also the friend of Swift and Pope—Henry St. John, better known by his title of the Lord Viscount Bolingbroke, although his era comes down to a later date, for he was not born till 1678, and he lived to 1751. Bolingbroke wrote no poetry, but his collected prose works fill five quarto volumes (without including his letters), and would thus entitle him by their quantity alone to be ranked as one of the most considerable writers of his time; of which we have abundant testimony that he was one of the most brilliant orators and talkers, and in every species of mere cleverness one of the most distinguished figures. His writings, being principally on subjects of temporary politics, have lost much of their interest; but a few of them, especially his Letters on the Study and Use of History, his Idea of a Patriot King, and his account and defence of his own conduct in his famous Letter to Sir William Windham, will still reward perusal even for the sake of their matter, while in style and manner almost everything he has left is of very remarkable merit. Bolingbroke's style, as we have elsewhere observed, "was a happy medium between that of the scholar and that of the man of society—or rather it was a happy combination of the best qualities of both, heightening the ease, freedom, fluency, and liveliness of elegant conversation with many of the deeper and richer tones of the eloquence of formal orations and of books. The example he thus set has probably had a very considerable effect in moulding the style of popular writing among us since his time."*

_{* Article on Bolingbroke in Penny Cyclopædia, v. 78.}

Garth; Blackmore.

In one of the passages in which he commemorates the friendship of Swift, Atterbury, and Bolingbroke, Pope records also the encouragement his earliest performances in rhyme received from a poet and man of wit of the opposite party, "well-natured Garth."* Sir Samuel Garth, who was an eminent physician and a zealous Whig, is the author of various poetical pieces published in the reigns of William and Anne, of which the one of greatest pretension is that entitled The Dispensary, a mock epic, in six short cantos, on the quarrels of his professional brethren, which appeared in 1699. The wit of this slight performance may have somewhat evaporated with age, but it cannot have been at any time very pungent. A much more voluminous, and also more ambitious, Whig poet of this Augustan age, as it is sometimes called, of our literature, was another physician, Sir Richard Blackmore. Blackmore made his début as a poet so early as the year 1696, by the publication of his Prince Arthur, which was followed by a succession of other epics, or long poems of a serious kind, each in six, ten, or twelve books, under the names of King Arthur, King Alfred, Eliza, the Redeemer, the Creation, &c., besides a Paraphrase of the Book of Job, a new version of the Psalms, a Satire on Wit, and various shorter effusions both in verse and prose. The indefatigable rhymester—"the everlasting Blackmore," as Pope calls him—died at last in 1729. Nothing can be conceived wilder or more ludicrous than this incessant discharge of epics; but Blackmore, whom Dryden charged with writing "to the rumbling of his coach's wheels," may be pronounced, without any undue severity, to have been not more a fool than a blockhead. His Creation, indeed, has been praised both by Addison and Johnson; but the politics of the author may be supposed to have blinded or

* See Prologue to the Satires, 135, &c.

mollified the one critic, and his piety the other; at least the only thing an ordinary reader will be apt to discover in this his *chef-d'œuvre*, that is not the flattest commonplace, is an occasional outbreak of the most ludicrous extravagance and bombast. Altogether this knight, droning away at his epics for above a quarter of a century, is as absurd a phenomenon as is presented to us in the history of literature. Pope has done him no more than justice in assigning him the first place among the contending "brayers" at the immortal games instituted by the goddess of the Dunciad:—

> But far o'er all, sonorous Blackmore's strain:
> Walls, steeples, skies, bray back to him again.
> In Tot'nam fields the brethren, with amaze,
> Prick all their ears up, and forget to graze;
> Long Chancery-lane retentive rolls the sound,
> And courts to courts return it round and round:
> Thames wafts it thence to Rufus' roaring hall,
> And Hungerford re-echoes bawl for bawl.
> All hail him victor in both gifts of song,
> Who sings so loudly and who sings so long.

DEFOE.

The Whigs, however, had to boast of one great writer of prose fiction, if, indeed, one who, although taking a frequent and warm part in the discussion of political subjects, really stood aloof from and above all parties, and may be said to have been in enlargement of view far in advance of all the public men of his time, can be properly claimed by any party. Nor does Daniel Defoe seem to have been recognized as one of themselves by the Whigs of his own day. He stood up, indeed, from first to last, for the principles of the Revolution against those of the Jacobites; but in the alternating struggle between the Whig and Tory parties for the possession of office he took little or no concern; he served and opposed administrations of either colour without reference to anything but their measures: thus we find him in 1706 assisting Godolphin and his colleagues to compass the union with Scotland; and in 1713 exerting himself with equal zeal in supporting Harley and Bolingbroke in the attempt to carry through their commercial treaty with France. He is believed to have first addressed himself to his countrymen through the press in 1683, when he was was only in his twenty-third year. From this time for a space of above thirty years he may be said never to have laid down his pen as a political writer; his publications in prose and verse, which are far too numerous to be here particularized, embracing nearly every subject which either the progress of events made of prominent importance during that time, or which was of eminent popular or social interest independently of times and circumstances. Many of these productions, written for a temporary purpose, or on the spur of some particular occasion, still retain a considerable value, even for their matter, either as directories of conduct or accounts of matters of fact; some, indeed, such as his History of the Union, are the works of highest authority we possess respecting the transactions to which they relate; all of them bear the traces of a sincere, earnest, manly character, and of an understanding unusually active, penetrating, and well-informed. Evidence enough there often is, no doubt, of haste and precipitation, but it is always the haste of a full mind; the subject may be rapidly and somewhat rudely sketched out, and the matter not always very artificially disposed, or set forth to the most advantage; but Defoe never wrote for the mere sake of writing, or unless when he really had something to state which he conceived it important that the public should know. He was too thoroughly honest to make a trade of politics.

Defoe's course and character as a political writer bear a considerable resemblance in some leading points to those of one of the most remarkable men of our own day, the late William Cobbett, who, however, had certainly much more passion and wilfulness than Defoe, whatever we may think of his claims to as much principle. But Defoe's political writings make the smallest part of his literary renown. At the age of fifty-eight—an age when other writers, without the tenth part of his amount of performance to boast of, have usually thought themselves entitled to close their labours—he commenced a new life of authorship with all the spirit and hopeful alacrity of five-and-twenty. A succession of works of fiction, destined, some of them, to take and keep the highest rank in that department of our literature, and to become popular books in every language of Europe, now proceeded from his pen with a rapidity evincing the easiest flow as well as the greatest fertility of imagination. Robinson Crusoe appeared in 1719; the Dumb Philosopher, the same year; Captain Singleton, in 1720; Duncan Campbell, the same year; Moll Flanders, in 1721; Colonel Jacque, in 1722; the Journal of the Plague, and probably, also, the Memoirs of a Cavalier (to which there is no date), the same year; the Fortunate Mistress, or Roxana, in 1724; the New Voyage Round the World, in 1725; and the Memoirs of Captain Carleton, in 1728. But these effusions of his inventive faculty seem to have been, after all, little more than the amusements of his leisure. In the course of the twelve years from 1719 to his death in 1731, besides his novels, he produced about twenty miscellaneous works, many of them of considerable extent. It may be pretty safely affirmed that no one who has written so much has written so well. No writer of fictitious narrative has ever excelled him in at least one prime excellence—the air of reality which he throws over the creations of his fancy; an effect proceeding from the strength of conception with which he enters into the scenes, adventures, and characters he undertakes to describe, and his perfect reliance upon his power of interesting the reader by the plainest possible manner of relating things essentially interesting. Truth and nature are never either improved by flowers of speech in Defoe, or smothered under that sort of adornment. In some of his political writings there are not wanting passages of considerable height of style, in which, excited by a fit occasion, he employs to good purpose the artifices of rhetorical embellishment and modulation: but in his works of imagination his almost constant characteristic is a simplicity and plainness, which, if there be any affectation about it all, is chargeable only with that of a homeliness sometimes approaching to rusticity. His writing, however, is always full of idiomatic nerve, and in a high degree graphic and expressive; and even its occasional slovenliness, whether the result of carelessness or design, aids the illusion by which the fiction is made to read so like a matter of fact. The truthful air of Defoe's fictions, we may just remark, is of quite a different character from that of Swift's, in which, although there is also much of the same vivid conception, and therefore minutely accurate delineation, of every person and thing introduced, a discerning reader will always perceive a smile lurking beneath the author's assumed gravity, telling him intelligibly enough that the whole is a joke. It is said, indeed, that, as the Journal of the Plague is quoted as an authentic narrative by Dr. Mead, and as Lord Chatham was, in all simplicity, in the habit of recommending the Memoirs of a Cavalier to his friends as the best account of the Civil Wars, and as those of Captain Carleton were read even by Samuel Johnson without a suspicion of their being other than a true history, so some Irish bishop was found with faith enough to believe in Gulliver's Travels, although not a little amazed by some things stated in the book. But it is not probable that there ever was any second instance, even on the Irish episcopal bench, of so high a pitch of innocence.

Dramatic Writers.

To this age, also, belong three of the greatest of our comic dramatists. Congreve, Vanbrugh, and Farquhar were born in the order in which we have named them, and also, we believe, successively presented themselves before the public as writers for the stage in the same order, although they reversed it in making their exits from the stage of life,

—Farquhar dying in 1707 at the age of twenty-nine, Vanbrugh in 1726 at that of fifty-four, Congreve not till 1729 in his fifty-ninth or sixtieth year.

Congreve's first play, The Old Bachelor, was brought out in 1693, the author having already, two or three years before, made himself known in the literary world by a novel called The Incognita, or Love and Duty Reconciled. The Old Bachelor was followed by The Double Dealer in 1694, and by Love for Love in 1695; the tragedy of The Mourning Bride was produced in 1697; and the comedy of The Way of the World, in 1700: a masquerade and an opera, both of slight importance, were the only dramatic pieces he wrote during the rest of his life. The comedy of Congreve has not much character, still less humour, and no nature at all; but blazes and crackles with wit and repartee, for the most part of an unusually pure and brilliant species,—not quaint, forced, and awkward, like what we find in some other attempts, in our dramatic literature and elsewhere, at the same kind of display, but apparently as easy and spontaneous as it is pointed, polished, and exact. His plots are also constructed with much artifice.

Sir John Vanbrugh is the author of ten or twelve comedies, of which the first, The Relapse, was produced in 1697, and of which The Provoked Wife, The Confederacy, and The Journey to London (which last, left unfinished by the author, was completed by Colley Cibber), are those of greatest merit. The wit of Vanbrugh flows rather than flashes; but its copious stream may vie in its own way with the dazzling fire-shower of Congreve's; and his characters have much more of real flesh and blood in their composition, coarse and vicious as almost all the more powerfully drawn among them are.

George Farquhar, the author of The Constant Couple and The Beaux' Stratagem, and of five or six other comedies, was a native of Ireland, in which country Congreve also spent his childhood and boyhood. Farquhar's first play, his Love in a Bottle, was brought out with great success at

Drury Lane in 1698; The Beaux' Stratagem, his last, was in the midst of its run when the illness during which it had been written terminated in the poor author's early death. The thoughtless and volatile, but good natured and generous, character of Farquhar is reflected in his comedies, which, with less sparkle, have more natural life and airiness, and are animated by a finer spirit of whim, than those of either Vanbrugh or Congreve. His morality, like theirs, is abundantly free and easy; but there is much more heart about his profligacy than in theirs, as well as much less grossness or hardness.

To these names may be added that of Colley Cibber, who has, however, scarcely any pretensions to be ranked as one of our classic dramatists, although, of about two dozen comedies, tragedies, and other pieces of which he is the author, his Careless Husband and one or two others may be admitted to be lively and agreeable. Cibber, who was born in 1671, produced his first play, the comedy of Love's Last Shift, in 1696, and was still an occasional writer for the stage after the commencement of the reign of George II.; one of his productions, indeed, his tragedy entitled Papal Tyranny, was brought out so late as the year 1745, when he himself performed one of the principal characters; and he lived till 1757. His well-known account of his own life, or his Apology for his Life, as he modestly or affectedly calls it, is an amusing piece of something higher than gossip; the sketches he gives of the various celebrated actors of his time are many of them executed, not perhaps with the deepest insight, but yet with much graphic skill in so far as regards those mere superficial characteristics that meet the ordinary eye.

The chief tragic writer of this age was Nicholas Rowe, the author of The Fair Penitent and Jane Shore, of five other tragedies, one comedy, and a translation in rhyme of Lucan's Pharsalia. Rowe, who was born in 1673, and died in 1718, was esteemed in his own day a great master of the pathetic, but is now regarded as little more than a smooth and occasionally sounding versifier.

MINOR POETS.

The age of the first two Georges, if we put aside what was done by Pope, or consider him as belonging properly to the preceding reign of Anne, was not very prolific in poetry of a high order; but there are several minor poets belonging to this time whose names live in our literature, and some of whose productions are still read. Matthew Green's poem entitled The Spleen originally appeared, we believe, in his lifetime in the first volume of Dodsley's Collection—although his other pieces, which are few in number and of little note, were only published by his friend Glover after the death of the author in 1737, at the age of forty-one. The Spleen, a reflective effusion in octo-syllabic verse, is somewhat striking from an air of originality in the vein of thought, and from the laboured concentration and epigrammatic point of the language; but, although it was much cried up when it first appeared, and the laudation has continued to be duly echoed by succeeding formal criticism, it may be doubted if many readers could now make their way through it without considerable fatigue, or if it be much read in fact at all. With all its ingenious or energetic rhetorical posture-making, it has nearly as little real play of fancy as charm of numbers, and may be most properly characterized as a piece of bastard or perverted Hudibrastic—an imitation of the manner of Butler to the very dance of his verse, only without the comedy—the same antics, only solemnized or made to carry a moral and serious meaning. The Grongar Hill of Dyer was published in 1726, when its author was in his twenty-seventh year; and was followed by The Ruins of Rome in 1740, and his most elaborate performance, The Fleece, in 1757, the year before his death. Dyer's is a natural and true note, though not one of much power or compass. What he has written is his own; not borrowed from or suggested by "others' books," but what he has himself seen, thought, and felt. He sees, too, with an artistic eye—while at the same time his pictures are full of the moral inspiration which alone makes description poetry. There is also considerable descriptive power in Somervile's blank verse poem of The Chase, in four Books, which was first published in 1735. Somervile, who was a Warwickshire squire, and the intimate friend of Shenstone, and who, besides his Chase, wrote various other pieces, now for the most part forgotten, died in 1742. Tickell, Addison's friend, who was born in 1686 and lived till 1740, is the author of a number of compositions, of which his Elegy on Addison and his ballad of Colin and Lucy are the best known. The ballad Gray has called "the prettiest in the world"—and if prettiness, by which Gray here probably means a certain easy simplicity and trimness, were the soul of ballad poetry, it might carry away a high prize. Nobody writes better grammar than Tickell. His style is always remarkably clear and exact, and the mere appropriateness and judicious collation of the words, aided by the swell of the verse in his more elaborate or solemn passages, have sometimes an imposing effect. Of his famous Elegy, the most opposite opinions have been expressed. Goldsmith has called it "one of the finest in our language;" and Johnson has declared that "a more sublime or elegant funeral poem is not to be found in the whole compass of English literature." So Lord Macaulay:—"Tickell bewailed his friend in an Elegy which would do honour to the greatest name in our literature, and which unites the energy and magnificence of Dryden to the tenderness and purity of Cowper."* Steele on the other hand has denounced it as being nothing more than "prose in rhyme." And it must be admitted that it is neither very tender nor very imaginative; yet rhyme too is part and parcel of poetry, and solemn thoughts, vigorously expressed and melodiously

* Essay on Addison.

enough versified, which surely we have here, cannot reasonably be refused that name, even though the informing power of passion or imagination may not be present in any very high degree.

The notorious Richard Savage is the author of several poetical compositions, published in the last fifteen or twenty years of his tempestuous and unhappy life, which he closed in Bristol jail in 1743, at the age of forty-six. Savage's poem called The Bastard has some vigorous lines, and some touches of tenderness as well as bursts of more violent passion; but, as a whole, it is crude, spasmodic, and frequently wordy and languid. His other compositions, some of which evince a talent for satire, of which assiduous cultivation might have made something, have all passed into oblivion. The personal history of Savage, which Johnson's ardent and expanded narrative has made universally known, is more interesting than his verse; but even that owes more than half its attraction to his biographer. He had, in fact, all his life, apparently, much more of another kind of madness than he ever had of that of poetry.

Fenton and Broome—the former of whom died in 1730 at the age of forty-seven, the latter in 1745, at what age is not known,—are chiefly remembered as Pope's coadjutors in his translation of the Odyssey. Johnson observes, in his Life of Fenton, that the readers of poetry have never been able to distinguish their Books from those of Pope; but the account he has given here and in the Life of Broome of the respective shares of the three, on the information, as he says, of Mr. Langton, who had got it from Spence, may be reasonably doubted. It differs, indeed, in some respects from that given in Spence's Anecdotes, since published. A critical reader will detect very marked varieties of style and manner in the different parts of the work. It is very clear, for instance, that the nineteenth and twentieth Books are not by Pope, and have not even received much of his revision: they are commonly attributed to Fenton, and we should think rightly. But it is impossible to believe, on the other hand, that the translator of these two Books is also the translator of the whole of the fourth Book, which is likewise assigned to Fenton in Johnson's statement. Could any one except Pope have written the following lines, which occur in that Book?—

> But, oh, beloved by heaven, reserved to thee,
> A happier lot the smiling fates decree:
> Free from that law, beneath whose mortal sway
> Matter is changed, and varying forms decay,
> Elysium shall be thine; the blissful plains
> Of utmost earth, where Rhadamanthus reigns.
> Joys ever young, unmixed with pain or fear,
> Fill the wide circle of the eternal year:
> Stern winter smiles on that auspicious clime,
> The fields are florid with unfading prime;
> From the bleak pole no winds inclement blow,
> Mould the round hail, or flake the fleecy snow;
> But from the breezy deep the blest inhale
> The fragrant murmurs of the western gale.
> This grace peculiar will the Gods afford
> To thee, the son of Jove, the beauteous Helen's lord.

Pope, indeed, may have inserted this and other passages in this and other Books, of which he did not translate the whole. Broome was a much more dexterous versifier than Fenton, and would come much nearer to Pope's ordinary manner: still we greatly doubt if the twenty-third Book in particular (which passes for Broome's) be not entirely Pope's, and also many parts of the second, the eighth, the eleventh, and the twelfth. On the other hand, the thirteenth, fourteenth, fifteenth, and twenty-fourth seem to us to be throughout more likely to be by him than by Pope. Pope himself seems to have looked upon Broome as rather a clever mimic of his own manner than as anything much higher. When they had quarrelled a few years after this, he introduced his old associate in the Dunciad, in a passage which originally ran:—

> See under Ripley rise a new Whitehall,
> While Jones and Boyle's united labours fall;
> While Wren with sorrow to the grave descends,
> Gay dies unpensioned with a hundred friends;
> Hibernian politics, O Swift, thy doom,
> And Pope's, translating ten whole years with Broome.

It was pretended, indeed, in a note, that no harm was meant to poor Broome by this delicate crucifixion of him. Yet he is understood to be the W. B. who, in the sixth chapter of the Art of Sinking in Poetry, entitled "Of the several kinds of geniuses in the Profound, and the marks and characters of each," heads the list of those described as "the Parrots, that repeat another's words in such a hoarse, odd voice, as makes them seem their own." And Broome, as Johnson has observed, is quoted more than once in the treatise as a proficient in the Bathos. Johnson adds, "I have been told that they were afterwards reconciled; but I am afraid their peace was without friendship." The couplet in the Dunciad, at least, was ultimately altered to—

> Hibernian politics, O Swift! thy fate,
> And Pope's, ten years to comment and translate.

Both Broome and Fenton published also various original compositions in verse, but nothing that the world has not very willingly let die. Fenton, however, although his contributions to the translation of the Odyssey neither harmonize well with the rest of the work, nor are to be commended taken by themselves, had more force and truth of poetical feeling than many of his verse-making contemporaries: one of his pieces, his ode to Lord Gower, is not unmusical, nor without a certain lyric glow and elevation.

Another small poet of this age is Ambrose Philips, whose Six Pastorals and tragedy of The Distressed Mother brought him vast reputation when they were first produced, but whose name has been kept in the recollection of posterity, perhaps, more by Pope's vindictive satire. An ironical criticism on the Pastorals in the Guardian, which took in Steele, who published it in the 40th number of that paper (for 27th April, 1713), was followed long afterwards by the unsparing ridicule of the Treatise on the Art of Sinking in Poetry, in which many of the illustrations are taken from the rhymes of poor Philips, who is held up in one place as the great master both of the infantine and the inane in style, and is elsewhere placed at the head of the class of writers designated the Tortoises, who are described as slow and dull, and, like pastoral writers, delighting much in gardens: "they have," it is added, "for the most part, a fine embroidered shell, and underneath it a heavy lump."* Philips, in some of his later effusions, had gone, in pursuit of what he conceived to be nature and simplicity, into a style of writing in short verses with not overmuch meaning, which his enemies parodied under the name of Namby-pamby. On the whole, however, he had no great reason to complain: if his poetry was laughed at by Pope and the Tories, it was both lauded, and very substantially rewarded, by the Whigs, who not only made Philips a lottery commissioner and a justice of peace for Westminster, but continued to push him forward till he became member for the county of Armagh in the Irish parliament, and afterwards judge of the Irish Prerogative Court. His success in life is alluded to in the same part of the Dunciad where Broome is brought in—in the line,

Lo! Ambrose Philips is preferred for wit!

This *Namby-pamby* Philips, who was born in 1671 and lived till 1749, must not be confounded with John Philips, the author of the mock-heroic poem of The Splendid Shilling (published in 1703), and also of a poem in two books, in serious blank verse, entitled Cider, which has the reputation of being a good practical treatise on the brewing of that drink. John Philips, who published likewise a poem on the battle of Blenheim, in rivalry of Addison, was a Tory poet, and the affectation of simplicity, at least, cannot be laid to his charge, for what he aims at imitating or appropriating is not what is called the language of nature, but the swell and pomp of Milton. His serious poetry, however, is not

---

* According to Johnson, Gay's Pastorals were written at Pope's instigation, in ridicule of those of Philips; "but," it is added, "the effect of reality and truth became conspicuous, even when the intention was to show them grovelling and degraded. These Pastorals became popular, and were read with delight, as just representations of rural manners and occupations, by those who had no interest in the rivalry of the poets, nor knowledge of the critical dispute."—Life of Gay.

worth much, at least as poetry. John Philips was born in 1676, and died in 1708.

Two or three more names may be merely mentioned. Leonard Welsted, who was born in 1689, and died in 1747, also, like Ambrose Philips, figures in the Dunciad and in the Treatise of Martinus Scriblerus, and produced a considerable quantity both of verse and prose, all now utterly forgotten. Thomas Yalden, who died a Doctor of Divinity in 1736, was a man of wit as well as the writer of a number of odes, elegies, hymns, fables, and other compositions in verse, of which one entitled a Hymn to Darkness, is warmly praised by Dr. Johnson, who has given the author a place in his Lives of the Poets. In that work too may be found an account of Hammond, the author of the Love Elegies, who died in 1742, in his thirty-second year, driven mad, and eventually sent to his grave, it is affirmed, by the inexorable cruelty of the lady, a Miss Dashwood, who, under the name of Delia, is the subject of his verses, and who, we are told, survived him for thirty-seven years without finding any one else either to marry or fall in love with her. The character, as Johnson remarks, that Hammond bequeathed her was not likely to attract courtship. Hammond's poetry, however, reflects but coldly the amorous fire which produced all this mischief; it is correct and graceful, but languid almost to the point of drowsiness. Gilbert West was born about 1705, and died in 1756: besides other verse, he published a translation of a portion of the odes of Pindar, which had long considerable reputation, but is not very Pindaric, though a smooth and sonorous performance. The one of his works that has best kept its ground is his prose tract entitled Observations on the Resurrection, a very able and ingenious disquisition, for which the university of Oxford made West a Doctor of Laws. Aaron Hill, who was born in 1685 and died in 1750, and who lies buried in Westminster Abbey, was at different periods of his life a traveller, a projector, a theatrical manager, and a literary man. He is the author of no fewer than seventeen dramatic pieces, original and translated, among which his versions of Voltaire's Zaire and Merope long kept possession of the stage. His poetry is in general both pompous and empty enough; and of all he has written, almost the only passage that is now much remembered is a satiric sketch of Pope, in a few lines, which have some imitative smartness, but scarcely any higher merit. Pope had offended him by putting him in the Dunciad, though the way in which he is mentioned is really complimentary to Hill.

Collins; Shenstone; Gray.

By far the greatest of all the poetical writers of this age who from the small quantity of their productions, or the brevity of each of them separately considered, are styled minor poets, is Collins. William Collins, born in 1720, died at the early age of thirty-six, and nearly all his poetry had been written ten years before his death. His volume of Odes, descriptive and allegorical, was published in 1746; his Oriental Eclogues had appeared some years before, while he was a student at Oxford. Only his unfinished Ode on the Popular Superstitions of the Highlanders was found among his papers after his death, and it is dated 1749. The six or seven last years of his short life were clouded with a depression of spirits which made intellectual exertion impossible. All that Collins has written is full of imagination, pathos, and melody. The defect of his poetry in general is that there is too little of earth in it: in the purity and depth of its beauty it resembles the bright blue sky. Yet Collins had genius enough for anything; and in his ode entitled The Passions he has shown with how strong a voice and pulse of humanity he could, when he chose, animate his verse, and what extensive and enduring popularity he could command.

Gray and Shentone were both born before Collins, though they both outlived him,—Shenstone dying at the age of fifty in 1763, Gray at that of fifty-five in 1771. Shenstone is remembered for his pastoral Ballad, his Schoolmistress, and an elegy or two; but there was very little potency of any kind in the music of his slender oaten pipe. Gray's famous Elegy written in a Country Churchyard, his two Pindarics, his Ode on Eton College, his Long Story, some translations from the Norse and Welsh, and a few other short pieces, which make up his contributions to the poetry of his native language, are all admirable for their exquisite finish, nor is a true poetical spirit ever wanting, whatever may be thought of the form in which it is sometimes embodied. When his two celebrated compositions, The Progress of Poesy and The Bard, appeared together in 1757, Johnson affirms that "the readers of poetry were at first content to gaze in mute amazement;" and, although the difficulty or impossibility of understanding them which was then, it seems, felt and confessed, is no longer complained of, much severe animadversion has been passed on them on other accounts. Still, whatever objections may be made to the artificial and unnatural character and over-elaboration of their style, the gorgeous brocade of the verse does not hide the true fire and fancy beneath, or even the real elegance of taste that has arrayed itself so ambitiously. But Gray often expresses himself, too, as naturally and simply in his poetry as he always does in his charming Letters and other writings in prose: the most touching of the verses in his Ode to Eton College, for instance, are so expressed; and in his Long Story he has given the happiest proof of his mastery over the lightest graces and gaieties of song.

YOUNG; THOMSON.

Of the remaining poetical names of this age the two most considerable are those of Young and Thomson. Dr. Edward Young, the celebrated author of the Night Thoughts, was born in 1681 and lived till 1765. He may be shortly characterized as, at least in manner, a sort of successor, under the reign of Pope and the new style established by him and Dryden, of the Donnes and the Cowleys of a former age. He had nothing, however, of Donne's subtle fancy, and as little of the gaiety and playfulness that occasionally break out among the quibbles and contortions of Cowley. On the other hand, he has much more passion and pathos than Cowley, and, with less elegance, perhaps makes a nearer approach in some of his greatest passages to the true sublime. But his style is radically an affected and false one; and of what force it seems to possess, the greater part is the result not of any real principle of life within it, but of mere strutting and straining. Nothing can be more unlike the poetry of the Night Thoughts than that of the Seasons. If Young is all art and effort, Thomson is all negligence and nature; so negligent, indeed, that he pours forth his unpremeditated song apparently without the thought ever occurring to him that he could improve it by any study or elaboration, any more than if he were some winged warbler of the woodlands, seeking and caring for no other listener except the universal air which the strain made vocal. As he is the poet of nature, so his poetry has all the intermingled rudeness and luxuriance of its theme. There is no writer who has drunk in more of the inmost soul of his subject. If it be the object of descriptive poetry to present us with pictures and visions the effect of which shall vie with that of the originals from which they are drawn, then Thomson is the greatest of all descriptive poets; for there is no other who surrounds us with so much of the truth of Nature, or makes us feel so intimately the actual presence and companionship of all her hues and fragrances. His spring blossoms and gives forth its beauty like a daisied meadow; and his summer landscapes have all the sultry warmth and green luxuriance of June; and his harvest fields and his orchards "hang the heavy head" as if their fruitage were indeed embrowning in the sun; and we see and hear the driving of his winter snows, as if the air around us were in confusion with their uproar. The beauty and purity of imagination, also, diffused over the melodious stanzas of the Castle of Indolence, make that poem one of the gems of the language. Thomson, whose Winter, the first portion of his Seasons, was published in 1726, died in 1748, in his forty-eighth year. Two years before had died his countryman, the Rev. Robert Blair, born in 1699, the author of the well-known poem in blank verse called The Grave, said to have been first published in 1743. It is remarkable for its masculine vigour of thought and expression, and for the imaginative solemnity with which it invests the most familiar truths; and it has always been one of our most popular religious poems.

ARMSTRONG; AKENSIDE; WILKIE; GLOVER.

Among the more eminent, again, of the second-rate writers of longer poems about this date, the latter part of the reign of George II., immediately after the death of Pope, may be noticed Dr. John Armstrong, who was born in Scotland in 1709, and whose Art of Preserving Health, published in 1744, has the rare merit of an original and characteristic style, distinguished by raciness and manly grace; and Dr. Mark Akenside, likewise a physician, the author, at the age of twenty-three, of The Pleasures of Imagination, published in the same year with Armstrong's poem, and giving another example of the treatment of a didactic subject in verse with great ingenuity and success. Akenside's rich, though diffuse, eloquence, and the store of fanciful illustration which he pours out, evidence a wonderfully full mind for so young a man. Neither Akenside nor Armstrong published any more verse after the accession of George III.; though the former lived till 1770, and the latter till 1779. Wilkie, the author of the rhyming epic called The Epigoniad, who was a Scotch clergyman and professor of natural philosophy at

St. Andrews, would also appear from the traditionary accounts we have of him to have been a person of some genius as well as learning, though in composing his said epic he seems not to have gone much farther for his model or fount of inspiration than to the more sonorous passages of Pope's Homer. The Epigoniad, published in 1753, can scarcely be said to have in any proper sense of the word long survived its author, who died in 1772. Nor probably was Glover's blank verse epic of Leonidas, which appeared so early as 1737, much read when he himself passed away from among men, in the year 1785, at the age of seventy-four—although it had had a short day of extraordinary popularity, and is a performance of considerable rhetorical merit. Glover, who was a merchant of London, and distinguished as a city political leader on the liberal side (a circumstance which helped the temporary success of his epic), also wrote two tragedies, Boadicea, which was brought out in 1753; Medea, which appeared in 1761: they have the reputation of being cold and declamatory, and have both been long ago consigned to oblivion. He is best remembered for his ballad of Admiral Hosier's Ghost—which he wrote when he was seven-and-twenty, and was accustomed, it seems, to sing to the end of his life,—though Hannah More, who tells us she heard him sing it in his last days, is mistaken in saying that he was then past eighty.

Scottish Poetry.

Thomson was the first Scotsman who won any conspicuous place for himself in English literature. He had been preceded, indeed, in the writing of English by two or three others of his countrymen; by Drummond of Hawthornden, who has been mentioned in a preceding page, and his contemporaries—the Earl of Stirling, who is the author of several rhyming tragedies and other poems, well versified, but not otherwise of much poetical merit, published between 1603 and 1637, the Earl of Ancrum, by whom we have some sonnets and other short pieces, and Sir Robert Ayton, to whom is commonly attributed the well-known song, "I do confess thou'rt smooth and fair," and who is also the author of a considerable number of other similar effusions, many of them of superior polish and elegance. At a later date, too, Sir George Mackenzie, as already noticed, had written some English prose; as, indeed, Drummond had also done, besides his poetry. But none of these writers, belonging to the century that followed the union of the crowns, can be considered as having either acquired any high or diffused reputation in his own time, or retained much hold upon posterity. Even Drummond is hardly remembered as anything more than a respectable sonnetteer; his most elaborate work, his prose History of the Jameses, has passed into as complete general oblivion as the tragedies and epics of Lord Stirling and the Essays of Sir George Mackenzie. If there be any other writer born in Scotland of earlier date than Thomson, who has still a living and considerable name among English authors, it is Bishop Burnet; but those of his literary performances by which he continues to be chiefly remembered, however important for the facts they contain, have scarcely any literary value. Leighton, the eloquent archbishop of Glasgow, although of Scotch descent, was himself born in London. The poetry of Thomson was the first produce of the next era, in which the two countries were really made one by their union under one legislature, and English became the literary language of the one part of the island as much as of the other.

The Scottish dialect, however, still continued to be employed in poetry. The great age of Scottish poetry, as we have seen, extends from about the beginning of the fifteenth to about the middle of the sixteenth century, the succession of distinguished names comprehending, among others, those of James I., and Henderson, and Holland, and Henry the Minstrel, and Gawin Douglas, and Dunbar, and Sir David

Lyndsay.* It is remarkable that this space of a hundred and fifty years exactly corresponds to the period of the decay and almost extinction of poetry in England which intervenes between Chaucer and Surrey. On the other hand, with the revival of English poetry in the latter part of the sixteenth century the voice of Scottish song almost died away. The principal names of the writers of Scottish verse that occur for a hundred and fifty years after the death of Lyndsay are those of Alexander Scot, who was Lyndsay's contemporary, but probably survived him, and who is the author of several short amatory compositions, which have procured him from Pinkerton the designation of the Scottish Anacreon; Sir Richard Maitland of Lethington, who died at a great age in 1586, and is less memorable as a poet than as a collector and preserver of poetry, the two famous manuscript volumes in the Pepysian Library, in which are found the only existing copies of so many curious old pieces, having been compiled under his direction, although his own compositions, which have, with proper piety, been printed by the Maitland Club at Glasgow, are also of some bulk, and are creditable to his good feeling and good sense; Captain Alexander Montgomery, whose allegory of The Cherry and the Slae, published in 1597, is remarkable for the facility and flow of the language, and long continued a popular favourite, its peculiar metre (which, however, is of earlier origin than this poem) having been on several occasions adopted by Burns; and Alexander Hume, who was a clergyman and died in 1609, having published a volume of Hymns, or Sacred Songs, in his native dialect, in 1599. Other Scottish poets of the sixteenth century, of whom nothing or next to nothing is known except the names and a few short pieces attributed to some of them, are John Maitland, Lord Thirlstane (second son of Sir Richard), Alexander Arbuthnot, who was a clergyman, Clapperton, Flemyng, John Blyth, Moffat, Fethy, Balnavis, Sempil, Norval, Allan Watson, George Bannatyne (the writer of the Bannatyne

* See Vol. 1. pp. 274—232.

manuscript in the Advocates' Library), who was a canon of the cathedral of Moray, and Wedderburn, the supposed author of the Compendious Book of Godly and Spiritual Songs, of which the first edition in all probability appeared in the latter part of this century, and also, according to one theory, of The Complaint of Scotland, published in 1548.* But it is possible that some of these names may belong to a date anterior to that of Lyndsay. King James, also, before his accession to the English throne, published in Edinburgh two collections of Scottish verse by himself; the first, in 1585, entitled The Essays of a Prentice in the Divine Art of Poesy; the other, in 1591, His Majesty's Poetical Exercises at vacant hours; but the royal inspiration is peculiarly weak and flat.

In the whole course, we believe, of the seventeenth century not even the name of a Scottish poet or versifier occurs. The next that appeared was Allan Ramsay, who was the contemporary of Thomson, and must be accounted the proper successor of Sir David Lyndsay, after the lapse of more than a century and a half. Ramsay was born in 1686, and lived till 1758. He belongs to the order of self-taught poets, his original profession having been that of a barber; his first published performance, his clever continuation of the old poem of Christ's Kirk on the Green (attributed by some to James I. of Scotland, by others to James V.) appeared in 1712; his Gentle Shepherd, in 1725; and he produced besides numerous songs and other shorter pieces from time to time. Ramsay's verse is in general neither very refined nor very imaginative, but it has always more or less in it of true poetic life. His lyrics, with all their frequent coarseness, are many of them full of rustic hilarity and humour; and his well-known pastoral, though its dramatic pretensions otherwise are slender enough, for nature and truth both in the characters and manners may rank with the happiest compositions of its class.

* See Vol. I. p. 241.

THE NOVELISTS, RICHARDSON, FIELDING, SMOLLETT.

A very remarkable portion of the literature of the middle of the last century is the body of prose fiction, the authors of which we familiarly distinguish as the modern English novelists, and which in some respects may be said still to stand apart from everything in the language produced either before or since. If there be any writer entitled to step in before Richardson and Fielding in claiming the honour of having originated the English novel, it is Daniel Defoe. But, admirable as Defoe is for his inventive power and his art of narrative, he can hardly be said to have left us any diversified picture of the social life of his time, and he is rather a great *raconteur* than a novelist, strictly and properly so called. He identifies himself, indeed, as perfectly as any writer ever did, with the imaginary personages whose adventures he details;—but still it is adventures he deals with rather than either manners or characters. It may be observed that there is seldom or ever anything peculiar or characteristic in the language of his heroes and heroines: some of them talk, or write, through whole volumes, but all in the same style; in fact, as to this matter, every one of them is merely a repetition of Defoe himself. Nor even in professed dialogue is he happy in individualizing his characters by their manner of expressing themselves; there may be the employment occasionally of certain distinguishing phrases, but the adaptation of the speech to the speaker seldom goes much beyond such mere mechanical artifices; the heart and spirit do not flash out as they do in nature; we may remember Robinson Crusoe's man Friday by his broken English, but it is in connexion with the fortunes of their lives only, of the full stream of incident and adventure upon which they are carried along, of the perils and perplexities in which they are involved, and the shifts they are put to, that we think of Colonel Jacque, or Moll Flanders, or even

of Robinson Crusoe himself. What character they have to
us is all gathered from the circumstances in which they are
placed; very little or none of it from either the manner or
the matter of their discourses. Even their conduct is for
the most part the result of circumstances; any one of them
acts, as well as speaks, very nearly as any other would have
done similarly situated. Great and original as he is in his
proper line, and admirable as the fictions with which he has
enriched our literature are for their other merits, Defoe has
created no character which lives in the national mind—no
Squire Western, or Trulliber, or Parson Adams, or Strap, or
Pipes, or Trunnion, or Lesmahago, or Corporal Trim, or
Uncle Toby. He has made no attempt at any such delineation. It might be supposed that a writer able to place himself and his readers so completely in the midst of the
imaginary scenes he describes would have excelled in treating a subject dramatically. But, in truth, his genius was
not at all dramatic. With all his wonderful power of interesting us by the air of reality he throws over his fictions,
and carrying us along with him whithersoever he pleases, he
has no faculty of passing out of himself in the dramatic
spirit, of projecting himself out of his own proper nature
and being into those of the creations of his brain. However
strong his conception was of other things, he had no strong
conception of character. Besides, with all his imagination
and invention, he had little wit and no humour—no remarkable skill in any other kind of representation except
merely that of the plain literal truth of things. Vivid and
even creative as his imagination was, it was still not poetical.
It looked through no atmosphere of ideal light at anything;
it saw nothing adorned, beautified, elevated above nature;
its gift was to see the reality, and no more. Its pictures,
therefore, partake rather of the character of fac-similes than
that of works of art in the true sense.

On turning our eyes from his productions to those either
of Fielding or Richardson, we feel at once the spell of quite
another sort of inventive or creative power. Yet no two

writers could well be more unlike than the two we have mentioned are to one another both in manner and in spirit. Intellectually and morally, by original constitution of mind as well as in the circumstances of their training and situation, the two great contemporary novelists stood opposed the one to the other in the most complete contrast. Fielding, a gentleman by birth, and liberally educated, had been a writer for the public from the time he was twenty: Richardson, who had nearly attained that age before Fielding came into the world (the one was born in 1689, the other in 1707), having begun life as a mechanic, had spent the greater part of it as a tradesman, and had passed his fiftieth year before he became an author. Yet, after they had entered upon the same new field of literature almost together, they found themselves rivals upon that ground for as long as either continued to write. To Richardson certainly belongs priority of date as a novelist: the first part of his Pamela was published in 1740, the conclusion in 1741; and Fielding's Joseph Andrews, originally conceived with the design of turning Richardson's work into ridicule, appeared in 1742. Thus, as if their common choice of the same species of writing, and their antipathies of nature and habit, had not been enough to divide them, it was destined that the two founders of the new school of fiction should begin their career by having a personal quarrel. For their works, notwithstanding all the remarkable points of dissimilarity between those of the one and those of the other, must still be considered as belonging to the same school or form of literary composition, and that a form which they had been the first to exemplify in our language. Unlike as Joseph Andrews was to Pamela, yet the two resembled each other more than either did any other English work of fiction. They were still our two first novels properly so called—our two first artistically constructed epics of real life. And the identity of the species of fictitious narrative cultivated by the two writers became more apparent as its character was more completely developed by their subsequent publications, and each proceeded in proving its capabilities in his own way, without reference to what had been done by the other. Fielding's Jonathan Wild appeared in 1743; Richardson's Clarissa Harlowe—the greatest of his works—was given to the world in 1748; and the next year the greatest birth of Fielding's genius—his Tom Jones—saw the light. Finally, Fielding's Amelia was published in 1751; and Richardson's Sir Charles Grandison in 1753. Fielding died at Lisbon in 1754, at the age of forty-seven; Richardson survived till 1761, but wrote nothing more.

Meanwhile, however, a third writer had presented himself upon the same field—Smollett, whose Roderick Random had appeared in 1748, his Peregrine Pickle in 1751, and his Count Fathom in 1754, when the energetic Scotsman was yet only in his thirty-fourth year. His Sir Launcelot Greaves followed in 1762, and his Humphrey Clinker in 1771, in the last year of the author's active life. Our third English novelist is as much a writer *sui generis* as either of his two predecessors, as completely distinguished from each of them in the general character of his genius as they are from each other. Of the three, Richardson had evidently by far the richest natural soil of mind; his defects sprung from deficiency of cultivation; his power was his own in the strictest sense; not borrowed from books, little aided even by experience of life, derived almost solely from introspection of himself and communion with his own heart. He alone of the three could have written what he did without having himself witnessed and lived through the scenes and characters described, or something like them which only required to be embellished and heightened, and otherwise artistically treated, in order to form an interesting and striking fictitious representation. His fertility of invention, in the most comprehensive meaning of that term, is wonderful,—supplying him on all occasions with a copious stream both of incident and of thought that floods the page, and seems as if it might so flow on and diffuse itself for ever. Yet it must be confessed that he has delineated for us rather human nature than human life—rather the heart and its universal passions, as modified merely by a few broad distinctions of temperament, of education, of external circumstances, than those subtler idiosyncracies which constitute what we properly call character. Many characters, no doubt, there are set before us in his novels, very admirably drawn and discriminated: Pamela, her parents, Mr. B., Mrs. Jewkes, Clarissa, Lovelace, Miss Howe, Sir Charles Grandison, Miss Byron, Clementina, are all delineations of this description for the most part natural, well worked out, and supported by many happy touches: but (with the exception, perhaps, of the last mentioned) they can scarcely be called original conceptions of a high order, creations at once true to nature and new to literature; nor have they added to that population of the world of fiction among which every reader of books has many familiar acquaintances hardly less real to his fancy and feelings than any he has met with in the actual world, and for the most part much more interesting. That which, besides the story, interests us in Richardson's novels, is not the characters of his personages but their sentiments—not their modes but their motives of action—the anatomy of their hearts and inmost natures, which is unfolded to us with so elaborate an inquisition and such matchless skill. Fielding, on the other hand, has very little of this, and Smollett still less. They set before us their pictures of actual life in much the same way as life itself would have set them before us if our experience had chanced to bring us into contact with the particular situations and personages delineated; we see, commonly, merely what we should have seen as lookers-on, not in the particular confidence of any of the figures in the scene; there are they all, acting or talking according to their various circumstances, habits, and humours, and we are welcome to look at them and listen to them as attentively as we please; but, if we want to know anything more of them than what is visible to all the world, we must find it out for ourselves in the best way we can, for neither they nor the author will ordinarily tell us a word of it. What both these writers have given us in their novels is for the most part their own actual experience of life, irradiated, of course, by the lights of fancy and genius, and so made something much more brilliant and attractive than it was in the reality, but still in its substance the product not of meditation but of observation chiefly. Even Fielding, with all his wit, or at least pregnancy of thought and style—for the quality in his writings to which we allude appears to be the result rather of elaboration than of instinctive perception—would probably have left us nothing much worth preserving in the proper form of a novel, if he had not had his diversified practical knowledge of society to draw upon and especially his extensive and intimate acquaintance with the lower orders of all classes, in painting whom he is always greatest and most at home. Within that field, indeed, he is the greatest of all our novelists. Yet he has much more refinement of literary taste than either Smollett or Richardson; and, indeed, of the works of all the three, his alone can be called classical works in reference to their formal character. Both his style and the construction of his stories display a care and artifice altogether unknown to the others, both of whom, writing on without plan or forethought, appear on all occasions to have made use alike of the first words and the first incidents that presented themselves. Smollett, a practised writer for the press, had the command, indeed, of a style the fluency of which is far from being without force, or rhetorical parade either; but it is animated by no peculiar expressiveness, by no graces either of art or of nature. His power consists in the cordiality of his conception and the breadth and freedom of his delineation of the humorous, both in character and in situation. The feeling of the humorous in Smollett always overpowers, or at least has a tendency to overpower, the merely satirical spirit; which is not the case with Fielding, whose humour has generally a sly vein of satire running through it, even when it is most gay and genial.

STERNE.

But he to whom belongs the finest spirit of whim among all our writers of this class is the immortal author of The Life and Opinions of Tristram Shandy. Sterne, born in Ireland in 1713, had already published one or two unregarded sermons when the first and second volumes of his most singular novel were brought out at York in the year 1759. The third and fourth volumes followed in 1761; the fifth and sixth in 1762; the seventh and eighth not till 1765; the ninth in 1767. The six volumes of his Yorick's Sermons had also come out in pairs in the intervals; his Sentimental Journey appeared in 1768; and his death took place the same year. Sterne has been charged with imitation and plagiarism; but surely originality is the last quality that can be denied to him. To dispute his possession of that is much the same as it would be to deny that the sun is luminous because some spots have been detected upon its surface. If Sterne has borrowed or stolen some few things from other writers, at least no one ever had a better right to do so in virtue of the amount that there is in his writings of what is really his own. If he has been much indebted to any predecessor, it is to Rabelais; but, except in one or two detached episodes, he has wholly eschewed the extravagance and grotesqueness in which the genius of Rabelais loves to disport itself, and the tenderness and humanity that pervade his humour are quite unlike anything in the mirth of Rabelais. There is not much humour, indeed, anywhere out of Shakespeare and Cervantes which resembles or can be compared with that of Sterne. It would be difficult to name any writer but one of these two who could have drawn Uncle Toby or Trim. Another common mistake about Sterne is, that the mass of what he has written consists of little better than nonsense or rubbish—that his beauties are but grains of gold glittering here and there in a heap of sand, or, at most, rare spots of green scattered over an arid waste. Of no writer could this be said with less correctness. Whatever he has done is wrought with the utmost care, and to the highest polish and perfection. With all his apparent caprices of manner, his language is throughout the purest idiomatic English; nor is there, usually, a touch in any of his pictures that could be spared without injury to the effect. And, in his great work, how completely brought out, how exquisitely finished, is every figure, from Uncle Toby, and Brother Shandy, and Trim, and Yorick, down to Dr. Slop, and Widow Wadman, and Mrs. Bridget, and Obadiah himself! Who would resign any one of them, or any part of any one of them?

Goldsmith.

It has been observed, with truth, that, although Richardson has on the whole the best claim to the title of inventor of the modern English novel, he never altogether succeeded in throwing off the inflation of the French romance, and representing human beings in the true light and shade of human nature. Undoubtedly the men and women of Fielding and Smollett are of more genuine flesh and blood than the elaborate heroes and heroines who figure in his pages. But both Fielding and Smollett, notwithstanding the fidelity as well as spirit of their style of drawing from real life, have for the most part confined themselves to some two or three departments of the wide field of social existence, rather abounding in strongly marked peculiarities of character than furnishing a fair representation of the common national mind and manners. And Sterne also, in his more aërial way, deals rather with the oddities and quaintnesses of opinion and habit that are to be met with among his countrymen than with the broad general course of our English way of thinking and living. Our first genuine novel of domestic life is Goldsmith's Vicar of Wakefield, written in 1761, when its author, born in Ireland in 1728, was as yet an obscure doer of all work for the booksellers, but not published till 1766, when his name had already obtained celebrity by his poem of The Traveller. Assuming the grace of confession, or the advantage of the first word, Goldsmith himself introduces his performance by observing, that there are a hundred faults in it; adding, that a hundred things might be said to prove them beauties. The case is not exactly as he puts it: the faults may have compensating beauties, but are incontrovertibly faults. Indeed, if we look only to what is more superficial or external in the work, to the construction and conduct of the story, and even to much of the exhibition of manners and character, its faults are unexampled and astounding. Never was there a story put together in such an inartificial, thoughtless, blundering way. It is little better than such a "concatenation accordingly" as satisfies one in a dream. It is not merely that everything is brought about by such sudden apparitions and transformations as only happen at the call of Harlequin's wand. Of this the author himself seems to be sensible, from a sort of defence which he sets up in one place: "Nor can I go on," he observes, after one of his sharp turns, "without a reflection on those accidental meetings which, though they happen every day, seldom excite our surprise but upon some extraordinary occasion. To what a fortuitous occurrence do we not owe every pleasure and convenience of our lives! How many seeming accidents must unite before we can be clothed or fed! The peasant must be disposed to labour, the shower must fall, the wind fill the merchant's sail, or numbers must want the usual supply." But, in addition to this, probability, or we might almost say possibility, is violated at every step with little more hesitation or compunction than in a fairy tale. Nothing happens, nobody acts, as things would happen, and as men and women would naturally act, in real life. Much of what goes on is entirely incredible and incomprehensible. Even the name of the book seems an absurdity. The Vicar leaves Wakefield in the beginning of the third chapter, and, it must be supposed, resigns his vicarage, of which we hear no more; yet the family is called the family of Wakefield throughout. This is of a piece with the famous bull that occurs in the ballad given in a subsequent chapter:—

> The dew, the blossoms on the tree,
> With charms *inconstant* shine;
> Their charms were his, but, woe to me,
> Their *constancy* was mine.

But why does the vicar, upon losing his fortune, give up his vicarage? Why, in his otherwise reduced circumstances, does he prefer a curacy of fifteen pounds to a vicarage of thirty-five? Are we expected to think this quite a matter of course (there is not a syllable of explanation), upon the same principle on which we are called upon to believe that he was overwhelmed with surprise at finding his old friend Wilmot not to be a monogamist?—the said friend being at that time actually courting a fourth wife. And it is all in the same strain. The whole story of the two Thornhills, the uncle and nephew, is a heap of contradictions and absurdities. Sir William Thornhill is universally known; and yet in his assumed character of Burchell, without even, as far as appears, any disguise of his person, he passes undetected in a familiar intercourse of months with the tenantry of his own estate. If, indeed, we are not to understand something even beyond this — that, while all the neighbours know him to be Sir William, the Primroses alone never learn that fact, and still continue to take him for Mr. Burchell. But what, after all, is Burchell's real history? Nothing that is afterwards stated confirms or explains the intimation he is made unintentionally to let fall in one of the commencing chapters, about his early life. How, by-the-by, does the vicar come to know, a few chapters afterwards, that Burchell has really been telling his own story in the account he had given of Sir William Thornhill? Compare chapters third and sixth. But, take any view we will, the uncle's treatment of his nephew remains unaccounted for. Still more unintelligible is his conduct in his self-adopted capacity of lover of one of the vicar's daughters, and guardian of the virtue and safety of both. The plainest, easiest way of saving them from all harm and all danger stares him in the face, and for no reason that can be imagined he leaves them to their fate. As for his accidental rescue of Sophia afterwards, the whole affair is only to be matched for wildness and extravagance in Jack the Giant-killer or some other of that class of books. It is beyond even the Doctor of Divinity appearing at the fair with his horse to sell, and in the usual forms putting him through his paces. But it is impossible to enumerate all the improbabilities with which the story is filled. Every scene, without any exception, in which the squire appears involves something out of nature or which passes understanding; — his position in reference to his uncle in the first place, the whole of his intercourse with the clergyman's family, his dining with them attended by his two women and his troop of servants in their one room, at other times his association there with young farmer Williams (suddenly provided by the author when wanted as a suitor for Olivia), the unblushing manner in which he makes his infamous proposals, the still more extraordinary indulgence with which they are forgiven and forgotten, or rather forgotten without his ever having asked or dreamt of asking forgiveness, all his audacious ruffianism in his attempts to possess himself of the two sisters at once, and finally, and above all, his defence of himself to his uncle at their meeting in the prison, which surely outrants anything ever before attempted in decent prose or rhyme. Nor must that superlative pair of lovers, the vicar's eldest son George and Miss Arabella Wilmot, be overlooked, with the singularly cool and easy way in which they pass from the most violent affection to the most entire indifference, and on the lady's part even transference of hand and heart to another, and back again as suddenly to mutual transport and confidence. If Goldsmith intended George for a representation of himself (as their adventures are believed to have been in some respects the same), we should be sorry to think the likeness a good one; for he is the most disagreeable character in the book. His very existence seems to have been entirely forgotten by his family, and by the author, for the first three years after he left home; and the story would have been all the better if he had never chanced to turn up again, or to be thought of, at all. Was ever such a letter read as the one he is made in duty and affection to write to his father in the twenty-eighth chapter! Yet there is that in the book which makes all this comparatively of little consequence; the inspiration and vital power of original genius, the charm of true feeling, some portion of the music of the great hymn of nature made audible to all hearts. Notwithstanding all its improbabilities, the story not only amuses us while we read, but takes root in the memory and affections as much almost as any story that was ever written. In truth, the critical objections to which it is obnoxious hardly affect its real merits and the proper sources of its interest. All of it that is essential lies in the development of the characters of the good vicar and his family, and they are one and all admirably brought out. He himself, simple and credulous, but also learned and clear-headed, so guileless and affectionate, sustaining so well all fortunes, so great both in suffering and in action, altogether so unselfish and noble-minded; his wife, of a much coarser grain, with her gooseberry-wine, and her little female vanities and schemes of ambition, but also made respectable by her love and reverence for her husband, her pride in, if not affection for, her children, her talent of management and housewifery, and the fortitude and resignation with which she too bears her part in their common calamities; the two girls, so unlike and yet so sister-like; the inimitable Moses, with his black ribbon, and his invincibility in argument and bargain-making; nor to be omitted the chubby-cheeked rogue little Bill, and the "honest veteran" Dick; the homely happiness of that fireside, upon which worldly misfortune can cast hardly a passing shadow; their little concerts, their dances; neighbour Flamborough's two rosy daughters, with their red top-knots; Moses's speculation in the green spectacles, and the vicar's own subsequent adventure (though running somewhat into the extravaganza style) with the same venerable arch-rogue, "with grey hair, and no flaps to his pocket-holes;" the immortal family picture; and, like a sudden thunderbolt falling in the sunshine, the flight of poor passion-driven Olivia, her few distracted words as she stept into the chaise, "O! what will my poor papa do when he knows I am undone!" and the heart-shivered old man's cry of anguish—"Now, then, my children, go and be miserable; for we shall never enjoy one hour more;"—these, and other incidents and touches of the same kind, are the parts of the book that are remembered; all the rest drops off, as so much mere husk, or other extraneous enwrapment, after we have read it; and out of these we reconstruct the story, if we will have one, for ourselves, or, what is better, rest satisfied with the good we have got, and do not mind though so much truth and beauty will not take the shape of a story, which is after all the source of pleasure even in a work of fiction which is of the lowest importance, for it scarcely lasts after the first reading. Part of the charm of this novel of Goldsmith's too consists in the art of writing which he has displayed in it. The style, always easy, transparent, harmonious, and expressive, teems with felicities in the more heightened passages. And, finally, the humour of the book is all good-humour. There is scarcely a touch of ill-nature or even of satire in it from beginning to end—nothing of either acrimony or acid. Johnson has well characterized Goldsmith in his epitaph as *sive risus essent movendi sive lacrymæ, affectuum potens at lenis dominator*—a ruler of our affections, and mover alike of our laughter and our tears, as gentle as he is prevailing. With all his loveable qualities, he had also many weaknesses and pettinesses of personal character; but his writings are as free from any ingredient of malignity, either great or small, as those of any man. As the author, too, of the

Traveller and the Deserted Village, published in 1765 and
1771, Goldsmith, who lived till 1774, holds a distinguished
place among the poetical writers of the middle portion of
the last century. He had not the skyey fancy of his predecessor Collins, but there is an earnestness and cordiality in
his poetry which the school of Pope, to which, in its form
at least, it belongs, had scarcely before reached, and which
make it an appropriate prelude to the more fervid song that
was to burst forth among us in another generation.

CHURCHILL.

But perhaps the writer who, if not by what he did himself, yet by the effects of his example, gave the greatest
impulse to our poetry at this time, was Churchill. Charles
Churchill, born in 1731, published his first poem, The
Rosciad, in 1761; and the rest of his pieces, his Apology to
the Critical Reviewers — his epistle to his friend Lloyd,
entitled Night — The Ghost, eventually extended to four
Books—The Prophecy of Famine—his Epistle to Hogarth—
The Conference—The Duellist—The Author—Gotham, in
three Books—The Candidate—The Farewell—The Times—
Independence—all within the next three years and a half.
He was suddenly carried off by an attack of fever in November, 1764. If we put aside Thomson, Churchill, after
all deductions, may be pronounced, looking to the
quantity as well as the quality of his productions, to be the
most considerable figure that appears in our poetry in the
half-century from Pope to Cowper. But that is, perhaps,
rather to say little for the said half-century than much for
Churchill. All that he wrote being not only upon topics of
the day, but addressed to the most sensitive or most excited
passions of the mob of readers, he made an immense impression upon his contemporaries, which, however, is now
worn very faint. Some looked upon him as Dryden come
to life again, others as a greater than Dryden. As for

Pope, he was generally thought to be quite outshone or eclipsed by the new satirist. Yet Churchill, in truth, with great rhetorical vigour and extraordinary fluency, is wholly destitute of either poetry or wit of any high order. He is only, at the most, a better sort of Cleveland, not certainly having more force or pungency than that old writer, but a freer flow and broader sweep in his satire. Of the true fervour and fusing power of Dryden he has nothing, any more than he has of what is best and most characteristic in Pope, to whose wit his stands in the relation or contrast of a wooden pin to a lancet. The most successful ten continuous lines he ever wrote in the same style are certainly not worth the ten worst of Pope's. But, indeed, he scarcely has anywhere ten lines, or two lines, without a blemish. In reading Pope, the constant feeling is that, of its kind, nothing could be better; in reading Churchill, we feel that nearly everything might be better, that, if the thought is good, the setting is defective, but generally that, whatever there may be of merit in either, there are flaws in both.

FALCONER; BEATTIE; MASON.

To the present date belongs Falconer's pleasing descriptive poem, The Shipwreck, the truth, nature, and pathos of which, without much imaginative adornment, have made it a general favourite. It was first published in 1762, and its author, who was a native of Scotland, was lost at sea in 1769, in his thirty-ninth year. Another poem of his age, by a countryman of Falconer's, is Beattie's Minstrel, the first book of which was published in 1770, the second in 1774. The Minstrel is an harmonious and eloquent composition, glowing with poetical sentiment; but its inferiority in the highest poetical qualities may be felt by comparing it with Thomson's Castle of Indolence, which is perhaps the other work in the language which it most nearly resembles, but which yet it resembles much in the same way as gilding does solid gold, or as coloured water might be made to resemble wine. We may also notice the celebrated Heroic Epistle to Sir William Chambers, which, with several other effusions in the same vein, appeared in 1773, and is now known to have been, what it was always suspected to be, the composition of Gray's friend, Mason, who commenced poet so early as 1748 by the publication of a satire on the University of Oxford, entitled Isis, and afterwards produced his tragedies of Elfrida in 1752 and Caractacus in 1759, and the four Books of his English Garden in 1772, 1777, 1779, and 1781, besides a number of odes and other shorter pieces, some of them not till towards the close of the century. Mason, who died, at the age of seventy-two, in 1797, enjoyed in his day a great reputation, which is now become very small. His satiric verse is in the manner of Pope, but without the wit; and the staple of the rest of his poetry too is mostly words.

The Wartons; Percy; Chatterton; Macpherson.

There is much more of fancy and true poetry, though less sound and less pretension, in the compositions of Thomas Warton, who first made himself known by a spirited reply to Mason's Isis in 1749, when he was only a young man of twenty-one, and afterwards produced many short pieces, all evidencing a genuine poetic eye and taste. Thomas Warton, however, who lived till 1790, chiefly owes the place he holds in our literature to his prose works—his Observations on the Fairy Queen, his edition of the Minor Poems of Milton, and, above all, his admirable History of English Poetry, which, unfinished as it is, is still perhaps our greatest work in the department of literary history. Of the three quarto volumes the first appeared in 1774, the second in 1778, the last in 1781. Dr. Joseph Warton, the elder brother of Thomas, is also the writer of some agreeable verses; but the book by which his name will live is his

Essay on the Genius and Writings of Pope, the first volume of which was published, anonymously, in 1756, the second not till 1782. He died in 1800, in his seventy-eighth year.

The Wartons may be regarded as the founders of a new school of poetic criticism in this country, which, romantic rather than classical in its spirit (to employ a modern nomenclature), and professing to go to nature for its principles instead of taking them on trust from the practice of the Greek and Roman poets, or the canons of their commentators, assisted materially in guiding as well as strengthening the now reviving love for our older national poetry. But perhaps the publication which was as yet at once the most remarkable product of this new taste, and the most effective agent in its diffusion, was Percy's celebrated Reliques of Ancient English Poetry, which first appeared in 1765. The reception of this book was the same that what is natural and true always meets with when brought into fair competition with the artificial; that is to say, when the latter is no longer new any more than the former:—

> "As one who, long in populous city pent,
> Forth issuing on a summer's morn to breathe
> Among the pleasant villages and farms
> Adjoined, from each thing met conceives delight,
> The smell of grain, or tedded grass, or kine,
> Or dairy, each rural sight, each rural sound;"

such pleasure took the reader of those rude old ballads in their simplicity, directness, and breezy freshness and force, thus suddenly coming upon him after being sated with mere polish and ornament. And connected with the same matter is the famous imposture of Rowley's poems, by which a boy of seventeen, the marvellous Chatterton, deceived in the first instance a large portion of the public, and, after the detection of the fraud, secured to himself a respectable place among the original poets of his country. Chatterton, who terminated his existence by his own hand in August, 1770, produced the several imitations of ancient English poetry which he attributed to Thomas Rowley, a monk of the fifteenth century, in that and the preceding year. But this was the age of remarkable forgeries of this description; Chatterton's poems of Rowley having been preceded, and perhaps in part suggested, by Macpherson's poems of Ossian. The first specimens of the latter were published in 1760, under the title of Fragments of Ancient Poetry, collected in the Highlands of Scotland, and translated from the Gaelic or Erse language; and they immediately excited both an interest and a controversy, neither the one nor the other of which has quite died away even to the present hour. One circumstance, which has contributed to keep up the dispute about Ossian so much longer than that about Rowley, no doubt, is, that there was some small portion of truth mixed up with Macpherson's deception, whereas there was none at all in Chatterton's; but the Ossianic poetry, after all that has been said about its falsehood of style and substance as well as of pretension, making it out to be thus a double lie, must still have some qualities wonderfully adapted to allure the popular taste. Both Chatterton and Macpherson wrote a quantity of modern English verse in their own names; but nothing either did in this way was worth much: they evidently felt most at ease in their masks.

Dramatic Writers.

The dramatic literature of the earlier part of the reign of George III. is very voluminous, but consists principally of comedies and farces of modern life, all in prose. Home, indeed, the author of Douglas, which came out in 1757, followed that first successful effort by about half a dozen other attempts in the same style, the last of which, entitled Alfred, was produced in 1778; but they were all failures. Horace Walpole's great tragedy, the Mysterious Mother, although privately printed in 1768, was never acted, and was not even published till many years after. The principal writers whose productions occupied the stage were Goldsmith, Garrick, and Foote, who all died in the earlier part of the reign of George III.; and Macklin, Murphy, Cumberland, Colman, Mrs. Cowley, and Sheridan, who mostly survived till after the commencement of the present century. Goldsmith's two capital comedies of the Good-Natured Man, and She Stoops to Conquer, were brought out, the former in 1768, the latter in 1773. But the most brilliant contributions made to our dramatic literature in this age were Sheridan's celebrated comedies of The Rivals, brought out in 1775, when the author was only in his twenty-fifth year, The Duenna, which followed the same year, and The School for Scandal, which crowned the reputation of the modern Congreve, in 1777. After all that had been written, indeed, meritoriously enough in many instances, by his contemporaries and immediate predecessors, these plays of Sheridan's were the only additions that had yet been made to the classic comedy of Congreve, Vanbrugh, and Farquhar; and perhaps we may say that they are still the last it has received. Sheridan's wit is as polished as Congreve's, and its flashes, if not quite so quick and dazzling, have a softer, a more liquid light; he may be said to stand between the highly artificial point and concentration of Congreve and the Irish ease and gaiety of Farquhar, wanting, doubtless, what is most characteristic of either, but also combining something of each. Sheridan had likewise produced all his other dramatic pieces—The Trip to Scarborough, The Critic, &c.—before 1780; although he lived for thirty-six years after that date.

Female Writers.

The direction of so large a portion of the writing talent of this age to the comic drama is an evidence of the extended diffusion of literary tastes and accomplishments among the class most conversant with those manners and forms of social life which chiefly supply the materials of modern comedy. To this period has been sometimes assigned the commencement of the pursuit of literature as a distinct profession in England; now, too, we may say, began its domestic cultivation among us—the practice of writing for the public as the occupation and embellishment of a part of that leisure which necessarily abounds in an advanced state of society, not only among persons possessing the means of living without exertion of any kind, but almost throughout the various grades of those who are merely raised above the necessity of labouring with their hands. Another indication of the same thing is the great increase that now took place in the number of female authors. To the names of Mrs. Cowley, Mrs. Sheridan, Mrs. Brooke, Mrs. Lennox, Miss Sophia Lee, and Miss Frances Burney, afterwards Madame D'Arblay, whose two first novels of Evelina and Cecilia appeared, the former in 1777, the latter in 1782, may be added, as distinguished in other kinds of writing than plays and novels, blind Anna Williams, Dr. Johnson's friend, whose volume of Miscellanies in prose and verse was published in 1766; the learned Miss Elizabeth Carter, whose translation of Epictetus, however, and we believe all her other works, had appeared before the commencement of the reign of George III., although she lived till the year 1806; her friend Miss Catherine Talbot, the writer of a considerable quantity both of prose and verse, now forgotten; Mrs. Montagu (originally Miss Elizabeth Robinson), the pupil of Dr. Conyers Middleton, and the founder of the Blue Stocking Club, whose once famous Essay on the Writings and Genius of Shakespeare was published in 1769, and who survived till the year 1800; Mrs. Chapone (Miss Hester Mulso), another friend of Miss Carter, and the favourite correspondent of Samuel Richardson, whose Letters on the Improvement of the Mind appeared in 1773; Mrs. Macaulay (originally Miss Catherine Sawbridge, finally Mrs. Graham), the notorious republican historian and pamphleteer, whose History of England from the Accession of James I. to the Restoration was published in a succession of volumes between the years 1763 and 1771, and then excited much attention, though now neglected; and the other female democratic writer, Miss Helen Maria Williams, who did not, however, begin to figure as a politician till after the French Revolution, her only publications that fall to be noticed in this place being some volumes of verse which she gave to the world in 1782 and the two or three following years. Mrs. Hannah More, Mrs. Barbauld, Mrs. Charlotte Smith, Mrs. Inchbald, and some other female writers who did not reach the height of their reputation till a later date, had also entered upon the career of authorship within the first quarter of a century of the reign of George III. And to the commencement of that reign is to be assigned perhaps the most brilliant contribution from a female pen that had yet been added to our literature, the collection of the Letters of Lady Mary Wortley Montagu, which, although written many years before, were first published in 1763, about a year after Lady Mary's death. The fourth volume, indeed, did not appear till 1767.

Periodical Essayists.

To the latter part of the reign of George II. belongs the revival of the Periodical Essay, which formed so distinguishing a feature of our literature in the age of Anne. Political writing, indeed, in this form had been carried on from the era of the Examiner, and the Englishman, and the Freeholder, and Defoe's Review and Mercator, and the British Merchant, with little, if any intermission, in various publications; the most remarkable being The Craftsman, in which Bolingbroke was the principal writer, and the papers of which, as first collected, and reprinted in seven volumes, extend from the 5th of December, 1726, to the 22nd of May, 1731; nor was the work dropped till it had gone on for some years longer. Some attempts had even been made during this interval to supply the place of the Tatler, Spectator, and Guardian, by periodical papers, ranging, in the same strain, over the general field of morals and manners: Ambrose Philips, for instance, and a number of his friends, in the year 1718 began the publication of a paper entitled "The Free-thinker, or Essays on Ignorance, Superstition, Bigotry, Enthusiasm, Craft, &c., intermixed with several pieces of wit and humour designed to restore the deluded part of mankind to the use of reason and common sense," which attracted considerable attention at the time, and was kept up till the numbers made a book of three volumes, which were more than once reprinted. The Museum was another similar work, which commenced in 1746, and also ran to three volumes—Horace Walpole, Akenside, the two Wartons, and other eminent writers, being among the contributors. But nothing of this kind that was then produced has succeeded in securing for itself a permanent place in our literature. The next of our periodical works after The Guardian that is recognized as one of the classics of the language is The Rambler, the first number of which appeared on Tuesday, the 20th of March, 1750, the last (the 208th) on Saturday, the 14th of March, 1752, and all the papers of which, at the rate of two a week, with the exception only of three or four, were the composition of Samuel Johnson, who may be said to have first become generally known as a writer through this publication. The Rambler was succeeded by The Adventurer, edited and principally written by Dr. Hawkesworth, which was also published twice a week, the first number having appeared on Tuesday, the 7th of November, 1752, the last (the 139th) on Saturday, the 9th of March, 1754. Meanwhile The World, a weekly paper, had been started under the conduct of Edward Moore, the author of the Fables for the Female Sex, the tragedy of The Gamester and other dramatic productions, assisted by Lord Lyttelton, the Earls of Chesterfield, Bath, and Cork, Horace Walpole, Soame Jenyns, and other contributors: the first number appeared on Thursday, the 4th of January, 1753; the 209th, and last, on the 30th of December, 1756. And contemporary with The World, during a part of this space, was The Connoisseur, established and principally written by George Colman, in conjunction with Bonnell Thornton, a writer possessed of considerable wit and humour, which, however, he dissipated for the most part upon ephemeral topics, being only now remembered for his share in a translation of Plautus, also undertaken in concert with his friend Colman, the first two of the five volumes of which were published in 1766, two years before his death, at the age of forty-four. The Connoisseur was, like The World, a weekly publication, and it was continued in 140 numbers, from Thursday, the 31st of January, 1754, to the 30th of September, 1756. Mrs. Frances Brooke's weekly periodical work entitled The Old Maid, which subsisted from November, 1755, to July in the following year, is not usually admitted into the collections of the English essayists. The next publication of this class which can be said still to hold a place in our literature is Johnson's Idler, which appeared once a week from Saturday, the 15th of April, 1758, to Saturday, the 5th of April, 1760. And with The Idler closes what may be called the second age of the English periodical essayists, which commences with The Rambler, and extends over the ten years from 1750 to 1760, the concluding decade of the reign of George II. After this occurs another long interval, in which that mode of writing was dropped, or at least no longer attracted either the favour of the public or the ambition of the more distinguished literary talent of the day; for no doubt attempts still continued to be made, with little or no success, by obscure scribblers, to keep up what had lately been so popular and so graced by eminent names. But we have no series of periodical papers of this time, of the same character with those already mentioned, that is still reprinted and read. Goldsmith's Citizen of the World, occupied as it is with the adventures and observations of an individual, placed in very peculiar circumstances, partakes more of the character of a novel than of a succession of miscellaneous papers; and both the letters composing that work and the other delightful essays of the same writer were published occasionally, not periodically or at regular intervals, and only as contributions to the newspapers or other journals of the day,—not by themselves, like the numbers of the Spectator, the Rambler, and the other works of that description that have been mentioned. Our next series of periodical essays, properly so called, was that which began to be published at Edinburgh, under the name of The Mirror, on Saturday, the 23rd of January, 1779, and was continued at the rate of a number a week till the 27th of May, 1780. The conductor and principal writer of The Mirror was the late Henry Mackenzie, who died in Edinburgh, at the age of eighty-six, in 1831, the author of The Man of Feeling, published anonymously in 1771, The Man of the World, 1773, and Julia de Roubigné, 1777, novels after the manner of Sterne, which are still universally read, and which have much of the grace and delicacy of style as well as of the pathos of that great master, although without any of his rich and peculiar humour. The Mirror was succeeded, after an interval of a few years, by The Lounger, also a weekly paper, the first number of which appeared on Saturday, the 5th of February, 1785, Mackenzie being again the leading contributor; the last (the 101st) on the 6th of January, 1787. But with these two publications the spirit of periodical essay-writing, in the style first made famous by Steele and Addison, expired also in Scotland, as it had already done a quarter of a century before in England.

POLITICAL WRITING.—WILKES; JUNIUS.

A hotter excitement, in truth, had dulled the public taste to the charms of those ethical and critical disquisitions, whether grave or gay, which it had heretofore found sufficiently stimulating; the violent war of parties, which, after a lull of nearly twenty years, was resumed on the accession of George III., made political controversy the only kind of writing that would now go down with the generality of readers; and first Wilkes's famous North Briton, and then the yet more famous Letters of Junius, came to take the place of the Ramblers and Idlers, the Adventurers and Connoisseurs. The North Briton, the first number of which appeared on Saturday, the 5th of June, 1762, was started in opposition to The Briton, a paper set up by Smollett in defence of the government on the preceding Saturday, the 29th of May, the day on which Lord Bute had been nominated first lord of the Treasury. Smollett and Wilkes had been friends up to this time; but the opposing papers were conducted in a spirit of the bitterest hostility, till the discontinuance of the Briton on the 12th of February, 1763, and the violent extinction of The North Briton on the 23rd of April following, fifteen days after the resignation of Bute, with the publication of its memorable "No. Forty-five." The celebrity of this one paper has preserved the memory of the North Briton to our day, in the same manner as in its own it produced several reimpressions of the whole work, which otherwise would probably have been as speedily and completely forgotten as the rival publication, and as the Auditors and Monitors, and other organs of the two factions, that in the same contention helped to fill the air with their din for a season, and then were heard of no more than any other quieted noise. Wilkes's brilliancy faded away when he proceeded to commit his thoughts to paper, as if it had dissolved itself in the ink. Like all convivial wits, or shining talkers, he was of course indebted for much of the effect he produced in society to the promptitude and skill with which he seized the proper moment for saying his good things, to the surprise produced by the suddenness of the flash, and to the characteristic peculiarities of voice, action, and manner with which the jest or repartee was set off, and which usually serve as signals or stimulants to awaken the sense of the ludicrous before its expected gratification comes; in writing, little or nothing of all this could be brought into play; but still some of Wilkes's colloquial impromptus that have been preserved are so perfect, considered in themselves, and without regard to the readiness with which they may have been struck out,—are so true and deep, and evince so keen a feeling at once of the ridiculous and of the real,—that one wonders at finding so little of the same kind of power in his more deliberate efforts. In all his published writings that we have looked into—and, what with essays, and pamphlets of one kind and another, they fill a good many volumes—we scarcely recollect anything that either in matter or manner rises above the veriest commonplace, unless perhaps it be a character of Lord Chatham, occurring in a letter addressed to the Duke of Grafton, some of the biting things in which are impregnated with rather a subtle venom. A few of his verses also have some fancy and elegance, in the style of Carew and Waller. But even his private letters, of which two collections have been published, scarcely ever emit a sparkle. And his House of Commons speeches, which he wrote beforehand and got by heart, are equally unenlivened. It is evident, indeed, that he had not intellectual lung enough for any protracted exertion or display. The soil of his mind was a hungry, unproductive gravel, with some gems imbedded in it. The author of the Letters of Junius made his *début* about four years after the expiration of The North Briton, what is believed to be his first communication having appeared in the Public Advertiser on the 28th of April, 1767; but the letters, sixty-nine in number, signed Junius, and forming the collection with which every reader is familiar, extend only over the space from the 21st of January, 1769, to the 2nd of November, 1771. Thus it appears that this celebrated writer had been nearly two years before the public before he attracted any considerable attention; a proof that the polish of his style was not really the thing that did most to bring him into notoriety; for, although we may admit that the composition of the letters signed Junius is more elaborate and sustained than that of the generality of his contributions to the same newspaper under the name of Brutus, Lucius, Atticus, and Mnemon, yet the difference is by no means so great as to be alone sufficient to account for the prodigious sensation at once excited by the former, after the slight regard with which the latter had been received for so long a time. What, in the first instance at least, more than his rhetoric, made the unknown Junius the object of universal interest, and of very general terror, was undoubtedly the quantity of secret intelligence he showed himself to be possessed of, combined with the unscrupulous boldness with which he was evidently prepared to use it. As has been observed, "ministers found, in these letters, proofs of some enemy, some spy, being amongst them." It was immediately perceived in the highest circle of political society that the writer was either actually one of the members of the government, or a person who by some means or other had found access to the secrets of the government. And this suspicion, generally diffused, would add tenfold interest to the mystery of the authorship of the letters, even where the feeling which it had excited was one of mere curiosity, as it would be, of course, with the mass of the public. But, although it was not his style alone, or even chiefly, that made Junius famous, it is probably that, more than anything else, which has preserved his fame to our day. More even than the secret, so long in being penetrated, of his real name: that might have given occasion to abundance of conjecture and speculation, like the problem of the Iron Mask and other similar enigmas; but it would not have prompted the reproduction of the letters in innumerable editions, and made them, what they long were, one of the most popular and generally read books in the language, retaining their hold upon the public mind to a degree which perhaps never was equalled by any other literary production having so special a reference, in the greater part of it, to topics of a temporary nature. The history of literature attests, as has been well remarked, that power of expression is a surer preservative of a writer's popularity than even strength of thought itself; that a book in which the former exists in a remarkable degree is almost sure to live, even if it should have very little else to recommend it. The style of Junius is wanting in some of the more exquisite qualities of eloquent writing; it has few natural graces, little variety, no picturesqueness; but still it is a striking and peculiar style, combining the charm of high polish with great nerve and animation, clear and rapid, and at the same time sonorous,—masculine enough, and yet making a very imposing display of all the artifices of antithetical rhetoric. As for the spirit of these famous compositions, it is a remarkable attestation to the author's power of writing that they were long universally regarded as dictated by the very genius of English liberty, and as almost a sort of Bible, or heaven-inspired exposition, of popular principles and rights. They contain, no doubt, many sound maxims, tersely and vigorously expressed; but of profound or far-sighted political philosophy, or even of ingenious disquisition having the semblance of philosophy, there is as little in the Letters of Junius as there is in the Diary of Dodington or of Pepys; and, as for the writer's principles, they seem to be as much the product of mere temper, and of his individual animosities and spites, as even of his partisan habits and passions. He defends the cause of liberty itself in the spirit of tyranny; there is no generosity, or even common fairness, in his mode of combating; the newest lie, or private scandal, of the day serves as well, and as frequently, as anything else to point his sarcasm, or to arm with its vivid lightning the thunder of declamatory invective that resounds through his pages.

JOHNSON.

The character of Junius was drawn, while the mysterious shadow was still occupying the public gaze with its handwriting upon the wall, by one of the most distinguished of

his contemporaries, in a publication which made a considerable noise at the time, but is now very much forgotten:—
"Junius has sometimes made his satire felt; but let not injudicious admiration mistake the venom of the shaft for the vigour of the bow. He has sometimes sported with lucky malice; but to him that knows his company it is not hard to be sarcastic in a mask. While he walks, like Jack the Giant-killer, in a coat of darkness, he may do much mischief with little strength. . . . . . Junius burst into notice with a blaze of impudence which has rarely glared upon the world before, and drew the rabble after him as a monster makes a show. When he had once provided for his safety by impenetrable secrecy, he had nothing to combat but truth and justice—enemies whom he knows to be feeble in the dark. Being then at liberty to indulge himself in all the immunities of invisibility; out of the reach of danger, he has been bold; out of the reach of shame, he has been confident. As a rhetorician, he has had the art of persuading when he seconded desire; as a reasoner, he has convinced those who had no doubt before; as a moralist, he has taught that virtue may disgrace; and, as a patriot, he has gratified the mean by insults on the high. Finding sedition ascendant, he has been able to advance it; finding the nation combustible, he has been able to inflame it. . . . . It is not by his liveliness of imagery, his pungency of periods, or his fertility of allusions that he detains the cits of London and the boors of Middlesex. Of style and sentiment they take no cognizance: they admire him for virtues like their own, for contempt of order and violence of outrage, for rage of defamation and audacity of falsehood. . . . . Junius is an unusual phenomenon, on which some have gazed with wonder, and some with terror; but wonder and terror are transitory passions. He will soon be more closely viewed, or more attentively examined; and what folly has taken for a comet, that from his flaming hair shook pestilence and war, inquiry will find to be only a meteor formed by the vapours of putrefying democracy, and kindled into flame by

the effervescence of interest struggling with conviction; which, after having plunged its followers into a bog, will leave us inquiring why we regard it." Thus wrote, in his ponderous but yet vigorous way, Samuel Johnson, in his pamphlet entitled Thoughts on the late Transactions respecting Falkland's Islands, published in 1771, in answer, as is commonly stated, to Junius's Forty-second Letter, dated the 30th of January in that year. Junius, although he continued to write for a twelvemonth longer, never took any notice of this attack; and Mrs. Piozzi tells us that Johnson "often delighted his imagination with the thoughts of having destroyed Junius." The lively lady, however, is scarcely the best authority on the subject of Johnson's *thoughts*, although we may yield a qualified faith to her reports of what he actually said and did. He may, probably enough, have thought, and said too, that he had beaten or silenced Junius, referring to the question discussed in his unanswered pamphlet; although, on the other hand, it does not appear that Junius was in the habit of ever noticing such general attacks as this: he replied to some of the writers who addressed him in the columns of the Public Advertiser, the newspaper in which his own communications were published, but he did not think it necessary to go forth to battle with any of the other pamphleteers by whom he was assailed, any more than with Johnson.

The great lexicographer winds up his character of Junius by remarking that he cannot think his style secure from criticism, and that his expressions are often trite, and his periods feeble. The style of Junius, nevertheless, was probably to a considerable extent formed upon Johnson's own. It has some strongly marked features of distinction, but yet it resembles the Johnsonian style much more than it does that of any other writer in the language antecedent to Johnson. Born in 1709, Johnson, after having while still resident in the country commenced his connexion with the press by some work in the way of translation and magazine writing, came to London along with his friend and pupil, the afterwards celebrated David Garrick, in March, 1737; and forthwith entered upon a career of authorship which extends over nearly half a century. His poem of London, an imitation of the Third Satire of Juvenal, appeared in 1738; his Life of Savage, in a separate form, in 1744 (having been previously published in the Gentleman's Magazine); his poem entitled The Vanity of Human Wishes, an imitation of Juvenal's Tenth Satire, in 1749; his tragedy of Irene (written before he came up to London) the same year; The Rambler, as already mentioned, between March, 1750, and March, 1752; his Dictionary of the English Language in 1755; The Idler between April, 1758, and April, 1760; his Rasselas in 1759; his edition of Shakespeare in 1765; his Journey to the Western Islands of Scotland in 1775; his Lives of the Poets in 1781; the intervals between these more remarkable efforts having given birth to many magazine articles, verses, and pamphlets, which cannot be here enumerated. His death took place on the 13th of December, 1784. All the works the titles of which have been given may be regarded as having taken and kept their place in our standard literature; and they form, in quantity at least, a respectable contribution from a single mind. But Johnson's mind is scarcely seen at its brightest if we do not add to the productions of his own pen the record of his colloquial wit and eloquence preserved by his admirable biographer, Boswell, whose renowned work first appeared, in two volumes quarto, in 1790; having, however, been preceded by the Journal of the Tour to the Hebrides, which was published the year after Johnson's death. It has been remarked, with truth, that his own works and Boswell's Life of him together have preserved a more complete portraiture of Johnson, of his intellect, his opinions, his manners, his whole man inward and outward, than has been handed down from one age to another of any other individual that ever lived. Certainly no celebrated figure of any past time still stands before our eyes so distinctly embodied as he does. If we will try, we shall find that all others are shadows, or mere outlines, in comparison; or, they seem to skulk about at a distance in the shade, while he is there fronting us in the full daylight, so that we see not only his worsted stockings and the metal buttons on his brown coat, but every feature of that massive countenance, as it is solemnized by meditation or lighted up in social converse, as his whole frame rolls about in triumphant laughter, or, as Cumberland saw the tender-hearted old man, standing beside his friend Garrick's open grave, at the foot of Shakespeare's monument, and bathed in tears. A noble heroic nature was that of this Samuel Johnson, beyond all controversy: not only did his failings lean to virtue's side— his very intellectual weaknesses and prejudices had something in them of strength and greatness; they were the exuberance and excess of a rich mind, not the stinted growth of a poor one. There was no touch of meanness in him: rude and awkward enough he was in many points of mere demeanour, but he had the soul of a prince in real generosity, refinement, and elevation. Of a certain kind of intellectual faculty, also, his endowment was very high. His quickness of penetration, and readiness in every way, were probably as great as had ever been combined with the same solid qualities of mind. Scarcely before had there appeared so thoughtful a sage, and so grave a moralist, with so agile and sportive a wit. Rarely has so prompt and bright a wit been accompanied by so much real knowledge, sagacity, and weight of matter. But, as we have intimated, this happy union of opposite kinds of power was most complete, and only produced its full effect, in his colloquial displays, when, excited and unformalized, the man was really himself, and his strong nature forced its way onward without regard to anything but the immediate object to be achieved. In writing he is still the strong man, working away valiantly, but, as it were, with fetters upon his limbs, or a burden on his back; a sense of the conventionalities of his position seems to oppress him; his style becomes artificial and ponderous; the whole process of his intellectual exertion loses much of its elasticity and life; and, instead of hard blows and flashes of flame, there is too often, it must be confessed, a mere raising of clouds of dust and the din of inflated common-place. Yet, as a writer, too, there is much in Johnson that is of no common character. It cannot be said that the world is indebted to him for many new truths, but he has given novel and often forcible and elegant expression to some old ones; the spirit of his philosophy is never other than manly and high-toned, as well as moral; his critical speculations, if not always very profound, are frequently acute and ingenious, and in manner generally lively, not seldom brilliant. Indeed, it may be said of Johnson, with all his faults and shortcomings, as of every man of true genius, that he is rarely or ever absolutely dull. Even his Ramblers, which we hold to be the most indigestible of his productions, are none of them mere leather or prunello; and his higher efforts, his Rasselas, his Preface to Shakespeare, and many passages in his Lives of the Poets, are throughout instinct with animation, and full of an eloquence which sometimes rises almost to poetry. Even his peculiar style, whatever we may allege against it, bears the stamp of the man of genius; it was thoroughly his own; and it not only reproduced itself, with variations, in the writings of some of the most distinguished of his contemporaries, from Junius's Letters to Macpherson's Ossian, but, whether for good or for evil, has perceptibly influenced our literature, and even in some degree the progress of the language, onwards to the present day. Some of the characteristics of the Johnsonian style, no doubt, may be found in older writers, but, as a whole, it must be regarded as the invention of Johnson. No sentence-making at once so uniformly clear and exact, and so elaborately stately, measured, and sonorous, had proceeded habitually from any previous English pen. The pomposity and inflation of Johnson's composition abated considerably in his own later writings, and, as the cumbering flesh fell off, the nerve and spirit increased: the most happily executed parts of the

Lives of the Poets offer almost a contrast to the oppressive rotundity of the Ramblers, produced thirty years before; and some eminent writers of a subsequent date, who have yet evidently formed their style upon his, have retained little or nothing of what, to a superficial inspection, seem the most marked characteristics of his manner of expression. Indeed, as we have said, there is perhaps no subsequent English prose-writer upon whose style that of Johnson has been altogether without its effect.*

BURKE.

But the greatest, undoubtedly, of all our writers of this age was Burke, one of the most remarkable men of any age. Edmund Burke was born in Dublin, in 1730; but he came over in 1750 to the British metropolis, and from this time he mostly resided in England till his death, in 1797. In 1756 he published his celebrated Vindication of Natural Society, an imitation of the style, and a parody on the philosophy, of Lord Bolingbroke; and the same year his Philosophical Inquiry into the Origin of our Ideas of the Sublime and Beautiful. In 1757 appeared anonymously his Account of the European Settlements in America. In 1759 came out the first volume of The Annual Register, of which he is known to have written, or superintended the writing of, the historical part for several years. His public life commenced in 1761, with the appointment of private secretary to the chief secretary for Ireland, an office which carried him back for about four years to his native country. In 1766 he became a member of the English House of Commons; and from that date almost to the hour of his death, besides his exertions as a front figure in the debates and

* Every reader who takes any interest in Johnson will remember the brilliant papers of Lord Macaulay in the Edinburgh Review, for September, 1831, and Mr. Carlyle, in the twenty-eighth number of Fraser's Magazine, for April, 1832.

other business of parliament, from which he did not retire till 1794, he continued to dazzle the world by a succession of political writings such as certainly had never before been equalled in brilliancy and power. We can mention only those of greatest note:—his Thoughts on the Cause of the Present Discontents, published in 1770; his Reflections on the Revolution in France, published in 1790; his Appeal from the New to the Old Whigs, in 1792; his Letter to a Noble Lord on his Pension, in 1796; his Letters on a Regicide Peace, in 1796 and 1797; his Observations on the Conduct of the Minority, in 1797; besides his several great speeches, revised and sent to the press by himself; that on American Taxation, in 1774; that on Conciliation with America, in 1775; that on the Economical Reform Bill, in 1780; that delivered in the Guildhall at Bristol previous to his election, the same year; that on Mr. Fox's India Bill, in 1783; and that on the Nabob of Arcot's Debts, in 1785. Those, perhaps the most splendid of all, which he delivered at the bar of the House of Lords in 1788 and 1789, on the impeachment of Mr. Hastings, have also been printed since his death from his own manuscript.

Burke was our first, and is still our greatest, writer on the philosophy of practical politics. The mere metaphysics of that science, or what we may call by that term for want of a better, meaning thereby all abstract speculation and theorizing on the general subject of government without reference to the actual circumstances of the particular country and people to be governed, he held from the beginning to the end of his life in undisguised, perhaps in undue, contempt. This feeling is as strongly manifested in his very first publication, his covert attack on Bolingbroke, as either in his writings and speeches on the contest with the American colonies or in those on the French Revolution. He was, as we have said, emphatically a practical politician, and, above all, an English politician. In discussing questions of domestic politics, he constantly refused to travel beyond the landmarks of the constitution as he found it established;

and the views he took of the politics of other countries were as far as possible regulated by the same principle. The question of a revolution, in so far as England was concerned, he did not hold to be one with which he had anything to do. Not only had it never been actually presented to him by the circumstances of the time; he did not conceive that it ever could come before him. He was, in fact, no believer in the possibility of any sudden and complete re-edification of the institutions of a great country; he left such transformations to Harlequin's wand and the machinists of the stage; he did not think they could take place in a system so mighty and so infinitely complicated as that of the political organization of a nation. A constitution, too, in his idea, was not a thing, like a steam-engine, or a machine for threshing corn, that could be put together and set up in a few weeks or months, and that would work equally well wherever it was set up; he looked upon it rather as something that must in every case grow and gradually evolve itself out of the soil of the national mind and character, that must take its shape in a great measure from the prevalent habits and feelings to which it was to be accommodated, that would not work or stand at all unless it thus formed an integral part of the social system to which it belonged. The notion of a constitution artificially constructed, and merely as it were fastened upon a country by bolts and screws, was to him much the same as the notion of a human body performing the functions of life with no other than such a separable artificial head stuck upon it. A constitution was with him a thing of life. It could no more be set up of a sudden than a full-grown tree could be ordered from the manufacturer's and so set up. Like a tree, it must have its roots intertwisted with the earth on which it stands, even as it has its branches extended over it. In the great fields of politics and religion, occupied as they are with men's substantial interests, Burke regarded inquiries into first principles as worse than vain and worthless, as much more likely to mislead and pervert than to afford instruction or

right guidance; and it is remarkable that this feeling, though
deepened and strengthened by the experience of his after-
life, and, above all, exasperated by the events to which his
attention was most strongly directed in his latest days into
an intense dread and horror of the confusion and wide-
spread ruin that might be wrought by the assumption of so
incompetent a power as mere human ratiocination to regu-
late all things according to its own conceit, was entertained and expressed by him with great distinctness at the
outset of his career. It was in this spirit, indeed, that he
wrote his Vindication of Natural Society, with the design of
showing how anything whatever might be either attacked
or defended with great plausibility by the method in which
the highest and most intricate philosophical questions were
discussed by Lord Bolingbroke. He "is satisfied," he says
in his Preface, "that a mind which has no restraint from a
sense of its own weakness, of its subordinate rank in the
creation, and of the extreme danger of letting the imagination loose upon some subjects, may very plausibly attack
everything the most excellent and venerable; that it would
not be difficult to criticise the Creation itself; and that, if
we were to examine the divine fabrics by our ideas of reason
and fitness, and to use the same method of attack by which
some men have assaulted revealed religion, we might, with
as good colour, and with the same success, make the
wisdom and power of God in his Creation appear to many
no better than foolishness." But, on the other hand, within
the boundary by which he conceived himself to be properly
limited and restrained, there never was either a more ingenious and profound investigator or a bolder reformer than
Burke. He had, indeed, more in him of the orator and of
the poet than of the mere reasoner; but yet, like Bacon,
whom altogether he greatly resembled in intellectual character, an instinctive sagacity and penetration generally led
him to see where the truth lay, and then his boundless ingenuity supplied him readily with all the considerations and
arguments which the exposition of the matter required, and

the fervour of his awakened fancy with striking illustration and impassioned eloquence in a measure hardly to be elsewhere found intermingled and incorporated with the same profoundness, extent, and many-sidedness of view. For in this Burke is distinguished from nearly all other orators, and it is a distinction that somewhat interferes with his mere oratorical power, that he is both too reflective and too honest to confine himself to the contemplation of only one side of any question he takes up: he selects, of course, for advocacy and inculcation the particular view which he holds to be the sound one, and often it will no doubt be thought by those who dissent from him that he does not do justice to some of the considerations that stand opposed to his own opinion; but still it is not his habit to overlook such adverse considerations; he shows himself at least perfectly aware of their existence, even when he possibly underrates their importance. For the immediate effect of his eloquence, as we have said, it might have been better if his mind had not been so Argus-eyed to all the various conflicting points of every case that he discussed—if, instead of thus continually looking before and after on all sides of him, and stopping, whenever two or more apparently opposite considerations came in his way, to balance or reconcile them, he could have surrendered himself to the one view with which his hearers were prepared strongly to sympathise, and carried them along with him in a whirlwind of passionate declamation. But, "born for the universe," and for all time, he was not made for such sacrifice of truth, and all high, enduring things, to the triumph of an hour. And he has not gone without his well-earned reward. If it was objected to him in his own day that, "too deep for his hearers," he

"still went on refining,
And thought of convincing while they thought of dining,"

that searching philosophy which pervades his speeches and writings, and is there wedded in such happy union to glowing words and poetic imagery, has rescued them alone from the neglect and oblivion that have overtaken all the other oratory and political pamphleteering of that day, however more loudly lauded at the time, and has secured to them an existence as extended as that of the language, and to their eloquence and wisdom whatever admiration and whatever influence and authority they may be entitled to throughout all coming generations. The writings of Burke are, indeed, the only English political writings of a past age that continue to be read in the present. And they are now perhaps more studied, and their value, both philosophical and oratorical, better and more highly appreciated, than even when they were first produced. They were at first probably received, even by those who rated them highest and felt their power the most, as little more than mere party appeals—which, indeed, to a considerable extent most of them were, for their author, from the circumstances of his position and of the time, was of necessity involved in the great battle of faction which then drew into its maelstrom everything littlest and greatest, meanest and loftiest—and, as was his nature, he fought that fight, while that was the work to be done, like a man, with his whole heart, and mind, and soul, and strength. But it can hardly be said in prosaic verity, as it has been said in the liveliness and levity of verse, that he "to party gave up what was meant for mankind." He gave up nothing to his party, except his best exertions for the time being, and for the end immediately in view, while he continued to serve under its banner. He separated himself from his party, and even from the friends and associates with whom he had passed his life, when, whether rightly or wrongly, he conceived that a higher duty than that of fidelity to his party-banner called upon him to take that course. For that Burke, in leaving the ranks of the opposition in the year 1790, or rather in declining to go along with the main body of the opposition in the view which they took at that particular moment of the French Revolution, acted from the most conscientious motives and the strongest convictions, we may assume to be now completely admitted by all whose opinions anybody thinks worth regarding. The notion that he was bought off by the ministry,—he who never to the end of his life joined the ministry, or ceased to express his entire disapprobation of their conduct of the war with France—he, by whom, in fact, they were controlled and coerced, not he by them—the old cry that he was paid to attack the French Revolution, by the pension, forsooth, that was bestowed upon him five years after—all this is now left to the rabid ignorance of your mere pothouse politician. Those who have really read and studied what Burke has written know that there was nothing new in the views he proclaimed after the breaking out of that mighty convulsion, nothing differing from or inconsistent with the principles and doctrines on the subject of government he had always held and expressed. In truth, he could not have joined in the chorus of acclamation with which Fox and many of his friends greeted the advent of the French Revolution without abandoning the political philosophy of his whole previous life. As we have elsewhere observed, "his principles were altogether averse from a purely democratic constitution of government from the first. He always, indeed, denied that he was a man of aristocratic inclinations, meaning by that one who favoured the aristocratic more than the popular element in the constitution: but he no more for all that ever professed any wish wholly to extinguish the former element than the latter. . . . . The only respect in which his latest writings really differ from those of early date is, that they evince a more excited sense of the dangers of popular delusion and passion, and urge with greater earnestness the importance of those restraining institutions which the author conceives, and always did conceive, to be necessary for the stability of governments and the conservation of society. But this is nothing more than the change of topic that is natural to a new occasion."* Or, as he has himself finely said, in defending his own consistency—"A man, who, among various objects of his equal regard, is secure of some, and full of anxiety for the fate of others, is apt to go to much

* Art. on Burke, in Penny Cyclopædia, vi. 35.

greater lengths in his preference of the objects of his immediate solicitude than Mr. Burke has ever done. A man so circumstanced often seems to undervalue, to vilify, almost to reprobate and disown, those that are out of danger. This is the voice of nature and truth, and not of inconsistency and false pretence. The danger of anything very dear to us removes, for the moment, every other affection from the mind. When Priam has his whole thoughts employed on the body of his Hector, he repels with indignation, and drives from him with a thousand reproaches, his surviving sons, who with an officious piety crowded about him to offer their assistance. A good critic would say that this is a master-stroke, and marks a deep understanding of nature in the father of poetry. He would despise a Zoilus, who would conclude from this passage that Homer meant to represent this man of affliction as hating, or being indifferent and cold in his affections to, the poor relics of his house, or that he preferred a dead carcase to his living children."*

As a specimen of Burke's spoken eloquence we will give from his Speech on the case of the Nabob of Arcot, delivered in the House of Commons on the 28th of February, 1785, the passage containing the description of Hyder Ali's devastation of the Carnatic:—

> When at length Hyder Ali found that he had to do with men who either would sign no convention, or whom no treaty and no signature could bind, and who were the determined enemies of human intercourse itself, he decreed to make the country possessed by these incorrigible and predestinated criminals a memorable example to mankind. He resolved, in the gloomy recesses of a mind capacious of such things, to leave the whole Carnatic an everlasting monument of vengeance, and to put perpetual desolation as a barrier between him and those against whom the faith which holds the moral elements of the world together was no protection. He became at length so confident of his force, so collected in his might, that he made no secret whatsoever of his dreadful resolution. Having terminated his disputes with every enemy, and every rival, who buried their mutual animosities in their common detestation against the creditors of the Nabob of Arcot,** he drew from every quarter

---

* Appeal from the New to the Old Whigs.
** The designs upon Hyder, which provoked this retaliation on his part, are represented in the speech as the scheme of the Nabob's English creditors.

whatever a savage ferocity could add to his new rudiments in the arts of destruction; and, compounding all the materials of fury, havoc, and desolation, into one black cloud, he hung for a while on the declivities of the mountains. Whilst the authors of all the evils were idly and stupidly gazing on this menacing meteor, which blackened all their horizon, it suddenly burst, and poured down the whole of its contents upon the plains of the Carnatic. Then ensued a scene of woe, the like of which no eye had seen, no heart conceived, and which no tongue can adequately tell. All the horrors of war before known or heard of were mercy to that new havoc. A storm of universal fire blasted every field, consumed every house, destroyed every temple. The miserable inhabitants, flying from their flaming villages, in part were slaughtered; others, without regard to sex, to age, to the respect of rank, or sacredness of function, fathers torn from children, husbands from wives, enveloped in a whirlwind of cavalry, and amidst the goading spears of drivers, and the trampling of pursuing horses, were swept into captivity in an unknown and hostile land. Those who were able to evade this tempest fled to the walled cities. But, escaping from fire, sword, and exile, they fell into the jaws of famine.

The alms of the settlement, in this dreadful exigency, were certainly liberal; and all was done by charity that private charity could do; but it was a people in beggary, a nation which stretched out its hands for food. For months together these creatures of sufferance, whose very excess and luxury in their most plenteous days had fallen short of the allowance of our austerest fasts, silent, patient, resigned, without sedition or disturbance, almost without complaint, perished by an hundred a day in the streets of Madras; every day seventy at least laid their bodies in the streets, or on the glacis of Tanjore, and expired of famine in the granary of India. I was going to awake your justice towards this unhappy part of our fellow-citizens by bringing before you some of the circumstances of this plague of hunger. Of all the calamities which beset and waylay the life of man, this comes the nearest to our heart, and is that wherein the proudest of us all feels himself to be nothing more than he is: but I find myself unable to manage it with decorum: these details are of a species of horror so nauseous and disgusting: they are so degrading to the sufferers and to the hearers; they are so humiliating to human nature itself; that, on better thoughts, I find it more advisable to throw a pall over this hideous object, and to leave it to your general conceptions.

For eighteen months without intermission, this destruction raged from the gates of Madras to the gates of Tanjore: and so completely did these masters in their art, Hyder Ali and his ferocious son, absolve themselves of their impious vow, that, when the British armies traversed, as they did, the Carnatic for hundreds of miles in all directions, through the whole line of their march they did not see one man, not one woman, not one child, not one four-footed beast of any description whatever. One dead, uniform silence reigned over the whole region.

It is a mistake to suppose that either imagination or passion is apt to become weaker as the other powers of the mind strengthen and acquire larger scope. The history of all the greatest poetical minds of all times and countries confutes this notion. Burke's imagination grew with his intellect, by which it was nourished, with his ever-extending realm of thought, with his constantly increasing experience of life and knowledge of every kind; and his latest writings are his most splendid as well as his most profound. Undoubtedly the work in which his eloquence is at once the most highly finished, and the most impregnated with philosophy and depth of thought, is his Reflections on the French Revolution. But this work is so generally known, at least in its most striking passages, that we may satisfy ourselves with a single short extract:—

> You will observe, that, from Magna Charta to the Declaration of Rights it has been the uniform policy of our constitution to claim and assert our liberties as an *entailed inheritance*, derived to us from our forefathers, and to be transmitted to our posterity; as an estate specially belonging to the people of this kingdom, without any reference whatever to any other more general or prior right. By this means our constitution preserves an unity in so great a diversity of its parts. We have an inheritable crown; an inheritable peerage; and a House of Commons and a people inheriting privileges, franchises, and liberties from a long line of ancestors.
>
> This policy appears to me to be the result of profound reflection; or rather the happy effect of following nature, which is wisdom without reflection, and above it. A spirit of innovation is generally the result of a selfish temper and confined views. People will not look forward to posterity, who never look backward to their ancestors. Besides, the people of England well know, that the idea of inheritance furnishes a sure principle of conservation, and a sure principle of transmission, without at all excluding a principle of improvement. It leaves acquisition free; but it secures what it acquires. Whatever advantages are obtained by a state proceeding on these maxims are locked fast as in a sort of family settlement; grasped as in a kind of mortmain for ever. By a constitutional policy, working after the pattern of nature, we receive, we hold, we transmit our government and our privileges, in the same manner in which we enjoy and transmit our property and our lives. The institutions of policy, the goods of fortune, the gifts of Providence, are handed down, to us and from us, in the same course and order. Our political system is placed in a just correspondence and symmetry with the order of the world, and with the mode of existence decreed to a permanent body composed of transitory parts; wherein, by the disposition of a stupendous wisdom, moulding together the great mysterious incorporation of the human race, the whole at one time is never old, or middle-aged, or young, but, in a condition of unchangeable constancy, moves on through the varied tenor of perpetual decay, fall, renovation, and progression. Thus, by preserving the method of nature in the conduct of the state, in what we improve we are never wholly new; in what we retain we are never wholly obsolete. By adhering in this manner, and on these principles, to our forefathers, we are guided, not by the superstition of antiquarians, but by the spirit of philosophic analogy. In this choice of inheritance we have given to our frame of polity the image of a relation in blood; binding up the constitution of our country with our dearest domestic ties; adopting our fundamental laws into the bosom of our family affections; keeping inseparable, and cherishing with the warmth of all their combined and mutually reflected charities, our state, our hearths, our sepulchres, and our altars.
>
> Through the same plan of a conformity to nature in our artificial institu-

tions, and by calling in the aid of her unerring and powerful instincts to fortify the fallible and feeble contrivances of our reason, we have derived several other, and those no small, benefits from considering our liberties in the light of an inheritance. Always acting as if in the presence of canonized forefathers, the spirit of freedom, leading in itself to misrule and excess, is tempered with an awful gravity. This idea of a liberal descent inspires us with a sense of habitual native dignity, which prevents that upstart insolence almost inevitably adhering to and disgracing those who are the first acquirers of any distinction. By this means our liberty becomes a noble freedom. It carries an imposing and majestic aspect. It has a pedigree and illustrating ancestors. It has its bearings and its ensigns armorial. It has its gallery of portraits; its monumental inscriptions; its records, evidences, and titles. We procure reverence to our civil institutions on the principle upon which nature teaches us to revere individual men; on account of their age, and on account of those from whom they are descended. All your sophisters cannot produce any thing better adapted to preserve a rational and manly freedom than the course that we have pursued, who have chosen our nature rather than our speculations, our breasts rather than our inventions, for the great conservatories and magazines of our rights and privileges.

The Reflections appeared in 1790. We shall not give any extract from the Letter to a Noble Lord on the attacks made upon him in the House of Lords by the Duke of Bedford and the Earl of Lauderdale, which, as it is one of the most eloquent and spirited, is also perhaps the most generally known of all Burke's writings. The following passage from another Letter, written in 1795 (the year before), to William Elliot, Esq., on a speech made in the House of Lords by the Duke of Norfolk, will probably be less familiar to many of our readers:—

I wish to warn the people against the greatest of all evils—a blind and furious spirit of innovation, under the name of reform. I was indeed well aware that power rarely reforms itself. So it is undoubtedly when all is quiet about it. But I was in hopes that provident fear might prevent fruitless penitence. I trusted that danger might produce at least circumspection; I flattered myself, in a moment like this, that nothing would be added to make authority top-heavy; that the very moment of an earthquake would not be the time chosen for adding a story to our houses. I hoped to see the surest of all reforms, perhaps the only sure reform, the ceasing to do ill. In the meantime, I wished to the people the wisdom of knowing how to tolerate a condition which none of their efforts can render much more than tolerable. It was a condition, however, in which every thing was to be found that could enable them to live to nature, and, if so they pleased, to live to virtue and to honour.

I do not repent that I thought better of those to whom I wished well than they will suffer me long to think that they deserved. Far from repenting, I would to God that new faculties had been called up in me, in favour not of this or that man, or this or that system, but of the general vital principle, that whilst in its vigour produced the state of things transmitted to us from our fathers; but which, through the joint operations of the abuses of authority and liberty, may perish in our hands. I am not of opinion that the race of men, and the commonwealths they create, like the bodies of individuals, grow effete, and languid, and bloodless, and ossify, by the necessities of their own conformation and the fatal operation of longevity and time. These analogies between bodies natural and politic, though they may sometimes illustrate arguments, furnish no argument of themselves. They are but too often used, under the colour of a specious philosophy, to find apologies for the despair of laziness and pusillanimity, and to excuse the want of all manly efforts when the exigencies of our country call for them most loudly.

How often has public calamity been arrested on the very brink of ruin by the seasonable energy of a single man! Have we no such man amongst us? I am as sure as I am of my being that one vigorous mind, without office, without situation, without public functions of any kind (at a time when the want of such a thing is felt, as I am sure it is), I say, one such man, confiding in the aid of God, and full of just reliance in his own fortitude, vigour, enterprise, and perseverance, would first draw to him some few like himself, and then that multitudes, hardly thought to be in existence, would appear, and troop about him.

If I saw this auspicious beginning, baffled and frustrated as I am, yet, on the very verge of a timely grave, abandoned abroad and desolate at home, stripped of my hoast, my hope, my consolation, my helper, my counsellor, and my guide (you know in part what I have lost, and would to God I could clear myself of all neglect and fault in that loss), yet thus, even thus, I would rake up the fire under all the ashes that oppress it. I am no longer patient of the public eye; nor am I of force to win my way, and to justle and elbow in a crowd. But, even in solitude, something may be done for society. The meditations of the closet have affected senates with a subtle frenzy, and inflamed armies with the brands of the furies. The cure might come from the same source with the distemper. I would add my part to those who would animate the people (whose hearts are yet right) to new exertions in the old cause.

Novelty is not the only source of zeal. Why should not a Maccabeus and his brethren arise to assert the honour of the ancient laws, and to defend the temple of their forefathers, with as ardent a spirit as can inspire any innovator to destroy the monuments of the piety and the glory of ancient ages? It is not a hazarded assertion, it is a great truth, that, when once things are gone out of their ordinary course, it is by acts out of the ordinary course they can alone be re-established. Republican spirit can only be combated by a spirit of the same nature: of the same nature, but informed with another principle, and pointed to another end. I would persuade a resistance both to the corruption and to the reformation that prevails. It will not be the weaker, but much the stronger, for combating both together. A victory over real corruptions would enable us to baffle the spurious and pretended reformations. I would not wish to excite, or even to tolerate, that kind of evil which invokes the powers of hell to rectify the disorders of the earth. No! I would add my voice, with better, and, I trust, more potent charms, to draw down justice, and wisdom, and fortitude from heaven, for the correction of human vice, and the recalling of human error from the devious ways into which it has been betrayed. I would wish to call the impulses of individuals at once to the aid and to the control of authority. By this, which I call the true republican spirit, paradoxical as it may appear, monarchies alone can be rescued from the imbecility of courts and the madness of the crowd. This republican spirit would not suffer men in high place to bring ruin on their country and on themselves. It would reform, not by destroying, but by saving the great, the rich, and the powerful. Such a republican spirit we, perhaps fondly, conceive to have animated the distinguished heroes and patriots of old, who knew no mode of policy but religion and virtue. These they would have paramount to all constitutions; they would not suffer monarchs, or senates, or popular assemblies, under pretences of dignity, or authority, or freedom, to shake off those moral riders which reason has appointed to govern every sort of rude power. These, in appearance loading them by their weight, do by that pressure augment their essential force. The momentum is increased by the extraneous weight. It is true in moral, as it is in mechanical science. It is true, not only in the draught but in the race. These riders of the great, in effect, hold the reins which guide them in their course, and wear the spur that stimulates them to the goals of honour and of safety. The great must submit to the dominion of prudence and of virtue, or none will long submit to the dominion of the great.

From the second of the Letters on a Regicide Peace, or to transcribe the full title, Letters addressed to a Member of the present Parliament on the Proposals for Peace with the Regicide Directory of France,* published in 1796, we give as our last extract the following remarkable observations on the conduct of the war:—

It is a dreadful truth, but it is a truth that cannot be concealed; in ability, in dexterity, in the distinctness of their views, the Jacobins are our superiors. They saw the thing right from the very beginning. Whatever were the first motives to the war among politicians, they saw that in its spirit, and for its objects, it was a *civil war*; and as such they pursued it. It is a war between the partisans of the ancient, civil, moral, and political order of Europe, against a sect of fanatical and ambitious atheists, which means to change them all. It is not France extending a foreign empire over other nations: it is a sect aiming at universal empire, and beginning with the conquest of France. The leaders of that sect secured the *centre of Europe*; and, that assured, they knew that, whatever might be the event of battles and sieges, their *cause* was victorious. Whether its territory had a little more or a little less peeled from its surface, or whether an island or two was detached from its commerce, to them was of little moment. The conquest of France was a glorious acquisition. That once well laid as a basis of empire, opportunities never could be wanting to regain or to replace what had been lost, and dreadfully to avenge themselves on the faction of their adversaries.

They saw it was a *civil war*. It was their business to persuade their adversaries that it ought to be a *foreign* war. The Jacobins everywhere set up a cry against the new crusade; and they intrigued with effect in the cabinet, in the field, and in every private society in Europe. Their task was not difficult. The condition of princes, and sometimes of first ministers too, is to be pitied. The creatures of the desk, and the creatures of favour, had no relish for the principles of the manifestoes.¹ They promised no governments, no regiments,

* There are four Letters in all; of which the two first appeared in 1796 (a surreptitious edition being also brought out at the same time by Owen, a bookseller of Piccadilly), the third was passing through the press when Burke died, in July, 1797, and the fourth, which is unfinished, and had been written, so far as it goes, before the three others, after his death.
¹ Of the Emperor and the King of Prussia, published in August, 1792.

no revenues from whence emoluments might arise by perquisite or by grant. In truth, the tribe of vulgar politicians are the lowest of our species. There is no trade so vile and mechanical as government in their hands. Virtue is not their habit. They are out of themselves in any course of conduct recommended only by conscience and glory. A large, liberal, and prospective view of the interests of states passes with them for romance; and the principles that recommend it for the wanderings of a disordered imagination. The calculators compute them out of their senses. The jesters and buffoons shame them out of everything grand and elevated. Littleness in object and in means to them appears soundness and sobriety. They think there is nothing worth pursuit but that which they can handle—which they can measure with a two-foot rule—which they can tell upon ten fingers.

Without the principles of the Jacobins, perhaps without any principles at all, they played the game of that faction..... They aimed, or pretended to aim, at *defending* themselves against a danger from which there can be no security in any *defensive* plan..... This error obliged them, even in their offensive operations, to adopt a plan of war, against the success of which there was something little short of mathematical demonstration. They refused to take any step which might strike at the heart of affairs. They seemed unwilling to wound the enemy in any vital part. They acted through the whole as if they really wished the conservation of the Jacobin power, as what might be more favourable than the lawful government to the attainment of the petty objects they looked for. They always kept on the circumference; and, the wider and remoter the circle was, the more eagerly they chose it as their sphere of action in this centrifugal war. The plan they pursued in its nature demanded great length of time. In its execution, they who went the nearest way to work were obliged to cover an incredible extent of country. It left to the enemy every means of destroying this extended line of weakness. Ill success in any part was sure to defeat the effect of the whole. This is true of Austria. It is still more true of England. On this false plan even good fortune, by further weakening the victor, put him but the further off from his object.

As long as there was any appearance of success, the spirit of aggrandisement, and consequently the spirit of mutual jealousy, seized upon all the coalesced powers. Some sought an accession of territory at the expense of France, some at the expense of each other, some at the expense of third parties; and, when the vicissitude of disaster took its turn, they found common distress a treacherous bond of faith and friendship.

The greatest skill, conducting the greatest military apparatus, has been employed; but it has been worse than uselessly employed, through the false policy of the war. The operations of the field suffered by the errors of the cabinet. If the same spirit continues when peace is made, the peace will fix and perpetuate all the errors of the war.....

Had we carried on the war on the side of France which looks towards the Channel or the Atlantic, we should have attacked our enemy on his weak or unarmed side. We should not have to reckon on the loss of a man who did not fall in battle. We should have an ally in the heart of the country, who, to one hundred thousand, would at one time have added eighty thousand men at the least, and all animated by principle, by enthusiasm, and by vengeance: motives which secured them to the cause in a very different manner from some of those allies whom we subsidized with millions. This ally (or rather this principal in the war), by the confession of the regicide himself, was more formidable to him than all his other foes united. Warring there, we should have led our arms to the capital of wrong. Defeated, we could not fail (proper precautions taken) of a sure retreat. Stationary, and only supporting the royalists, an impenetrable barrier, an impregnable rampart, would have been formed between the enemy and his naval power. We are probably the only nation who have declined to act against an enemy, when it might have been done, in his own country; and who, having an armed, a powerful, and a long victorious ally in that country, declined all effectual co-operation, and suffered him to perish for want of support. On the plan of a war in France, every advantage that our allies might obtain would be doubtful in its effect. Disasters on the one side might have a fair chance of being compensated by victories on the other. Had we brought the main of our force to bear upon that quarter, all the operations of the British and imperial crowns would have been combined. The war would have had system, correspondence, and a certain connection. But, as the war has been pursued, the operations of the two crowns have not the smallest degree of mutual bearing or relation.[1]

METAPHYSICAL AND ETHICAL WRITERS.

The most remarkable metaphysical and speculative works which had appeared in England since Locke's Essay were, Dr. Samuel Clarke's Sermons on the Evidences of Natural and Revealed Religion, 1705, in which he expounded his famous à priori argument for the existence of a God; Berkeley's Theory of Vision, 1709; his Principles of Human Knowledge, 1710, in which he announced his argument against the existence of matter; his Dialogue between Hylas and Philonous, 1713; his Alciphron, or the Minute Philosopher, 1732; his Analyst, 1734; the Earl of Shaftesbury's Characteristics of Men, Manners, Opinions, and Times, first published in the form in which we now have them in 1713, after the author's death; Mandeville's Fable of the Bees, or Private Vices Public Benefits, 1714; Dr. Francis Hutcheson's Inquiry into the Ideas of Beauty and Virtue, 1725; Andrew Baxter's Inquiry into the Nature of the Human Soul, 1730 (?); Bishop Butler's Sermons preached at the Rolls Chapel, 1726; and his Analogy of Religion, Natural and Revealed, to the Constitution and Course of Nature, 1736. David Hume, who was born in 1711, and died in 1776, and

[1] These prophetic views are very similar to those that were urged twelve years later in a memorable article in the Edinburgh Review, known to be by a great living orator. (See No. XXV., Don Cevallos on the French Usurpation of Spain.)

who has gained the highest place in two very distinct fields of intellectual and literary enterprise, commenced his literary life by the publication of his Treatise on Human Nature, in 1739. The work, which, as he has himself stated, was projected before he left college, and written and published not long after, fell, to use his own words, "dead-born from the press;" nor did the speculations it contained attract much more attention when republished ten years after in another form under the title of Philosophical Essays concerning Human Understanding; but they eventually proved perhaps more exciting and productive, at least for a time, both in this and in other countries, than any other metaphysical views that had been promulgated in modern times. Hume's Inquiry concerning the Principles of Morals appeared in 1752, his Natural History of Religion in 1755; and with the latter publication he may be regarded as having concluded the exposition of his sceptical philosophy. Among the most distinguished writers on mind and morals that appeared after Hume within the first quarter of a century of the reign of George III. may be mentioned Hartley, whose Observations on Man, in which he unfolded his hypothesis of the association of ideas, were published in 1749; Lord Kames (Henry Home), whose Essays on the Principles of Morality and Natural Religion were published in 1752; Adam Smith, whose Theory of Moral Sentiments was published in 1759; Reid, whose Inquiry into the Human Mind on the Principles of Common Sense was published in 1764; Abraham Tucker (calling himself Edward Search, Esq.), the first part of whose Light of Nature Pursued was published in 1768, the second in 1778, after the author's death; and Priestley, whose new edition of Hartley's work, with an Introductory Dissertation, was published in 1775; his Examination of Dr. Reid's Inquiry, the same year; and his Doctrine of Philosophical Necessity, in 1777. We may add to the list Campbell's very able Dissertation on Miracles, in answer to Hume, which appeared in 1763; and Beattie's Essay on Truth, noticed in a former page, which appeared in 1770, and was also, as everybody knows, an attack upon the philosophy of the great sceptic.

HISTORICAL WRITERS:—HUME; ROBERTSON; GIBBON.

In the latter part of his literary career Hume struck into altogether another line, and the subtle and daring metaphysician suddenly came before the world in the new character of an historian. He appears, indeed, to have nearly abandoned metaphysics very soon after the publication of his Philosophical Essays. In a letter to his friend Sir Gilbert Elliott, which, though without date, seems from its contents, according to Mr. Stewart, to have been written about 1750 or 1751, he says, "I am sorry that our correspondence should lead us into these abstract speculations. I have thought, and read, and composed very little on such questions of late. Morals, politics, and literature have employed all my time." The first volume of his History of Great Britain, containing the Reigns of James I. and Charles I., was published, in quarto, at Edinburgh, in 1754; the second, containing the Commonwealth and the Reigns of Charles II. and James II., at London, in 1757. According to his own account the former was received with "one cry of reproach, disapprobation, and even detestation;" and after the first ebullitions of the fury of his assailants were over, he adds, "what was still more mortifying, the book seemed to sink into oblivion: Mr. Miller told me that in a twelvemonth he sold only forty-five copies of it." He was so bitterly disappointed, that, he tells us, had not the war been at that time breaking out between France and England, he had certainly retired to some provincial town of the former kingdom, changed his name, and never more returned to his native country. However, after a little time, in the impracticability of executing this scheme of expatriation, he resolved to pick up courage and persevere, the more especially as his second volume was considerably advanced. That, he informs us, "happened to give less displeasure to the Whigs, and was better received: it not only rose itself, but helped to buoy up its unfortunate brother." The work, indeed, seems to have now rapidly attained extraordinary popularity. Two more volumes, comprehending the reigns of the princes of the House of Tudor, appeared in 1759; and the remaining two, completing the History from the Invasion of Julius Cæsar to the accession of Henry VII., in 1762. And several new editions of all the volumes were called for in rapid succession. Hume makes as much an epoch in our historical as he does in our philosophical literature. His originality in the one department is as great as in the other; and the influence he has exerted upon those who have followed him in the same path has been equally extensive and powerful in both cases. His History, notwithstanding some defects which the progress of time and of knowledge is every year making more considerable, or at least enabling us better to perceive, and some others which probably would have been much the same at whatever time the work had been written, has still merits of so high a kind as a literary performance that it must ever retain its place among our few classical works in this department, of which it is as yet perhaps the greatest. In narrative clearness, grace, and spirit, at least, it is not excelled, scarcely equalled, by any other completed historical work in the language; and it has besides the high charm, indispensable to every literary performance that is to endure, of being impressed all over with the peculiar character of the author's own mind, interesting us even in its most prejudiced and objectionable passages (perhaps still more, indeed, in some of these than elsewhere) by his tolerant candour and gentleness of nature, his charity for all the milder vices, his unaffected indifference to many of the common objects of human passion, and his contempt for their pursuers, never waxing bitter or morose, and often impregnating his style and manner with a vein of the quietest but yet truest and richest humour. One effect which we may probably ascribe in great part to the example of Hume was the attention that immediately began to be turned to historic composition in a higher spirit than had heretofore been felt among us, and that ere long added to the possessions of the language in that department the celebrated performances of Robertson and Gibbon. Robertson's History of Scotland during the Reigns of Queen Mary and of King James VI. was published at London in 1759; his History of the Reign of the Emperor Charles V., in 1769; and his History of America, in 1776. Robertson's style of narration, lucid, equable, and soberly embellished, took the popular ear and taste from the first. A part of the cause of this favourable reception is slily enough indicated by Hume, in a letter which he wrote to Robertson himself on the publication of the History of Scotland:—"The great success of your book, besides its real merit, is forwarded by its prudence, and by the deference paid to established opinions. It gains also by its being your first performance, and by its surprising the public, who are not upon their guard against it. By reason of these two circumstances justice is more readily done to its merit, which, however, is really so great, that I believe there is scarce another instance of a first performance being so near perfection."* The applause, indeed, was loud and universal, from Horace Walpole to Lord Lyttelton, from Lord Mansfield to David Garrick. Nor did it fail to be renewed in equal measure on the appearance both of his History of Charles V. and of his History of America. But, although in his own day he probably bore away the palm from Hume in the estimation of the majority, the finest judgments even then discerned, with Gibbon, that there was something higher in "the careless inimitable graces" of the latter than in his rival's more elaborate regularity, flowing and perspicuous as it usually is; and, as always happens, time has brought the general opinion into accordance with this feeling of the wiser few. The first volume of Gibbon's History of the Decline and Fall of the

* Account of the Life and Writings of Robertson, by Dugald Stewart.

Roman Empire appeared in 1776, a few months before the death of Hume, and about a year before the publication of Robertson's America; the second and third followed in 1781; the three additional volumes, which completed the work, not till 1788. Of the first volume, the author tells us, "the first impression was exhausted in a few days; a second and third edition were scarcely adequate to the demand; and a scarcely diminished interest followed the great undertaking to its close, notwithstanding the fear which he expresses in the preface to his concluding volumes that "six ample quartos must have tried, and may have exhausted the indulgence of the public." A performance at once of such extent, and of so sustained a brilliancy throughout, perhaps does not exist in ancient or modern historical literature; but it is a hard metallic brilliancy, which even the extraordinary interest of the subject and the unflagging animation of the writer, with the great skill he shows in the disposition of his materials, do not prevent from becoming sometimes fatiguing and oppressive. Still the splendour, artificial as it is, is very imposing; it does not warm, as well as illuminate, like the light of the sun, but it has at least the effect of a theatrical blaze of lamps and cressets; while it is supported everywhere by a profusion of real erudition such as would make the dullest style and manner interesting. It is remarkable, however, that, in regard to mere language, no one of these three celebrated historical writers, the most eminent we have yet to boast of, at least among those that have stood the test of time, can be recommended as a model. No one of the three, in fact, was of English birth and education. Gibbon's style is very impure, abounding in Gallicisms; Hume's, especially in the first edition of his History, is, with all its natural elegance, almost as much infested with Scotticisms; and, if Robertson's be less incorrect in that respect, it is so unidiomatic as to furnish a still less adequate exemplification of genuine English eloquence. Robertson died at the age of seventy-one, in 1793; Gibbon, in 1794, at the age of fifty-seven.

POLITICAL ECONOMY; THEOLOGY; CRITICISM AND BELLES LETTRES.

Besides his metaphysical and historical works, upon which his fame principally rests, the penetrating and original genius of Hume also distinguished itself in another field, that of economical speculation, which had for more than a century before his time to some extent engaged the attention of inquirers in this country. There are many ingenious views upon this subject scattered up and down in his Political Discourses, and his Moral and Political Essays. Other contributions, not without value, to the science of political economy, for which we are indebted to the middle of the last century, are the Rev. R. Wallace's Essay on the Numbers of Mankind, published at Edinburgh in 1753: and Sir James Steuart's Inquiry into the Principles of Political Economy, which appeared in 1767. But these and all other preceding works on the subject have been thrown into the shade by Adam Smith's celebrated Inquiry into the Nature and Causes of the Wealth of Nations, which, after having been long expected, was at last given to the world in the beginning of the year 1776. It is interesting to learn that this crowning performance of his friend was read by Hume, who died before the close of the year in which it was published: a letter of his to Smith is preserved, in which after congratulating him warmly on having acquitted himself so as to relieve the anxiety and fulfil the hopes of his friends, he ends by saying, "If you were here at my fireside, I should dispute some of your principles. . . . But these, and a hundred other points, are fit only to be discussed in conversation. I hope it will be soon, for I am in a very bad state of health, and cannot afford a long delay." Smith survived till July, 1790.

A few other names, more or less distinguished in the literature of this time, we must content ourselves with merely mentioning:—in theology, Warburton, Lowth, Horsley,

Jortin, Madan, Gerard, Blair, Geddes, Lardner, Priestley; in critical and grammatical disquisition, Harris, Monboddo, Kames, Blair, Jones; in antiquarian research, Walpole, Hawkins, Burney, Chandler, Barrington, Steevens, Pegge, Farmer, Vallancey, Grose, Gough; in the department of the belles lettres and miscellaneous speculation, Chesterfield, Hawkesworth, Brown, Jenyns, Bryant, Hurd, Melmoth, Potter, Francklin, &c.

THE LATTER PART OF THE EIGHTEENTH CENTURY.

COWPER.

THE death of Samuel Johnson, in the end of the year 1784, makes a pause, or point of distinction, in our literature, hardly less notable than the acknowledgment of the independence of America, the year before, makes in our political history. It was not only the end of a reign, but the end of kingship altogether, in our literary system. For King Samuel has had no successor; nobody since his day, and that of his contemporary Voltaire, who died in 1778, at the age of eighty-five, has sat on a throne of literature either in England or in France.

It is a remarkable fact that, if we were to continue our notices of the poets of the last century in strict chronological order, the first name we should have to mention would be that of a writer who more properly belongs to what may almost be called our own day. Crabbe, whose Tales of the Hall, the most striking production of his powerful and original genius, appeared in 1819, and who died so recently as 1832, published his first poem, The Library, in 1781: some extracts from it are given in the Annual Register for that year. But Crabbe's literary career is divided into two parts by a chasm or interval, during which he published nothing, of nearly twenty years; and his proper era is the present century.

One remark, however, touching this writer may be made

here: his first manner was evidently caught from Churchill more than from any other of his predecessors. And this was also the case with his contemporary Cowper, the poetical writer whose name casts the greatest illustration upon the last twenty years of the eighteenth century. William Cowper, born in 1731, twenty-three years before Crabbe,—we pass over his anonymous contributions to his friend the Rev. Mr. Newton's collection of the Olney Hymns, published in 1776, —gave to the world the first volume of his poems, containing those entitled Table-Talk, The Progress of Error, Truth, Expostulation, Hope, Charity, Conversation, and Retirement, in 1782; his famous History of John Gilpin appeared the following year, without his name, in a publication called The Repository; his second volume, containing The Task, Tirocinium, and some shorter pieces, was published in 1785; his translations of the Iliad and the Odyssey in 1791; and his death took place on the 25th of April, 1800. It is recorded that Cowper's first volume attracted little attention: it certainly appears to have excited no perception in the mind or eye of the public of that day that a new and great light had arisen in the poetical firmament. The Annual Register for 1781, as we have said, gives extracts from Crabbe's Library; a long passage from his next poem, The Village, is given in the volume for 1783; the volume for 1785 in like manner treats its readers to a quotation from The Newspaper, which he had published in that year; but, except that the anonymous History of John Gilpin is extracted in the volume for 1783 from the Repository, we have nothing there of Cowper's till we come to the volume for 1786, which contains two of the minor pieces published in his second volume. Crabbe was probably indebted for the distinction he received in part to his friend and patron Burke, under whose direction the Register was compiled; but the silence observed in regard to Cowper may be taken as not on that account the less conclusive as to the little or next to no impression his first volume made. Yet surely there were both a force and a freshness of manner in the new aspirant that might have

been expected to draw some observation. Nor had there
of late been such plenty of good poetry produced in England as to make anything of the kind a drug in the market.
But here, in fact, lay the main cause of the public inattention. The age was not poetical. The manufacture of verse
was carried on, indeed, upon a considerable scale, by the
Hayleys and the Whiteheads and the Pratts and others
(spinners of sound and weavers of words not for a moment
to be compared in inventive and imaginative faculty, or in
faculty of any kind, any more than for the utility of their
work, with their contemporaries the Arkwrights and Cartwrights); but the production of poetry had gone so much
out, that, even in the class most accustomed to judge of
these things, few people knew it when they saw it. It has
been said that the severe and theological tone of this poetry
of Cowper's operated against its immediate popularity; and
that was probably the case too; but it could only have been
so, at any rate to the same extent, in a time at the least as
indifferent to poetry as to religion and morality. For, certainly, since the days of Pope, nothing in the same style had
been produced among us to be compared with these poems
of Cowper's for animation, vigour, and point, which are
among the most admired qualities of that great writer, any
more than for the cordiality, earnestness, and fervour which
are more peculiarly their own. Smoother versification we
had had in great abundance; more pomp and splendour of
rhetorical declamation, perhaps, as in Johnson's paraphrases
from Juvenal; more warmth and glow of imagination, as in
Goldsmith's two poems, if they are to be considered as
coming into the competition. But, on the whole, verse of
such bone and muscle had proceeded from no recent writer,
—not excepting Churchill, whose poetry had little else than
its coarse strength to recommend it, and whose hasty and
careless workmanship Cowper, while he had to a certain
degree been his imitator, had learned, with his artistical
feeling, infinitely to surpass. Churchill's vehement invective with its exaggerations and personalities, made him the

most popular poet of his day: Cowper, neglected at first, has taken his place as one of the classics of the language. Each has had his reward—the reward he best deserved, and probably most desired.

As the death of Samuel Johnson closes one era of our literature, so the appearance of Cowper as a poet opens another. Notwithstanding his obligations both to Churchill and Pope, a main characteristic of Cowper's poetry is its originality. Compared with almost any one of his predecessors, he was what we may call a natural poet. He broke through conventional forms and usages in his mode of writing more daringly than any English poet before him had done, at least since the genius of Pope had bound in its spell the phraseology and rhythm of our poetry. His opinions were not more his own than his manner of expressing them. His principles of diction and versification were announced, in part, in the poem with which he introduced himself to the public, his Table-Talk, in which, having intimated his contempt for the "creamy smoothness" of modern fashionable verse, where sentiment was so often

> sacrificed to sound,
> And truth cut short to make a period round,

he exclaims,

> Give me the line that ploughs its stately course
> Like a proud swan, conquering the stream by force;
> That, like some cottage beauty, strikes the heart,
> Quite unindebted to the tricks of art.

But, although he despised the "tricks" of art, Cowper, like every great poet, was also a great artist; and, with all its in that day almost unexampled simplicity and naturalness, his style is the very reverse of a slovenly or irregular one. If his verse be not so highly polished as that of Pope,—who, he complains, has

> Made poetry a mere mechanic art,
> And every warbler has his tune by heart,—

it is in its own way nearly as "well disciplined, complete, compact," as he has described Pope's to be. With all his avowed admiration of Churchill, he was far from being what he has called that writer—

> Too proud for art, and trusting in mere force.

On the contrary, he has in more than one passage descanted on "the pangs of a poetic birth"—on

> the shifts and turns,
> The expedients and inventions multiform,
> To which the mind resorts, in chase of terms,
> Though apt, yet coy, and difficult to win;—

and the other labours to be undergone by whoever would attain to excellence in the work of composition. Not, however, that, with all this elaboration, he was a slow writer. Slowness is the consequence of indifference, of a writer not being excited by his subject—not having his heart in his work, but going through it as a mere task; let him be thoroughly in earnest, fully possessed of his subject and possessed by it, and, though the pains he takes to find apt and effective expression for his thoughts may tax his whole energies like wrestling with a strong man, he will not write slowly. He is in a state of active combustion—consuming away, it may be, but never pausing. Cowper is said to have composed the six thousand verses, or thereby, contained in his first volume, in about three months.

Not creative imagination, nor deep melody, nor even, in general, much of fancy or grace or tenderness, is to be met with in the poetry of Cowper; but yet it is not without both high and various excellence. Its main charm, and that which is never wanting, is its earnestness. This is a quality which gives it a power over many minds not at all alive to the poetical; but it is also the source of some of its strongest attractions for those that are. Hence its truth both of landscape-painting, and of the description of character and states of mind; hence its skilful expression of such emotions and passions as it allows itself to deal with; hence the force and fervour of its denunciatory eloquence, giving to some passages as fine an inspiration of the moral sublime as is perhaps anywhere to be found in didactic poetry. Hence, we may say, even the directness, simplicity and manliness of Cowper's diction—all that is best in the form, as well as in the spirit, of his verse. It was this quality, or temper of mind, in short, that principally made him an original poet; and, if not the founder of a new school, the pioneer of a new era, of English poetry. Instead of repeating the unmeaning conventionalities and faded affectations of his predecessors, it led him to turn to the actual nature within him and around him, and there to learn both the truths he should utter and the words in which he should utter them.

After Cowper had found, or been found out by, his proper audience, the qualities in his poetry that at first had most repelled ordinary readers rather aided its success. In particular, as we have said, its theological tone and spirit made it acceptable in quarters to which poetry of any kind had rarely penetrated, and where it may perhaps be affirmed that it keeps its ground chiefly perforce of this its most prosaic peculiarity; although, at the same time, it is probable that the vigorous verse to which his system of theology and morals has been married by Cowper has not been without effect in diffusing not only a more indulgent toleration but a truer feeling and love for poetry throughout what is called the religious world. Nor is it to be denied that the source of Cowper's own most potent inspiration is his theological creed. The most popular of his poems, and also certainly the most elaborate, is his Task; it abounds in that delineation of domestic and every-day life which interests everybody, in descriptions of incidents and natural appearances with which all are familiar, in the expression of sentiments and convictions to which most hearts readily respond: it is a poem, therefore, in which the greatest number of readers find the greatest number of things to attract and attach them. Besides, both in the form and in the matter, it has less of what is felt to be strange and sometimes repulsive by the generality; the verse flows, for the most part, smoothly enough, if not with much variety of music; the diction is, as usual with Cowper, clear, manly, and expressive, but at the same time, from being looser and more diffuse, seldomer harsh or difficult than it is in some of his other compositions; above all, the doctrinal strain is pitched upon a lower key, and, without any essential point being given up, both morality and religion certainly assume a countenance and voice considerably less rueful and vindictive. But, although The Task has much occasional elevation and eloquence, and some sunny passages, it perhaps nowhere rises to the passionate force and vehemence to which Cowper had been carried by a more burning zeal in some of his earlier poems. Take, for instance, the following fine burst in that entitled Table-Talk:—

> Not only vice disposes and prepares
> The mind, that slumbers sweetly in her snares,
> To stoop to tyranny's usurped command,
> And bend her polished neck beneath his hand
> (A dire effect, by one of Nature's laws,
> Unchangeably connected with its cause);
> But Providence himself will intervene
> To throw his dark displeasure o'er the scene.
> All are his instruments: each form of war,
> What burns at home, or threatens from afar,
> Nature in arms, her elements at strife,
> The storms that overset the joys of life,
> Are but his rods to scourge a guilty land,
> And waste it at the bidding of his hand.
> He gives the word, and mutiny soon roars
> In all her gates, and shakes her distant shores;
> The standards of all nations are unfurled;
> She has one foe, and that one foe the world:
> And, if he doom that people with a frown,
> And mark them with a seal of wrath pressed down,
> Obduracy takes place; callous and tough
> The reprobated race grows judgment-proof;
> Earth shakes beneath them, and heaven wars above;
> But nothing scares them from the course they love.
> To the lascivious pipe, and wanton song,
> That charm down fear, they frolic it along,
> With mad rapidity and unconcern,
> Down to the gulf from which is no return.
> They trust in navies, and their navies fail—
> God's curse can cast away ten thousand sail!
> They trust in armies and their courage dies;
> In wisdom, wealth, in fortune, and in lies;
> But all they trust in withers, as it must,
> When He commands, in whom they place no trust.

> Vengeance at last pours down upon their coast
> A long-despised, but now victorious, host;
> Tyranny sends the chain, that must abridge
> The noble sweep of all their privilege;
> Gives liberty the last, the mortal shock;
> Slips the slave's collar on, and snaps the lock.

And, even when it expresses itself in quite other forms, and with least of passionate excitement, the fervour which inspires these earlier poems occasionally produces something more brilliant or more graceful than is anywhere to be found in The Task. How skilfully and forcibly executed, for example, is the following moral delineation in that called Truth:—

> The path to bliss abounds with many a snare;
> Learning is one, and wit, however rare.
> The Frenchman first in literary fame—
> (Mention him, if you please. Voltaire?—The same)
> With spirit, genius, eloquence, supplied,
> Lived long, wrote much, laughed heartily, and died.
> The Scripture was his jest-book, whence he drew
> *Bon mots* to gall the Christian and the Jew;
> An infidel in health; but what when sick?
> Oh—then a text would touch him at the quick.
> View him in Paris in his last career;
> Surrounding throngs the demigod revere;
> Exalted on his pedestal of pride,
> And fumed with frankincense on every side,
> He begs their flattery with his latest breath,
> And, smothered in 't at last, is praised to death.
>   You cottager, who weaves at her own door,
> Pillow and bobbins all her little store;
> Content though mean, and cheerful if not gay,
> Shuffling her threads about the livelong day,
> Just earns a scanty pittance, and at night
> Lies down secure, her heart and pocket light;
> She, for her humble sphere by nature fit,
> Has little understanding, and no wit,
> Receives no praise; but, though her lot be such,
> (Toilsome and indigent) she renders much;
> Just knows, and knows no more, her Bible true—
> A truth the brilliant Frenchman never knew;
> And in that charter reads with sparkling eyes
> Her title to a treasure in the skies.
>   O happy peasant! O unhappy bard!
> His the mere tinsel, hers the rich reward;
> He praised perhaps for ages yet to come,
> She never heard of half a mile from home;
> He lost in errors his vain heart prefers,
> She safe in the simplicity of hers.

Still more happily executed, and in a higher style of art, is the following version, so elaborately finished, and yet so severely simple, of the meeting of the two disciples with their divine Master on the road to Emmaus, in the piece entitled Conversation:—

> It happened on a solemn eventide,
> Soon after He that was our surety died,
> Two bosom friends, each pensively inclined,
> The scene of all those sorrows left behind,
> Sought their own village, busied as they went
> In musings worthy of the great event:
> They spake of him they loved, of him whose life,
> Though blameless, had incurred perpetual strife,
> Whose deeds had left, in spite of hostile arts,
> A deep memorial graven on their hearts.
> The recollection, like a vein of ore,
> The farther traced, enriched them still the more:
> They thought him, and they justly thought him, one
> Sent to do more than he appeared to have done;
> To exalt a people, and to place them high
> Above all else; and wondered he should die.
> Ere yet they brought their journey to an end,
> A stranger joined them, courteous as a friend,
> And asked them, with a kind, engaging air,
> What their affliction was, and begged a share.
> Informed, he gathered up the broken thread,
> And, truth and wisdom gracing all he said,
> Explained, illustrated, and searched so well
> The tender theme on which they chose to dwell,
> That, reaching home, The night, they said, is near
> We must not now be parted,—sojourn here.
> The new acquaintance soon became a guest,
> And, made so welcome at their simple feast, .
> He blessed the bread, but vanished at the word,
> And left them both exclaiming, 'Twas the Lord!
> Did not our hearts feel all he deigned to say?
> Did not they burn within us by the way?

For one thing, Cowper's poetry, not organ-toned, or informed with any very rich or original music, any more than soaringly imaginative or gorgeously decorated, is of a style that requires the sustaining aid of rhyme: in blank verse it is apt to overflow in pools and shallows. And this is one among other reasons why, after all, some of his short poems, which are nearly all in rhyme, are perhaps what he has done best. His John Gilpin, universally known and universally enjoyed by his countrymen, young and old, educated and uneducated, and perhaps the only English poem of which this can be said, of course at once suggests itself as standing alone in the collection of what he has left us for whimsical conception and vigour of comic humour; but there is a quieter exercise of the same talent, or at least of a kindred sense of the ludicrous and sly power of giving it expression, in others of his shorter pieces. For tenderness and pathos, again, nothing else that he has written, and not much that is elsewhere to be found of the same kind in English poetry, can be compared with his Lines on receiving his Mother's Picture:—

> O that those lips had language! Life has passed
> With me but roughly since I heard thee last.
> Those lips are thine—thy own sweet smile I see,
> The same that oft in childhood solaced me:
> Voice only fails, else how distinct they say,
> "Grieve not, my child, chase all thy fears away!"
> The meek intelligence of those clear eyes
> (Blest be the art that can immortalize,
> The art that baffles Time's gigantic claim
> To quench it) here shines on me still the same.
> Faithful remembrancer of one so dear,
> O welcome guest, though unexpected here!
> Who bidd'st me honour with an artless song
> Affectionate, a mother lost so long.
> I will obey, not willingly alone,
> But gladly, as the precept were her own:
> And, while that face renews my filial grief,
> Fancy shall weave a charm for my relief,
> Shall steep me in Elysian reverie,
> A momentary dream that thou art she.
> My mother! when I learned that thou wast dead,
> Say, wast thou conscious of the tears I shed?
> Hovered thy spirit o'er thy sorrowing son,
> Wretch even then, life's journey just begun?
> Perhaps thou gav'st me, though unfelt, a kiss;
> Perhaps a tear, if souls can melt in bliss—
> Ah that maternal smile! it answers—Yes.
> I heard the bell tolled on thy burial day,
> I saw the hearse that bore thee slow away,
> And, turning from my nursery window, drew
> A long, long sigh, and wept a last adieu!
> But was it such?—It was.—Where thou art gone,
> Adieus and farewells are a sound unknown:
> May I but meet thee on that peaceful shore,
> The parting word shall pass my lips no more!

Thy maidens, grieved themselves at my concern,
Oft gave me promise of thy quick return.
What ardently I wished I long believed,
And, disappointed still, was still deceived;
By expectation every day beguiled,
Dupe of to-morrow even from a child,
Thus many a sad to-morrow came and went,
Till, all my stock of infant sorrow spent,
I learned at last submission to my lot,
But, though I less deplored thee, ne'er forgot.
 Where once we dwelt our name is heard no more,
Children not thine have trod my nursery floor;
And where the gardener Robin, day by day,
Drew me to school along the public way,
Delighted with my bauble coach, and wrapped
In scarlet mantle warm, and velvet-capped,
'Tis now become a history little known
That once we called the pastoral house our own.
Short-lived possession! but the record fair,
That memory keeps of all thy kindness there,
Still outlives many a storm, that has effaced
A thousand other themes less deeply traced.
Thy nightly visits to my chamber made,
That thou might'st know me safe and warmly laid;
Thy morning bounties ere I left my home,
The biscuit, or confectionary plum;
The fragrant waters on my cheeks bestowed
By thy own hand, till fresh they shone and glowed:
All this, and, more endearing still than all,
Thy constant flow of love, that knew no fall,
Ne'er roughened by those cataracts and breaks,
That humour interposed too often makes;
All this still legible in memory's page,
And still to be so to my latest age,
Adds joy to duty, makes me glad to pay
Such honours to thee as my numbers may;
Perhaps a frail memorial, but sincere,
Not scorned in heaven, though little noticed here.
 Could Time, his flight reversed, restore the hours,
When, playing with thy vesture's tissued flowers,
The violet, the pink, and jessamine,
I pricked them into paper with a pin,
(And thou wast happier than myself the while,
Would'st softly speak, and stroke my head, and smile)
Could those few pleasant days again appear,
Might one wish bring them, would I wish them here?
I would not trust my heart;—the dear delight
Seems so to be desired, perhaps I might.—
But no:—what here we call our life is such,
So little to be loved, and thou so much,
That I should ill requite thee to constrain
Thy unbound spirit into bonds again.
 Thou, as a gallant bark from Albion's coast
(The storms all weather'd and the ocean crossed),

> Shoots into port at some well-havened isle,
> Where spices breathe, and brighter seasons smile,
> There sits quiescent on the floods, that show
> Her beauteous form reflected clear below,
> While airs impregnated with incense play
> Around her, fanning light her streamers gay;
> So thou, with sails how swift! hast reached the shore
> "Where tempests never beat, nor billows roar."[1]
> And thy loved consort on the dangerous tide
> Of life long since has anchored by thy side.
> But me, scarce hoping to attain that rest,
> Always from port withheld, always distressed—
> Me howling blasts drive devious, tempest-tossed,
> Sails ripped, seams opening wide, and compass lost;
> And day by day some current's thwarting force
> Sets me more distant from a prosperous course.
> Yet O the thought that thou art safe, and he!
> That thought is joy, arrive what may to me.
> My boast is not, that I deduce my birth
> From loins enthroned, and rulers of the earth;
> But higher far my proud pretensions rise—
> The son of parents passed into the skies.
> And now farewell.—Time unrevoked has run
> His wonted course; yet what I wished is done.
> By contemplation's help, not sought in vain,
> I seem to have lived my childhood o'er again;
> To have renewed the joys that once were mine,
> Without the sin of violating thine;
> And, while the wings of fancy still are free,
> And I can view this mimic show of thee,
> Time has but half succeeded in his theft—
> Thyself removed, thy power to soothe me left.

This is no doubt, as a whole, Cowper's finest poem, at once springing from the deepest and purest fount of passion, and happy in shaping itself into riches and sweeter music than he has reached in any other. It shows what his real originality, and the natural spirit of art that was in him, might have done under a better training and more favourable circumstances of personal situation, or perhaps in another age. Generally, indeed, it may be said of Cowper, that the more he was left to himself, or trusted to his own taste and feelings, in writing, the better he wrote. In so far as regards the form of composition, the principal charm of what he has done best is a natural elegance, which is most perfect in what he has apparently written with the least

[1] Garth.

labour, or at any rate with the least thought of rules or models. His Letters to his friends, not written for publication at all, but thrown off in the carelessness of his hours of leisure and relaxation, have given him as high a place among the prose classics of his country as he holds among our poets. His least successful performances are his translations of the Iliad and Odyssey, throughout which he was straining to imitate a style not only unlike his own, but, unfortunately, quite as unlike that of his original—for these versions of the most natural of all poetry, the Homeric, are, strangely enough, attempted in the manner of the most artificial of all poets, Milton.

DARWIN.

Neither, however, did this age of our literature want its artificial poetry. In fact, the expiration or abolition of that manner among us was brought about not more by the example of a fresh and natural style given by Cowper, than by the exhibition of the opposite style, pushed to its extreme, given by his contemporary Darwin. Our great poets of this era cannot be accused of hurrying into print at an immature age. Dr. Erasmus Darwin, born in 1721, after having risen to distinguished reputation as a physician, published the Second Part of his Botanic Garden, under the title of The Loves of the Plants, in 1789: and the First Part, entitled The Economy of Vegetation, two years after. He died in 1802. The Botanic Garden, hard, brilliant, sonorous, may be called a poem cast in metal—a sort of Pandemonium palace of rhyme, not unlike that raised long ago in another region,—

> where pilasters round
> Were set, and Doric pillars, overlaid
> With golden architrave; nor did there want
> Cornice, or frieze, with bossy sculptures graven;
> The roof was fretted gold.

The poem, however, did not rise exactly "like an exhalation." "The verse," writes its author's sprightly biographer, Miss Anna Seward, "corrected, polished, and modulated with the most sedulous attention; the notes involving such great diversity of matter relating to natural history; and the composition going forward in the short recesses of professional attendance, *but chiefly in his chaise, as he travelled from one place to another;* the Botanic Garden could not be the work of one, two, or three years; it was *ten* from its primal lines to its first publication." If this account may be depended on, the Doctor's supplies of inspiration must have been vouchsafed to him at the penurious rate of little more than a line a day. At least, therefore, it cannot be said of him, as it was said of his more fluent predecessor in both gifts of Apollo, Sir Richard Blackmore, that he wrote "to the rumbling of his chariot wheels." The verse, nevertheless, does in another way smack of the travelling-chaise, and of "the short recesses of professional attendance." Nothing is done in passion and power; but all by filing, and scraping, and rubbing, and other painstaking. Every line is as elaborately polished and sharpened as a lancet; and the most effective paragraphs have the air of a lot of those bright little instruments arranged in rows, with their blades out, for sale. You feel as if so thick an array of points and edges demanded careful handling, and that your fingers are scarcely safe in coming near them. Darwin's theory of poetry evidently was, that it was all a mechanical affair— only a higher kind of pin-making. His own poetry, however, with all its defects, is far from being merely mechanical. The Botanic Garden is not a poem which any man of ordinary intelligence could have produced by sheer care and industry, or such faculty of writing as could be acquired by serving an apprenticeship to the trade of poetry. Vicious as it is in manner, it is even there of an imposing and original character; and a true poetic fire lives under all its affectations, and often blazes up through them. There is not much, indeed, of pure soul or high imagination in

Darwin; he seldom rises above the visible and material; but he has at least a poet's eye for the perception of that, and a poet's fancy for its embellishment and exaltation. No writer has surpassed him in the luminous representation of visible objects in verse; his descriptions have the distinctness of drawings by the pencil, with the advantage of conveying, by their harmonious words, many things that no pencil can paint. His images, though they are for the most part tricks of language rather than transformations or new embodiments of impassioned thought, have often at least an Ovidian glitter and prettiness, or are striking from their mere ingenuity and novelty—as, for example, when he addresses the stars as "flowers of the sky," or apostrophizes the glowworm as "Star of the earth, and diamond of the night." These two instances, indeed, thus brought into juxtaposition, may serve to exemplify the principle upon which he constructs such decorations: it is, we see, an economical principle; for, in truth, the one of these figures is little more than the other reversed, or inverted. Still both are happy and effective enough conceits—and one of them is applied and carried out so as to make it more than a mere momentary light flashing from the verse. The passage is not without a tone of grandeur and meditative pathos:—

> Roll on, ye stars! exult in youthful prime,
> Mark with bright curves the printless steps of time;
> Near and more near your beamy cars approach,
> And lessening orbs on lessening orbs encroach;—
> Flowers of the Sky! ye too to age must yield,
> Frail as your silken sisters of the field!
> Star after star from heaven's high arch shall rush,
> Suns sink on suns, and systems systems crush,
> Headlong, extinct, to one dark centre fall,
> And death and night and chaos mingle all!
> —Till o'er the wreck, emerging from the storm,
> Immortal Nature lifts her changeful form,
> Mounts from her funeral pyre on wings of flame,
> And soars and shines, another and the same.

There is also a fine moral inspiration, as well as the usual rhetorical brilliancy, in the following lines:—

> Hail, adamantine Steel! magnetic Lord!
> King of the prow, the ploughshare, and the sword!
> True to the pole, by thee the pilot guides
> His steady helm amid the struggling tides,
> Braves with broad sail the immeasurable sea,
> Cleaves the dark air, and asks no star but thee!

BURNS.

It was in October or November of the year 1786 that the press of the obscure country town of Kilmarnock gave to the world, in an octavo volume, the first edition of the Poems, chiefly in the Scottish Dialect, of Robert Burns. A second edition was printed at Edinburgh early in the following year. Burns, born on the 25th of January, 1759, had composed most of the pieces contained in the publication in the two years preceding its appearance: his life—an April day of sunshine and storm—closed on the 21st of July, 1796; and in his last nine or ten years he may have about doubled the original quantity of his printed poetry. He was not quite thirty-seven and a half years old when he died—about a year and three months older than Byron. Burns is the greatest peasant-poet that has ever appeared; but his poetry is so remarkable in itself that the circumstances in which it was produced hardly add anything to our admiration. It is a poetry of very limited compass—not ascending towards any "highest heaven of invention," nor even having much variety of modulation, but yet in its few notes as true and melodious a voice of passion as was ever heard. It is all light and fire. Considering how little the dialect in which he wrote had been trained to the purposes of literature, what Burns has done with it is miraculous. Nothing in Horace, in the way of curious felicity of phrase, excels what we find in the compositions of this Ayrshire ploughman. The words are almost always so apt and full of life, at once so natural and expressive, and so graceful and musical in their animated simplicity, that, were the matter ever so trivial, they would of themselves turn it into poetry. And the same native artistic feeling manifests itself in everything else. One characteristic that belongs to whatever Burns has written is that, of its kind or in its own way, it is a perfect production. It is perfect in the same sense in which every production of nature is perfect, the humblest weed as well as the proudest flower; and in which, indeed, every true thing whatever is perfect, viewed in reference to its species and purpose. His poetry is, throughout, real emotion melodiously uttered. As such, it is as genuine poetry as was ever written or sung. Not, however, although its chief and best inspiration is passion rather than imagination, that any poetry ever was farther from being a mere Æolian warble addressing itself principally to the nerves. Burns's head was as strong as his heart; his natural sagacity, logical faculty, and judgment were of the first order; no man, of poetical or prosaic temperament, ever had a more substantial intellectual character. And the character of his poetry is like that of the mind and the nature out of which it sprung—instinct with passion, but not less so with power of thought—full of light, as we have said, as well as of fire. More of matter and meaning, in short, in any sense in which the terms may be understood, will be found in no verses than there is in his. Hence the popularity of the poetry of Burns with all classes of his countrymen—a popularity more universal, probably, than any other writer ever gained, at least so immediately; for his name, we apprehend, had become a household word among all classes in every part of Scotland even in his own lifetime. Certainly at the present day, that would be a rare Lowland Scotchman, or Scotchwoman either, who should be found never to have heard of the name and fame of Robert Burns, or even to be altogether ignorant of his works. It has happened, however, from this cause, that he is not perhaps, in general, estimated by the best of his productions. Nobody, of course, capable of appreciating any of the characteristic qualities of Burns's poetry will ever think of quoting even the best of the few verses he has written in English, as evidence of his poetic genius. In these he is Samson shorn of his hair, and become as any other man. But even such poems as his Cotter's Saturday Night, and his tale of Tam o' Shanter, convey no adequate conception of what is brightest and highest in his poetry. The former is a true and touching description in a quiet and subdued manner, suitable to the subject, but not adapted to bring out much of his illuminating fancy and fusing power of passion: the other is a rapid, animated, and most effective piece of narrative, with some vigorous comedy, and also some scene-painting in a broad, dashing style, but exhibiting hardly more of the peculiar humour of Burns than of his pathos. Of a far rarer merit, much richer in true poetic light and colour, and of a much more original and distinctive inspiration, are many of his poems which are much less frequently referred to, at least out of his own country. Take, for instance, that entitled To a Mouse, on turning her up in her Nest with the Plough, November, 1785:—

> Wee,[1] sleekit,[2] cow'rin,[3] timorous beastie,[4]
> O what a panic 's in thy breastie![4]
> Thou need na[5] start awa[6] sa hastie,
>   Wi' bickerin' brattle![7]
> I wad be laith[8] to rin[9] an' chase thee,
>   Wi' murderin' pattle.[10]
>
> I'm truly sorry man's dominion
> Has broken nature's social union,
> An' justifies that ill opinion
>   Which makes thee startle
> At me, thy poor earth-born companion,
>   An' fellow mortal.
>
> I doubt na, whiles,[11] but thou may thieve;
> What then? Poor beastie, thou maun[12] live!
> A daimen icker[13] in a thrave[14]
>   'S a sma'[15] request:
> I 'll get a blessin' wi' the lave,[16]
>   An' never miss 't.

[1] Little. [2] Sleek. [3] Cowering. [4] Diminutives of "beast," and "breast." [5] Not. [6] Away. [7] With scudding fury. [8] Would (should) be loth. [9] Run. [10] With murderous ploughstaff. [11] Sometimes. [12] Must. [13] An occasional ear of corn. [14] A double shock. [15] Is a small. [16] Remainder.

Thy wee bit housie,[1] too, in ruin!
Its silly wa's the win's are strewin'![2]
An' naething, now, to big a new ane,[3]
    O' foggage[4] green!
An' bleak December's winds ensuin',
    Baith snell[5] and keen!

Thou saw the fields laid bare an' waste,
An' weary winter comin' fast;
An' cozie[6] here, beneath the blast,
    Thou thought to dwell;
Till crash! the cruel coulter passed
    Out through thy cell.

That wee bit heap o' leaves an' stibble[7]
Has cost thee monie[8] a weary nibble!
Now thou 's[9] turned out, for a' thy trouble,
    But house or hald,[10]
To thole[11] the winter's sleety dribble;
    An' cranreuch cald.[12]

But, Mousie,[13] thou art no thy lane[14]
In proving foresight may be vain:
The best-laid schemes o' mice an' men
    Gang aft a-gley,[15]
An' leave us nought but grief and pain,
    For promised joy.

Still thou art blest compared wi' me!
The present only toucheth thee:
But och![16] I backward cast my ea'[17]
    On prospects drear;
An' forward, though I canna[18] see,
    I guess an' fear.

A simple and common incident poetically conceived has never been rendered into expression more natural, delicately graceful, and true. Of course, however, our glossarial interpretations can convey but a very insufficient notion of the aptness of the poet's language to those to whom the Scottish dialect is not familiar. Such a phrase as "bickering brattle," for instance, is not to be translated. The epithet "bickering" implies that sharp, explosive, fluttering

---

[1] Triple diminutive of *house*—untranslatable into English.
[2] Its weak walls the winds are strewing.
[3] Nothing now to build a new one. [4] Moss. [5] Biting.
[6] Snug. [7] Very small quantity of leaves and stubble. [8] Many.
[9] Thou is (art). [10] Without house or hold. [11] Endure.
[12] Hoar-frost cold.
[13] Diminutive of "mouse." [14] Not alone. [15] Go oft awry.
[16] Ah. [17] Eye. [18] Cannot.

violence, or impetuosity, which belongs to any sudden and rapid progressive movement of short continuance, and it expresses the noise as well as the speed. It is no doubt the same word with the old English "bickering," but used in a more extensive sense: a "bicker" means commonly a short irregular fight, or skirmish: but Milton has "bickering flame," where, although the commentators interpret the epithet as equivalent to *quivering*, we apprehend it includes the idea of *crackling* also. Darwin has borrowed the phrase: "bursts," he says, "through bickering flames." Nor is it possible to give the effect of the diminutives, in which the Scottish language is almost as rich as the Italian. While the English, for example, has only its *manikin*, the Scotch has its *mannie, mannikie, bit mannie, bit mannikie, wee bit mannie, wee bit mannikie, little wee bit mannie, little wee bit mannikie;* and so with *wife, wifie, wifikie,* and many other terms. Almost every substantive noun has at least one diminutive form, made by the affix *ie,* as *mousie, housie.* We ought to notice also, that the established or customary spelling in these and other similar instances does not correctly represent the pronunciation:—the vowel sound is the soft one usually indicated by *oo;* as if the words were written *moosie, hoosie, coorin,* &c. It is an advantage that the Scottish dialect possesses, somewhat akin to that possessed by the Greek in the time of Homer, that, from having been comparatively but little employed in literary composition, and only imperfectly reduced under the dominion of grammar, many of its words have several forms, which are not only convenient for the exigencies of verse, but are used with different effects or shades of meaning. In particular, the English form is always available when wanted; and it is the writer's natural resource when he would rise from the light or familiar style to one of greater elevation or earnestness. Thus, in the above verses, while expressing only half-playful tenderness and commiseration, Burns writes "Now thou 's turned out" (pronounce *oot*), in his native dialect; but it is in the regular English form, "Still thou art blest," that he gives utterance to the deeper pathos and solemnity of the concluding verse.

The proper companion to this short poem is that addressed To a Mountain Daisy, on turning one down with the Plough, in April 1786; but in that the execution is not so pure throughout, and the latter part runs somewhat into common-place. The beginning, however, is in the poet's happiest manner:—

> Wee, modest, crimson-tipped flow'r,
> Thou's[1] met me in an evil hour;
> For I maun crush amang the stour[2]
>   Thy tender stem;
> To spare thee now is past my pow'r,
>   Thou bonnie[3] gem.
>
> Alas! its no[4] thy neebor[5] sweet,
> The bonnie lark, companion meet!
> Bending thee 'mang the dewy weet[6]
>   Wi' spreckled[7] breast,
> When upward springing, blythe, to greet
>   The purpling east.
>
> Cauld blew the bitter-biting north
> Upon thy early, humble, birth;
> Yet cheerfully thou glinted[8] forth
>   Amid the storm.
> Scarce reared above the parent earth
>   Thy tender form.
>
> The flaunting flowers our gardens yield
> High sheltering woods and wa's maun[9] shield;
> But thou beneath the random bield[10]
>   O' clod or stane[11]
> Adorns the histie[12] stibble-field,
>   Unseen, alane.
>
> There, in thy scanty mantle clad,
> Thy snawy[13] bosom sun-ward spread,
> Thou lifts thy unassuming head
>   In humble guise;
> But now the share uptears thy bed,
>   And low thou lies!

[1] Thou hast.   [2] Dust (pronounce *floor, hoor, stoor, poor*).
[3] Lovely.   [4] Not.   [5] Neighbour.   [6] Wet.   [7] Speckled.
[8] Peeped, or rather glanced (glanced'st).   [9] Walls must.
[10] Shelter.   [11] Stone.   [12] Dry and rugged.
[13] Snowy.

> Such is the fate of artless maid,
> Sweet floweret of the rural shade!
> By love's simplicity betrayed,
>   And guileless trust,
> Till she, like thee, all soiled is laid
>   Low i' the dust.
>
> Such is the fate of simple bard,
> On life's rough ocean luckless-starred!
> Unskilful he to note the card
>   Of prudent lore,
> Till billows rage, and gales blow hard,
>   And whelm him o'er!
>
> Such fate to suffering worth is given,
> Who long with wants and woes has striven,
> By human pride or cunning driven
>   To misery's brink,
> Till, wrenched of every stay but heaven,
>   He, ruined, sink!
>
> Even thou who mourn'st the Daisy's fate,
> That fate is thine—no distant date;
> Stern Ruin's ploughshare drives, elate,
>   Full on thy bloom,
> Till crushed beneath the furrow's weight
>   Shall be thy doom!

The most brilliant comic power, again, animates the pieces entitled Scotch Drink, Death and Dr. Hornbook, the Holy Fair, the Ordination, and others of his more irreverent or reckless effusions. As a picture of manners, however, his Hallowe'en is Burns's greatest performance—with its easy vigour, its execution absolutely perfect, its fulness of various and busy life, the truth and reality throughout, the humour diffused over it like sunshine and ever and anon flashing forth in changeful or more dazzling light, the exquisite feeling and rendering both of the whole human spirit of the scene, and also of its accessories in what we can scarcely call or conceive of as inanimate nature while reading such lines as the following:—

> Whiles[1] ow'r[2] a linn[3] the burnie[4] plays,
> As through the glen[5] it wimpled;[6]
> Whiles round a rocky scar[7] it strays;
> Whiles in a wiel[8] it dimpled;

[1] Sometimes. [2] Over. [3] Waterfall.
[4] Rivulet. [5] Dale. [6] Nimbly meandered.
[7] Cliff. [8] Small whirlpool.

Whiles glittered to the nightly rays,
  Wi' bickering, dancing dazzle;
Whiles cookit¹ underneath the braes,
  Below the spreading hazel.

But this poem is too long for quotation, and s besides well known to every reader who knows anything of Burns. We will rather present our English readers with one or two shorter pieces that may serve to illustrate another quality of the man and of his poetry—the admirable sagacity and good sense, never separated from manliness and a high spirit, that made so large a part of his large heart and understanding. All the more considerate nature of Burns speaks in the following Epistle to a Young Friend, dated May, 1786:—

I lang hae² thought, my youthfu' friend,
  A something to have sent you,
Though it should serve nae³ other end
  Than just a kind memento;
But how the subject-theme may gang
  Let time and chance determine;
Perhaps it may turn out a sang,
  Perhaps turn out a sermon.

Ye'll try the world soon, my lad,
  And, Andrew dear, believe me,
Ye'll find mankind an unco squad,⁴
  And muckle⁵ they may grieve ye:
For care and trouble set your thought,
  Ev'n when your end 's attained:
And a'⁶ your views may come to nought,
  Where every nerve is strained.

I'll no⁷ say men are villains a'⁸;
  The real, hardened wicked,
Wha hae nae⁸ check but human law,
  Are to a few restricked;⁹
But oh! mankind are unco¹⁰ weak,
  An' little to be trusted;
If *self* the wavering balance shake,
  It's rarely right adjusted!

Yet they wha fa'¹¹ in fortune's strife,
  Their fate we should na¹² censure:
For still the important *end* of life
  They equally may answer:

¹ Slily disappeared by dipping down, skulked. [Dr. Currie interprets it, "appeared and disappeared hy fits."] ² Long have. ³ No.
⁴ Strange crew. ⁵ Much. ⁶ All. ⁷ Not. ⁸ Who have no.
⁹ Restricted. ¹⁰ Very, strangely. ¹¹ Who fall. ¹² Not.

A man may hae an honest heart,
  Though poortith¹ hourly stare him;
A man may tak² a neebor's³ part,
  Yet hae nae cash to spare him.

Aye free aff han'⁴ your story tell,
  When wi' a bosom crony;⁵
But still keep something to yoursel⁶
  You scarcely tell to ony.⁷
Conceal yoursel as weel's⁸ ye can
  Frae⁹ critical dissection;
But keek¹⁰ through every other man
  Wi' sharpened, slee¹¹ inspection.

The sacred lowe¹² o' weel-placed love,
  Luxuriantly indulge it;
But never tempt the illicit rove,
  Though naething should divulge it:
I wave the quantum o' the sin,
  The hazard of concealing;
But oh! it hardens a' within,
  And petrifies the feeling!

To catch dame Fortune's golden smile,
  Assiduous wait upon her;
And gather gear by every wile
  That's justified by honour;
Not for to hide it in a hedge,
  Not for a train attendant;
But for the glorious privilege
  Of being independent.

The fear o' hell 's a hangman's whip
  To haud¹³ the wretch in order;
But where ye feel your honour grip,
  Let that aye be your border;
Its slightest touches—instant pause;
  Debar a' side pretences;
And resolutely keep its laws,
  Uncaring consequences.

The great Creator to revere
  Must sure become the creature;
But still the preaching cant forbear,
  And even the rigid feature:
Yet ne'er with wits profane to range
  Be complaisance extended;
An Atheist's laugh 's a poor exchange
  For Deity offended.

¹ Poverty. ² Take. ³ Neighbour's.
⁴ Off-hand. ⁵ Intimate associate. ⁶ Yourself. ⁷ Any.
⁸ As well as. ⁹ From. ¹⁰ Look slily. ¹¹ Sly.
¹² Flame. ¹³ Hold.

> When ranting round in pleasure's ring
> Religion may be blinded;
> Or, if she gie[1] a random sting,
> It may be little minded;
> But when on life we're tempest-driven—
> A conscience but a canker—
> A correspondence fixed wi' heaven
> Is sure a noble anchor.
>
> Adieu, dear, amiable youth!
> Your heart can ne'er be wanting;
> May prudence, fortitude, and truth,
> Erect your brow undaunting!
> In ploughman phrase, "God send you speed,"
> Still daily to grow wiser;
> And may you better reck the rede[2]
> Than ever did the adviser.

This poem, it will be observed, is for the greater part in English; and it is not throughout written with all the purity of diction which Burns never violates in his native dialect. For instance, in the fourth stanza the word "censure" is used to suit the exigencies of the rhyme, where the sense demands some such term as deplore or regret; for, although we might censure the man himself who fails to succeed in life (which, however, is not the idea here), we do not censure, that is blame or condemn, his fate; we can only lament it; if we censure anything, it is his conduct. In the same stanza, the expression "stare him" is, we apprehend, neither English nor Scotch: usage authorizes us to speak of poverty staring a man in the face, but not of it staring him, absolutely. Again, in the tenth stanza, we have "Religion may be blinded," apparently, for may be blinked, disregarded, or looked at as with shut eyes.[3] We notice these things, to prevent an impression being left with the English reader that they are characteristic of Burns. No such vices of style, we repeat, are to be found in his Scotch, where the diction is uniformly as natural and correct as it is appropriate and expressive.

---

[1] Give.
[2] "Himself the primrose path of dalliance treads,
And recks not his own read."—Shakespeare, Hamlet.
[3] Unless, indeed, we may interpret the word as meaning deprived of the power of seeing.

In a far more elevated and impassioned strain is the poem entitled The Vision. It is too long to be quoted entire; but the following extracts will be sufficiently intelligible:—

> The sun had closed the winter day,
> The curlers quat¹ their roaring play,
> An' hungered mawkin² ta'en her way
>   To kail-yards³ green,
> While faithless snaws⁴ ilk⁵ step betray
>   Whare⁶ she has been.
>
> The thresher's weary flingin' tree⁷
> The lee-lang⁸ day had tired me;
> And, whan⁹ the day had closed his e'e¹⁰
>   Far i' the west,
> Ben i' the spence,¹¹ right pensivelie,
>   I gaed¹² to rest.
>
> There, lanely,¹³ by the ingle-cheek,¹⁴
> I sat and eyed the spewing reek,¹⁵
> That filled wi' hoast-provoking smeek¹⁶
>   The auld clay beggin':¹⁷
> An' heard the restless rattons¹⁸ squeak
>   About the riggin'.¹⁹
>
> All in this mottie,²⁰ misty clime,
> I backward mused on wasted time,
> How I had spent my youthfu' prime,
>   An' done nae thing
> But stringin' blethers²¹ up in rhyme,
>   For fools to sing.
>
> Had I to guid advice but harkit,²²
> I might, by this,²³ hae led a market,
> Or strutted in a bank an' clarkit²⁴
>   My cash account:
> While here, half-mad, half-fed, half-sarkit,²⁵
>   Is a' the amount.
>
> I started, muttering Blockhead! Coof!²⁶
> And heaved on high my waukit loof,²⁷
> To swear by a' yon starry roof,
>   Or some rash aith,²⁸
> That I henceforth would be rhyme-proof
>   Till my last breath—

¹ Quitted. ² The hare. ³ Colewort gardens.
⁴ Snows. ⁵ Every. ⁶ Where [pronounce *whar*].
⁷ Flail. ⁸ Live-long. ⁹ When. ¹⁰ Eye.
¹¹ Within in the sitting apartment. ¹² Went. ¹³ Lonely.
¹⁴ Fireside. ¹⁵ Smoke issuing out. ¹⁶ Cough-provoking smoke.
¹⁷ The old clay building, or house. ¹⁸ Rats. ¹⁹ The roof of the house.
²⁰ Full of motes. ²¹ Nonsense, idle words. ²² Hearkened.
²³ By this time. ²⁴ Written. ²⁵ Half-shirted.
²⁶ Fool. ²⁷ My palm thickened (with labour). ²⁸ Oath.

When click! the string the snick[1] did draw;
And jee! the door gaed to the wa';
An' by my ingle-lowe I saw,
  Now bleezin'[2] bright,
A tight, outlandish hizzie,[3] braw,
  Come full in sight.

Ye need na doubt I held my whisht;[4]
The infant aith, half-formed, was crushed;
I glowr'd as eerie's I'd been dushed[5]
  In some wild glen;
When sweet, like modest worth, she blushed
  And steppit ben.[6]

Green, slender, leaf-clad holly boughs
Were twisted, gracefu', round her brows;
I took her for some Scottish Muse
  By that same token;
An' come to stop those reckless vows
  Would soon been[7] broken.

A hair-brained, sentimental trace
Was strongly marked in her face,
A wildly witty, rustic grace
  Shone full upon her;
Her eye, even turned on empty space,
  Beamed keen with honour.

With musing, deep, astonished stare,
I viewed the heavenly-seeming fair;
A whispering throb did witness bear
  Of kindred sweet:
When, with an elder sister's air,
  She did me greet:—

"All hail! my own inspired bard!
In me thy native Muse regard!
Nor longer mourn thy fate is hard,
  Thus poorly low!
I come to give thee such reward
  As we bestow.

"Know the great Genius of this land
Has many a light aërial band,
Who, all beneath his high command,
  Harmoniously,
As arts or arms they understand,
  Their labours ply.

 * * * * * *

---

[1] Latch. [2] Blazing. [3] Hussy. [4] Silence.
[5] I stared as frightened as if I had been attacked by a butting ram.
[6] Walked into the room. [7] Which would soon have been.

"Of these am I—Coila my name;
And this district as mine I claim,
Where once the Campbells, chiefs of fame,
    Held ruling power:—
I marked thy embryo tuneful flame
    Thy natal hour.

"With future hope I oft would gaze
Fond on thy little early ways,
Thy rudely carolled chiming phrase
    In uncouth rhymes,
Fired at the simple, artless lays
    Of other times.

"I saw thee seek the sounding shore,
Delighted with the dashing roar;
Or, when the North his fleecy store
    Drove through the sky,
I saw grim nature's visage hoar
    Struck thy young eye.

"Or, when the deep-green-mantled earth
Warm cherished every floweret's birth,
And joy and music pouring forth
    In every grove,
I saw thee eye the general mirth
    With boundless love.

"When ripened fields and azure skies
Called forth the reapers' rustling noise
I saw thee leave their evening joys,
    And lonely stalk
To vent thy bosom's swelling rise
    In pensive walk.

"When youthful love, warm-blushing, strong
Keen-shivering shot thy nerves along,
Those accents, grateful to thy tongue,
    The adored name,
I taught thee how to pour in song,
    To soothe thy flame.

"I saw thy pulse's maddening play
Wild send thee pleasure's devious way,
Misled by fancy's meteor ray,
    By passion driven;
But yet the light that led astray
    Was light from heaven.

"To give my counsels all in one,
Thy tuneful flame still careful fan:
Preserve the dignity of man
    With soul erect;
And trust the universal plan
    Will all protect.

> "And wear thou this"—she solemn said,
> And bound the holly round my head:
> The polished leaves and berries red
>   Did rustling play;
> And, like a passing thought, she fled
>   In light away.

These extracts, as extracts in every case must be, are only indications or hints of what is to be found in the body of poetry from which they are taken; and in this instance, from various causes, the impression so conveyed may probably be more than usually inadequate—for the strangeness of the dialect must veil much of the effect to an English reader, even when the general sense is apprehended; and, besides, their length, their peculiarly Scottish spirit and character, and other considerations have prevented us from quoting the most successful of Burns's pieces in some of the styles in which he most excelled. But still what we have transcribed may serve to give a more extended and a truer notion of what his poetry really is than is commonly entertained by strangers, among whom he is mostly known and judged of from two or three of his compositions, which perhaps of all that he has produced are the least marked by the peculiar character of his genius. Even out of his own country, his Songs, to be sure, have taken all hearts—and they are the very flame-breath of his own. No truer poetry exists in any language, or in any form. But it is the poetry of the heart much more than of either the head or the imagination. Burns's songs do not at all resemble the exquisite lyrical snatches with which Shakespeare, and also Beaumont and Fletcher, have sprinkled some of their dramas—enlivening the busy scene and progress of the action as the progress of the wayfarer is enlivened by the voices of birds in the hedgerows, or the sight and scent of wild-flowers that have sprung up by the road-side. They are never in any respect exercises of ingenuity, but always utterances of passion, and simple and direct as a shout of laughter or a gush of tears. Whatever they have of fancy, whatever they have of melody, is born of real emotion—is merely the natural expression of the poet's feeling at the moment, seeking and finding vent in musical words. Since "burning Sappho" loved and sung in the old isles of Greece, not much poetry has been produced so thrillingly tender as some of the best of these songs. Here, for example, is one, rude enough perhaps in language and versification,—but every line, every cadence is steeped in pathos:—

> Ye banks, and braes, and streams around
>   The castle o' Montgomery,
> Green be your woods, and fair your flowers,
>   Your waters never drumlie![1]
> There summer first unfauld her robes,
>   And there the langest tarry!
> For there I took the last farewell
>   O' my sweet Highland Mary.
>
> How sweetly bloomed the gay green birk,[2]
>   How rich the hawthorn's blossom,
> As underneath their fragrant shade
>   I clasp'd her to my bosom!
> The golden hours on angel wings
>   Flew o'er me and my dearie;
> For dear to me as light and life
>   Was my sweet Highland Mary.
>
> Wi' mony a vow and locked embrace
>   Our parting was fu' tender;
> And, pledging aft to meet again,
>   We tore oursels asunder;
> But oh! fell death's untimely frost,
>   That nipt my flower sae early!
> Now green's the sod, and cauld's the clay,
>   That wraps my Highland Mary!
>
> O pale, pale now those rosy lips
>   I aft hae kissed sae fondly!
> And closed for aye the sparkling glance
>   That dwelt on me sae kindly!
> And mouldering now in silent dust
>   That heart that lo'ed[3] me dearly!
> But still within my bosom's core
>   Shall live my Highland Mary.

These compositions are so universally known, that it is needless to give any others at full length; but we may throw together a few verses and half-verses gathered from several of them:—

[1] Turbid with mud.   [2] Birch.   [3] Loved.

When o'er the hill the eastern star
　Tells bughtin'[1] time is near, my Joe;
And owsen[2] frae the furrowed field
　Return sae dowf[3] and weary, O;
Down by the burn, where scented birks
　Wi' dew are hanging clear, my Joe,
I'll meet thee on the lea-rig,[4]
　My ain[5] kind dearie, O.

In mirkest[6] glen, at midnight hour,
　I'd rove, and ne'er be eerie,[7] O,
If through that glen I gaed[8] to thee,
　My ain kind dearie, O.
Although the night were ne'er sae wild,
　And I were ne'er sae weary, O,
I'd meet thee on the lea-rig,
　My ain kind dearie, O.

. . . . .

———

I hae sworn by the heavens to my Mary,
　I hae sworn by the heavens to be true;
And sae may the heavens forget me,
　When I forget my vow!

O plight me your faith, my Mary,
　And plight me your lily-white hand;
O plight me your faith, my Mary,
　Before I leave Scotia's strand.

We hae plighted our troth, my Mary,
　In mutual affection to join;
And cursed be the cause that shall part us!
　The hour, and the moment o' time!

———

O poortith[9] cauld, and restless love,
　Ye wreck my peace between ye;
Yet poortith a' I could forgive,
　An' 'twere na for my Jeanie.

O why should fate sic[10] pleasure have
　Life's dearest bands untwining?
Or why sae sweet a flower as love
　Depend on fortune's shining?

. . . . .

To thy bosom lay my heart,
　There to throb and languish;
Though despair had wrung its core,
　That would heal its anguish.

[1] Folding.	[2] Oxen.	[3] Dull, spiritless.
[4] Grassy ridge.	[5] Own.	[6] Darkest.
[7] Frightened by dread of spirits.	[8] Went.	[9] Poverty.　[10] Such.

Take away those rosy lips,
  Rich with balmy treasure;
Turn away thine eyes of love,
  Lest I die with pleasure.

. . . . .

Here's a health to ane I lo'e dear,
  Here's a health to ane I lo'e dear;
Thou art sweet as the smile when fond lovers meet,
  And soft as their parting tear, Jessy!

Although thou maun[1] never be mine,
  Although even hope is denied,
'Tis sweeter for thee despairing
  Than aught in the world beside, Jessy!

. . . . .

Ae[2] fond kiss, and then we sever;
Ae fareweel, alas, for ever!
Had we never loved sae kindly,
Had we never loved sae blindly,
Never met, or never parted,
We had ne'er been broken-hearted.
Fare thee weel, thou first and fairest!
Fare thee weel, thou best and dearest!

Ae fond kiss, and then we sever;
Ae fareweel, alas, for ever!

. . . . .

In all, indeed, that he has written best, Burns may be said to have given us himself,—the passion or sentiment which swayed or possessed him at the moment,—almost as much as in his songs. In him the poet was the same as the man. He could describe with admirable fidelity and force incidents, scenes, manners, characters, or whatever else, which had fallen within his experience or observation; but he had little proper dramatic imagination, or power of going out of himself into other natures, and, as it were, losing his personality in the creations of his fancy. His blood was too hot, his pulse beat too tumultuously, for that; at least he was during his short life too much the sport both of his own passions and of many other stormy influences to acquire such power of intellectual self-command and self-sup-

[1] Must.   [2] One.

pression. What he might have attained to if a longer earthly existence had been granted to him—or a less tempestuous one—who shall say? Both when his genius first blazed out upon the world, and when its light was quenched by death, it seemed as if he had been born or designed to do much more than he has done. Having written what he wrote before his twenty-seventh year, he had doubtless much more additional poetry in him than he gave forth between that date and his death at the age of thirty-seven —poetry which might now have been the world's for ever if that age had been worthy of such a gift of heaven as its glorious poet.

THE NINETEENTH CENTURY.

It might almost seem as if there were something in the impressiveness of the great chronological event formed by the termination of one century and the commencement of another that had been wont to act with an awakening and fructifying power upon literary genius in these islands. Of the three last great sunbursts of our literature, the first, making what has been called the Elizabethan age of our dramatic and other poetry, threw its splendour over the last quarter of the sixteenth and the first of the seventeenth century; the second, famous as the Augustan age of Anne, brightened the earlier years of the eighteenth; the nineteenth century was ushered in by the third. At the termination of the reign of George III., in the year 1820, there were still among us, not to mention minor names, at least nine or ten poetical writers, each (whatever discordance of opinion there might be about either their relative or their absolute merits) commanding universal attention from the reading world to whatever he produced:—Crabbe (to take them in the order of their seniority), Wordsworth, Coleridge, Southey, Scott, Campbell, Moore, Byron, Shelley, and perhaps we ought to add Keats, though more for the shining promise of his great but immature genius than for what he had actually done. Many other voices there were from which divine words were often heard, but these were oracles to whom all listened, whose inspiration all men acknowledged. It is such crowding and clustering of remarkable writers that has chiefly distinguished the great literary ages in every country: there are eminent writers at other times, but they come singly or in small numbers, as Lucretius, the noblest of the Latin poets, did before the Augustan age of Roman literature; as our own Milton and Dryden did in the interval between our Elizabethan age and that of Anne; as Goldsmith, and Burke, and Johnson, and then Cowper and Burns, in twos and threes, or one by one, preceded and as it were led in the rush and crush of our last revival. For such single swallows, though they do not make, do yet commonly herald the summer; and accordingly those remarkable writers who have thus appeared between one great age of literature and another have mostly, it may be observed, arisen not in the earlier but in the later portion of the interval—have been not the lagging successors of the last era, but the precursors of the next. However the fact is to be explained or accounted for, it does indeed look as if Nature in this, as in other things, had her times of production and of comparative rest and inactivity—her autumns and her winters—or, as we may otherwise conceive it, her alternations of light and darkness, of day and night. After a busy and brilliant period of usually some thirty or forty years, there has always followed in every country a long term during which the literary spirit, as if overworked and exhausted, has manifested little real energy or power of life, and even the very demand and taste for the highest kind of literature, for depth, and subtlety, and truth, and originality, and passion, and beauty, has in a great measure ceased with the supply—a sober and slumbrous twilight of imitation and mediocrity, and little more than mechanical dexterity in bookmaking, at least with the generality of the most popular and applauded writers.

After all, the reawakening of our English literature, on each of the three occasions we have mentioned, was probably brought about mainly by the general political and social circumstances of the country and of the world at the time. The poetical and dramatic wealth and magnificence of the era of Elizabeth and James came, no doubt, for the most part, out of the passions that had been stirred and the strength that had been acquired in the mighty contests and convulsions which filled, here and throughout Europe, the middle of the sixteenth century; another breaking up of old institutions and re-edification of the state upon a new foundation and a new principle, the work of the last sixty years of the seventeenth century, if it did not contribute much to train the wits and fine writers of the age of Anne, at least both prepared the tranquillity necessary for the restoration of elegant literature, and disposed the public mind for its enjoyment; the poetical dayspring, finally, that came with our own century was born with, and probably in some degree out of, a third revolution, which shook both established institutions and the minds and opinions of men throughout Europe as much almost as the Reformation itself had done three centuries and a half before. It is also to be observed that on each of these three occasions the excitement appears to have come to us in part from a foreign literature which had undergone a similar reawakening, or put forth a new life and vigour, shortly before our own: in the Elizabethan age the contagion or impulse was caught from the literature of Italy; in the age of Anne from that of France; in the present period from that of Germany.

THE LAST AGE OF THE GEORGES.

WORDSWORTH.

This German inspiration operated most directly, and produced the most marked effect, in the poetry of Wordsworth. Wordsworth, who was born in 1770, has preserved in the editions of his collected works some of his verses written so long ago as 1786; and he also continued to the last to reprint the two earliest of his published poems, entitled An Evening Walk, addressed to a Young Lady, from the Lakes of the North of England, and Descriptive Sketches, taken during a pedestrian tour among the Alps, both of which first appeared in 1793. The recollection of the former of these poems probably suggested to somebody, a few years later, the otherwise not very intelligible designation of the Lake School, which has been applied to this writer and his imitators, or supposed imitators. But the Evening Walk and the Descriptive Sketches, which are both written in the usual rhyming ten-syllabled verse, are perfectly orthodox poems, according to the common creed, in spirit, manner, and form. The peculiarities which are conceived to constitute what is called the Lake manner first appeared in the Lyrical Ballads; the first volume of which was published in 1798, the second in 1800.

In the Preface to the second volume of the Lyrical Ballads, the author himself described his object as being to ascertain how far the purposes of poetry might be fulfilled "by fitting to metrical arrangement a selection of the real language of men in a state of vivid sensation." It might, perhaps, be possible to defend this notion by the aid of certain assumptions as to what is implied in, or to be understood by, a state of vivid sensation, which it may be contended is only another phrase for a state of poetical excitement: undoubtedly the language of a mind in such a state, selected, or corrected, and made metrical, will be poetry. It is almost a truism to say so. Nay, we might go farther, and assert that, in the circumstances supposed, the selection and the adaptation to metrical arrangement would not be necessary; the language would flow naturally into something of a musical shape (that being one of the conditions of poetical expression), and, although it might be improved by correction, it would have all the essentials of poetry as it was originally produced. But what is evidently meant is, that the real or natural language of any and every mind when simply in a state of excitement or passion is necessarily poetical. The respect in which the doctrine differs from that commonly held is, that it assumes mere passion or vivid sensation to be in all men and in all cases substantially identical with poetical excitement, and the language in which passion expresses itself to be consequently always poetry, at least after it has undergone some purification or pruning, and been reduced to metrical regularity. As for this qualification, we may remark that it must be understood to mean nothing more than that the language of passion is improved with reference to poetical effect by being thus trained and regulated: otherwise the statement would be contradictory and would refute itself; for, if passion, or vivid sensation, always speaks in poetry, the metrical arrangement and the selection are unnecessary and unwarrantable; if these operations be indispensable, the language of vivid sensation is not always poetry. But surely it is evident from the nature of the thing that it is altogether a misconception of what poetry is to conceive it to be nothing more than the language naturally prompted by passion or strong emotion. If that were all, all men, all women, and all children would be poets. Poetry, in the first place, is an art, just as painting is an art; and the one is no more to be practised solely under the guidance of strong emotion than the other. Secondly, poetical emotion is something as distinct from mere ordinary passion or excitement as is musical emotion, or the feeling of the picturesque or the beautiful or the grand in painting or in architecture; the one may and often does exist where there exists nothing of the other. Nobody has ever thought of defining music to be merely the natural vocal utterance of men in a state of vivid sensation, or painting to be nothing more than their natural way of expressing themselves when in such a state by lines and colours: no more is poetry simply their real language, or expression by words, when in such a state. It makes no difference that words are a mode of expression of which men have much more generally the use than they have the use of either colours or musical sounds; if all men could sing or could handle the brush, they still would not all be musicians and painters whenever they were in a passion.

It is true that even in the rudest minds emotion will tend to make the expression more vivid and forcible; but it will not for all that necessarily rise to poetry. Emotion or excitement alone will not produce that idealization in which poetry consists. To have that effect the excitement must be of a peculiar character, and the mind in which it takes place must be peculiarly gifted. The mistake has probably arisen from a confusion of two things which are widely different—the real language of men in a state of excitement, and the imaginative imitation of such language in the artistic delineation of the excitement. The latter alone will necessarily or universally be poetical; the former may be the veriest of prose. It may be said, indeed, that it is not men's real language, but the imitation of it, which is meant to be called poetry by Wordsworth and his followers—that, of course, their own poetry, even when most conformable to their own theory, can only consist of what *they conceive* would be the real language of persons placed in the circumstances of those from whom it professes to proceed. But this explanation, besides that it leaves the theory we are examining, considered as an account or definition of poetry, as narrow and defective as ever, still assumes that poetical imitation is nothing more than transcription, or its equivalent—such invention as comes as near as possible to what literal transcription would be; which is the very misapprehension against which we are arguing. It is equally false, we contend, to say that poetry is nothing more than either the real language of men in a state of excitement, or the mere imitation, the closer the better, of that real language. The imitation must be an idealized imitation—an intermingling of the poet with his subject by which it receives a new character; just as, in painting, a great portrait, or other picture from nature, is never a fac-simile copy, but always as much a reflection from the artist's own spirit as from the scene or object it represents. The realm of nature and the realm of art, although counterparts, are nevertheless altogether distinct the one from the other; and both painting and poetry belong to the latter, not to the former.

We cannot say that Wordsworth's theory of poetry has been altogether without effect upon his practice, but it has shown itself rather by some deficiency of refinement in his general manner than by very much that he has written in express conformity with its requisitions. We might affirm, indeed, that its principle is as much contradicted and confuted by the greater part of his own poetry as it is by that of all languages and all times in which poetry has been written, or by the universal past experience of mankind in every age and country. He is a great poet, and has enriched our literature with much beautiful and noble writing, whatever be the method or principle upon which he constructs, or fancies that he constructs, his compositions. His Laodamia, without the exception of a single line, his Lonely Leech-gatherer, with the exception of very few lines; his Ruth, his Tintern Abbey, his Feast of Brougham, the Water Lily, the greater part of the Excursion, most of the Sonnets, his great Ode on the Intimations of Immortality in Early Childhood, and many of his shorter lyrical pieces, are nearly as unexceptionable in diction as they are deep and true in feeling, judged according to any rules or principles of art that are now patronized by anybody. It is true, indeed, that it will not do to look at anything that Wordsworth has written through the spectacles of that species of criticism which was in vogue among us in the last century; we believe that in several of the pieces we have named even that narrow and superficial doctrine (if it could be recalled from the tomb) would find little or nothing to object to, but we fear it would find as little to admire; it had no feeling or understanding of the poetry of any other era than its own, —neither of that of Homer, nor that of the Greek dramatists, nor that of our own Elizabethan age,—and it certainly would not enter far into the spirit either of that of Wordsworth or of any of his eminent contemporaries or successors. It is part, and a great part, of what the literature of Germany has done for us within the last sixty years, that it has given a wider scope and a deeper insight to our perception and mode of judging of the poetical in all its forms and manifestations; and the poetry of Wordsworth has materially aided in establishing this revolution of taste and critical doctrine, by furnishing the English reader with some of the earliest and many of the most successful or most generally appreciated examples and illustrations of the precepts of the new faith. Even the errors of Wordsworth's poetical creed and practice, the excess to which he has sometimes carried his employment of the language of the uneducated classes, and his attempts to extract poetical effects out of trivial incidents and humble life, were fitted to be rather serviceable than injurious in the highly artificial state of our poetry when he began to write. He may not have succeeded in every instance in which he has tried to glorify the familiar and elevate the low, but he has nevertheless taught us that the domain of poetry is much wider and more various than it used to be deemed, that there is a great deal of it to be found where it was formerly little the fashion to look for anything of the kind, and that the poet does not absolutely require for the exercise of his art and the display of his powers what are commonly called illustrious or distinguished characters, and an otherwise dignified subject, any more than long and learned words. Among his English contemporaries Wordsworth stands foremost and alone as the poet of common life. It is not his only field, nor perhaps the field in which he is greatest; but it is the one which is most exclusively his own. He has, it is true, no humour or comedy of any kind in him (which is perhaps the explanation of the ludicrous touches that sometimes startle us in his serious poetry), and therefore he is not, and seldom attempts to be, what Burns was for his countrymen, the poetic interpreter, and, as such, refiner as well as embalmer, of the wit and merriment of the common people: the writer by whom that title is to be won is yet to arise, and probably from among the people themselves: but of whatever is more tender or more thoughtful in the spirit of ordinary life in England the poetry of Wordsworth is the truest and most comprehensive transcript we possess. Many of his verses, embodying as they do the philosophy as well as the sentiment of this every-day human experience, have a completeness and impressiveness, as of texts, mottoes, proverbs, the force of which is universally felt, and has already worked them into the texture and substance of the language to a far greater extent, we apprehend, than has happened in the case of any contemporary writer.

Wordsworth, though only a few years deceased, for he survived till 1850, nearly sixty years after the publication of his first poetry, is already a classic; and, extensively as he is now read and appreciated, any review of our national literature would be very incomplete without at least a few extracts from his works illustrative of the various styles in which he has written. As a specimen of what may be called his more peculiar manner, or that which is or used to be more especially understood by the style of the Lake School of poetry, we will begin with the well-known verses entitled The Fountain, a Conversation, which, in his own classification, are included among what he designates Poems of Sentiment and Reflection, and are stated to have been composed in 1799:—

> We talked with open heart, and tongue
> Affectionate and true,
> A pair of friends, though I was young,
> And Matthew seventy-two.
>
> We lay beneath a spreading oak,
> Beside a mossy seat;
> And from the turf a fountain broke,
> And gurgled at our feet.
>
> "Now, Matthew!" said I, "let us match
> This water's pleasant tune
> With some old Border-song, or catch
> That suits a summer's noon;
>
> Or of the church-clock and the chimes
> Sing here, beneath the shade,
> That half-mad thing of witty rhymes
> Which you last April made!"
>
> In silence Matthew lay, and eyed
> The spring beneath the tree;
> And thus the dear old man replied,
> The grey-haired man of glee:
>
> "No check, no stay, this streamlet fears;
> How merrily it goes!
> 'Twill murmur on a thousand years,
> And flow as now it flows.
>
> And here, on this delightful day,
> I cannot choose but think
> How oft, a vigorous man, I lay
> Beside this fountain's brink.
>
> My eyes are dim with childish tears,
> My heart is idly stirred,
> For the same sound is in my ears
> Which in those days I heard.
>
> Thus fares it still in our decay:
> And yet the wiser mind
> Mourns less for what age takes away
> Than what it leaves behind.
>
> The blackbird amid leafy trees,
> The lark above the hill,
> Let loose their carols when they please,
> Are quiet when they will.
>
> With nature never do they wage
> A foolish strife; they see
> A happy youth, and their old age
> Is beautiful and free:

> But we are pressed by heavy laws;
> And often, glad no more,
> We wear a face of joy, because
> We have been glad of yore.
>
> If there be one who need bemoan
> His kindred laid in earth,
> The household hearts that were his own,
> It is the man of mirth.
>
> My days, my friend, are almost gone,
> My life has been approved,
> And many love me; but by none
> Am I enough beloved."
>
> "Now, both himself and me he wrongs,
> The man who thus complains!
> I live and sing my idle songs
> Upon these happy plains,
>
> And, Matthew, for thy children dead
> I 'll be a son to thee!"
> At this he grasped my hand, and said,
> "Alas! that cannot be!"
>
> We rose up from the fountain-side;
> And down the smooth descent
> Of the green sheep-track did we glide;
> And through the wood we went;
>
> And, ere we came to Leonard's Rock,
> He sang those witty rhymes
> About the crazy old church-clock,
> And the bewildered chimes.

The following, entitled The Affliction of Margaret, dated 1804, and classed among the Poems founded on the Affections, is more impassioned, but still essentially in the same style:—

> Where art thou, my beloved son,
> Where art thou, worse to me than dead?
> Oh find me, prosperous or undone!
> Or, if the grave be now thy bed,
> Why am I ignorant of the same,
> That I may rest; and neither blame
> Nor sorrow may attend thy name?
>
> Seven years, alas! to have received
> No tidings of an only child;
> To have despaired, have hoped, believed,
> And been for evermore beguiled;
> Sometimes with thoughts of very bliss!
> I catch at them, and then I miss;
> Was ever darkness like to this?

He was among the prime in worth,
An object beauteous to behold;
Well born, well bred; I sent him forth
Ingenuous, innocent, and bold:
If things ensued that wanted grace,
As hath been said, they were not base;
And never blush was on my face.

Ah! little doth the young one dream,
When full of play and childish cares,
What power is in his wildest scream,
Heard by his mother unawares!
He knows it not, he cannot guess:
Years to a mother bring distress;
But do not make her love the less.

Neglect me! no, I suffered long
From that ill thought; and, being blind,
Said. "Pride shall help me in my wrong:
Kind mother have I been, as kind
As ever breathed:" and that is true;
I've wet my path with tears like dew,
Weeping for him when no one knew.

My son, if thou be humbled, poor,
Hopeless of honour and of gain,
Oh! do not dread thy mother's door;
Think not of me with grief and pain:
I now can see with better eyes;
And worldly grandeur I despise,
And Fortune with her gifts and lies.

Alas! the fowls of heaven have wings,
And blasts of heaven will aid their flight.
They mount—how short a voyage brings
The wanderers back to their delight!
Chains tie us down by land and sea;
And wishes, vain as mine, may be
All that is left to comfort thee.

Perhaps some dungeon hears thee groan,
Maimed, mangled, by inhuman men;
Or thou, upon a desert thrown,
Inheritest the lion's den;
Or hast been summoned to the deep,
Thou, thou and all thy mates, to keep
An incommunicable sleep.

I look for ghosts; but none will force
Their way to me:—'tis falsely said
That there was ever intercourse
Between the living and the dead;
For, surely, then I should have sight
Of him I wait for day and night
With love and longings infinite.

> My apprehensions come in crowds;
> I dread the rustling of the grass;
> The very shadows of the clouds
> Have power to shake me as they pass;
> I question things, and do not find
> One that will answer to my mind;
> And all the world appears unkind.
>
> Beyond participation lie
> My troubles, and beyond relief:
> If any chance to heave a sigh,
> They pity me, and not my grief.
> Then come to me, my Son, or send
> Some tidings that my woes may end;
> I have no other earthly friend!

Here is another from the same class, and still in the same style, dated 1798. The verses are very beautiful; they bear some resemblance to the touching old Scotch ballad called Lady Anna Bothwell's Lament, beginning

> Balow, my boy, lie still and sleep;
> It grieves me sair to see thee weep—

of which there is a copy in Percy's Reliques, and others, differing considerably from that, in other collections:—

> Her eyes are wild, her head is bare,
> The sun has burned her coal-black hair;
> Her eyebrows have a rusty stain,
> And she came far from over the main.
> She has a baby on her arm,
>   Or else she were alone:
> And underneath the haystack warm,
>   And on the greenwood stone,
> She talked and sung the woods among,
> And it was in the English tongue.
>
> "Sweet babe, they say that I am mad,
> But nay, my heart is far too glad;
> And I am happy when I sing
> Full many a sad and doleful thing:
> Then, lovely baby, do not fear!
> I pray thee, have no fear of me;
> But safe as in a cradle, here,
> My lovely baby, shalt thou be:
> To thee I know too much I owe;
> I cannot work thee any woe.
>
> A fire was once within my brain;
> And in my head a dull, dull pain;
> And fiendish faces, one, two, three,
> Hung at my breast, and pulled at me;

But then there came a sight of joy
It came at once to do me good;
I waked and saw my little boy,
My little boy of flesh and blood;
Oh joy for me that sight to see!
For he was there, and only he.

Suck, little babe, oh suck again!
It cools my blood, it cools my brain;
Thy lips I feel them, baby! they
Draw from my heart the pain away.
Oh! press me with thy little hand;
It loosens something at my chest;
About that tight and deadly band
I feel thy little fingers prest.
The breeze I see is in the tree:
It comes to cool my babe and me.

Oh! love me, love me, little boy!
Thou art thy mother's only joy;
And do not dread the waves below
When o'er the sea-rock's edge we go;
The high crag cannot work me harm,
Nor leaping torrents when they howl;
The babe I carry on my arm
He saves for me my precious soul;
Then happy lie; for blest am I;
Without me my sweet babe would die.

Then do not fear, my boy! for thee
Bold as a lion will I be;
And I will always be thy guide,
Through hollow snows and rivers wide.
I'll build an Indian bower; I know
The leaves that make the softest bed;
And if from me thou wilt not go,
But still be true till I am dead,
My pretty thing, then thou shalt sing
As merry as the birds in spring.

Thy father cares not for my breast,
'Tis thine, sweet baby, there to rest;
'Tis all thine own!—and, if its hue
Be changed, that was so fair to view,
'Tis fair enough for thee, my dove!
My beauty, little child, is flown,
But thou wilt live with me in love;
And what if my poor cheek be brown?
'Tis well for thee, thou canst not see
How pale and wan it else would be.

Dread not their taunts, my little life;
I am thy father's wedded wife;
And underneath the spreading tree
We two will live in honesty.

If his sweet boy he could forsake,
With me he never would have stayed;
From him no harm my babe can take;
But he, poor man! is wretched made;
And every day we two will pray
For him that's gone and far away.

I'll teach my boy the sweetest things,
I'll teach him how the owlet sings.
My little babe! thy lips are still,
And thou hast almost sucked thy fill.
——Where art thou gone, my own dear child?
What wicked looks are those I see?
Alas! alas! that look so wild,
It never, never came from me:
If thou art mad, my pretty lad,
Then I must be for ever sad.

Oh! smile on me, my little lamb!
For I thy own dear mother am.
My love for thee has well been tried:
I 've sought thy father far and wide.
I know the poisons of the shade,
I know the earth-nuts fit for food:
Then, pretty dear, be not afraid:
We 'll find thy father in the wood.
Now laugh and be gay, to the woods away!
And there, my babe, we'll live for aye."

But much, perhaps we might say the greater part, of Wordsworth's poetry is in a very different style or manner. Take, for example, his noble Laodamia, dated 1814, and in the later editions placed among what he calls Poems of the Imagination, though formerly classed as one of the Poems founded on the Affections:—

"With sacrifice before the rising morn
Vows have I made by fruitless hope inspired;
And from the infernal Gods, 'mid shades forlorn
Of night, my slaughtered Lord have I required:
Celestial pity I again implore:—
Restore him to my sight—great Jove, restore!"

So speaking, and by fervent love endowed
With faith, the suppliant heavenward lifts her hands;
While, like the sun emerging from a cloud,
Her countenance brightens—and her eye expands;
Her bosom heaves and spreads, her stature grows;
And she expects the issue in repose.

O terror! what hath she perceived? O joy!
What doth she look on? Whom doth she behold?
Her Hero slain upon the beach of Troy?
His vital presence? his corporeal mould?
It is—if sense deceive her not—'tis He!
And a God leads him, winged Mercury!

Mild Hermes spake—and touched her with his wand
That calms all fear; "Such grace hath crowned thy prayer,
Laodamia! that at Jove's command
Thy husband walks the paths of upper air:
He comes to tarry with thee three hours' space;
Accept the gift, behold him face to face!"

Forth sprang the impassioned Queen her Lord to clasp;
Again that consummation she assayed;
But unsubstantial form eludes her grasp
As often as that eager grasp was made.
The Phantom parts—but parts to re-unite,
And re-assume his place before her sight.

"Protesilaus, lo! thy guide is gone!
Confirm, I pray, the Vision with thy voice:
This is our palace,—yonder is thy throne;
Speak, and the floor thou tread'st on will rejoice.
Not to appal me have the Gods bestowed
This precious boon; and blest a sad abode."

"Great Jove, Laodamia! doth not leave
His gifts imperfect:—Spectre though I be,
I am not sent to scare thee or deceive;
But in reward of thy fidelity.
And something also did my worth obtain;
For fearless virtue bringeth boundless gain.

Thou knowest, the Delphic oracle foretold
That the first Greek who touched the Trojan strand
Should die; but me the threat could not withhold;
A generous cause a victim did demand;
And forth I leapt upon the sandy plain;
A self-devoted chief—by Hector slain."

"Supreme of Heroes—bravest, noblest, best!
Thy matchless courage I bewail no more,
Which then, when tens of thousands were deprest
By doubt, propelled thee to the fatal shore:
Thou found'st—and I forgive thee—here thou art—
A nobler counsellor than my poor heart.

But thou, though capable of sternest deed,
Wert kind as resolute, and good as brave;
And he, whose power restores thee, hath decreed
That thou should'st cheat the malice of the grave;
Redundant are thy locks, thy lips as fair
As when their breath enriched Thessalian air.

No Spectre greets me,—no vain Shadow this;
Come, blooming Hero, place thee by my side!
Give, on this well-known couch, one nuptial kiss
To me, this day, a second time thy bride!"
Jove frowned in heaven: the conscious Parcae threw
Upon those roseate lips a Stygian hue.

"This visage tells thee that my doom is past:
Nor should the change be mourned, even if the joys
Of sense were able to return as fast
And surely as they vanish.—Earth destroys
Those raptures duly—Erebus disdains:
Calm pleasures there abide—majestic pains.

Be taught, O faithful Consort, to control
Rebellious passion: for the Gods approve
The depth, and not the tumult of the soul;
A fervent, not ungovernable love.
Thy transports moderate; and meekly mourn
When I depart, for brief is my sojourn."—

"Ah, wherefore?—Did not Hercules by force
Wrest from the guardian monster of the tomb
Alcestis, a reanimated corse,
Given back to dwell on earth in vernal bloom?
Medea's spells dispersed the weight of years,
And Aeson stood a youth 'mid youthful peers.

The Gods to us are merciful—and they
Yet further may relent: for mightier far
Than strength of nerve and sinew, or the sway
Of magic potent over sun and star,
Is love, though oft to agony distrest,
And though his favourite seat be feeble woman's breast.

But if thou goest I follow"—"Peace!" he said—
She looked upon him and was calmed and cheered;
The ghastly colour from his lips had fled;
In his deportment, shape, and mien appeared
Elysian beauty, melancholy grace,
Brought from a pensive, though a happy place.

He spake of love, such love as Spirits feel
In worlds whose course is equable and pure;
No fears to beat away—no strife to heal—
The past unsighed for, and the future sure;
Spake of heroic acts in graver mood
Revived, with finer harmony pursued;

Of all that is most beauteous—imaged there
In happier beauty; more pellucid streams,
An ampler ether, a diviner air,
And fields invested with purpureal gleams;
Climes which the sun, who sheds the brightest day
Earth knows, is all unworthy to survey.

Yet there the soul shall enter which hath earned
That privilege by virtue.—"Ill," said he,
"The end of man's existence I discerned,
Who from ignoble games and revelry
Could draw, when we had parted, vain delight,
While tears were thy best pastime day and night:

And while my youthful peers before my eyes
(Each hero following his peculiar bent)
Prepared themselves for glorious enterprise
By martial sports,—or, seated in the tent,
Chieftains and kings in council were detained;
What time the fleet at Aulis lay enchained.

The wished-for wind was given:—I then revolved
The oracle upon the silent sea;
And, if no worthier led the way, resolved
That, of a thousand vessels, mine should be
The foremost prow in pressing to the strand,—
Mine the first blood that tinged the Trojan sand.

Yet bitter, oftimes bitter, was the pang
When of thy loss I thought, beloved wife!
On thee too fondly did my memory hang,
And on the joys we shared in mortal life,—
The paths which we had trod—these fountains, flowers;
My new-planned cities, and unfinished towers.

But should suspense permit the foe to cry,
'Behold, they tremble!—haughty their array,
Yet of their number no one dares to die!'
In soul I swept the indignity away:
Old frailties then recurred:—but lofty thought,
In act embodied, my deliverance wrought.

And thou, though strong in love, art all too weak
In reason, in self-government too slow;
I counsel thee by fortitude to seek
Our blest reunion in the shades below.
The invisible world with thee hath sympathised;
Be thy affections raised and solemnised.

Learn, by a mortal yearning, to ascend—
Seeking a higher object. Love was given,
Encouraged, sanctioned, chiefly for that end;
For this the passion to excess was driven—
That self might be annulled; her bondage prove
The fetters of a dream, opposed to love."¹

---

¹ The reader of Milton will remember the same idea in the Eighth Book of Paradise Lost:—

"Love refines
The thoughts, and heart enlarges; hath his seat
In reason, and is judicious: is the scale
By which to heavenly love thou may'st ascend."

> Aloud she shrieked! for Hermes reappears!
> Round the dear shade she would have clung—'tis vain;
> The hours are past—too brief had they been years;
> And him no mortal effort can detain:
> Swift, towards the realms that know not earthly day,
> He through the portal takes his silent way,
> And on the palace floor a lifeless corse she lay.
>
> She—who, though warned, exhorted, and reproved,
> Thus died, from passion desperate to a crime—
> By the just Gods, whom no weak pity moved,
> Was doomed to wear out her appointed time,
> Apart from happy ghosts, that gather flowers
> Of blissful quiet 'mid unfading bowers.
>
> Yet tears to mortal suffering are due;
> And mortal hopes defeated and o'erthrown
> Are mourned by man,—and not by man alone,
> As fondly he believes.—Upon the side
> Of Hellespont (such faith was entertained)
> A knot of spiry trees for ages grew
> From out the tomb of him for whom she died;
> And ever, when such stature they had gained
> That Ilium's walls were subject to their view,
> The trees' tall summits withered at the sight;
> A constant interchange of growth and blight.

In the same grand strain is very much especially of Wordsworth's later poetry. Neither puerility nor over familiarity of diction, with whatever other faults they may be chargeable, can well be attributed to either the Excursion, or the Sonnets, or the Odes. But it is, on the other hand, a misconception to imagine that this later poetry is for the most part enveloped in a haze through which the meaning is only to be got at by initiated eyes. Nothing like this is the case. The Excursion, published in 1814, for instance, with the exception of a very few passages, is a poem that he who runs may read, and the greater part of which may be apprehended by readers of all classes as readily as almost any other poetry in the language. We may say the same even of The Prelude, or Introduction to the Recluse (intended to consist of three Parts, of which The Excursion is the second, the first remaining in manuscript, and the third having been only planned), which was begun in 1799 and completed in 1805, although not published till a few months after the author's death in 1850; an

elaborate poem, in fourteen books, of eminent interest as
the poet's history of himself, and of the growth of his own
mind, as well as on other accounts, and long before characterized by Coleridge, to whom it is addressed, as

> "An Orphic song indeed,
> A song divine of high and passionate thoughts
> To their own music chanted."*

COLERIDGE.

In all that constitutes artistic character the poetry of
Coleridge is a contrast to that of Wordsworth. Coleridge,
born in 1772, published the earliest of his poetry that is now
remembered in 1796, in a small volume containing also some
pieces by Charles Lamb, to which some by Charles Lloyd
were added in a second edition the following year. It was
not till 1800, after he had produced and printed separately
his Ode to the Departing Year (1796), his noble ode entitled
France (1797), his Fears in Solitude (1798), and his translations of both parts of Schiller's Wallenstein, that he was
first associated as a poet and author with Wordsworth, in the
second volume of whose Lyrical Ballads, published in 1800,
appeared, as the contributions of an anonymous friend,
Coleridge's Ancient Mariner, Foster Mother's Tale, Nightingale, and Love. "I should not have requested this assistance," said Wordsworth, in his preface, "had I not believed
that the poems of my friend would, in a great measure, have
the same tendency as my own, and that, though there would

---

* In reference, no doubt, to Wordsworth's own lines, in the First Book of
the Poem :—
> "Some philosophic song
> Of Truth that cherishes our daily life;
> With meditations passionate from deep
> Recesses in man's heart, immortal verse
> Thoughtfully fitted to the Orphean lyre."

And here, again, we have the echo of Milton's line, in the Third Book of
Paradise Lost :—
> "With other notes than to the Orphean lyre."

be found a difference, there would be found no discordance, in the colours of our style; as our opinions on the subject of poetry do almost entirely coincide." Coleridge's own account, however, is somewhat different. In his Biographia Literaria, he tells us that, besides the Ancient Mariner, he was preparing for the conjoint publication, among other poems, the Dark Ladie and the Christabel, in which he should have more nearly realized his ideal than he had done in his first attempt, when the volume was brought out with so much larger a portion of it the produce of Wordsworth's industry than his own, that his few compositions, "instead of forming a balance, appeared rather an interpolation of heterogeneous matter;" and then he adds, in reference to the long preface in which Wordsworth had expounded his theory of poetry, "With many parts of this preface in the sense attributed to them, and which the words undoubtedly seem to authorize, I never concurred; but, on the contrary, objected to them as erroneous in principle and contradictory (in appearance at least) both to other parts of the same preface, and to the author's own practice in the greater number of the poems themselves."

Coleridge's poetry is remarkable for the perfection of its execution, for the exquisite art with which its divine spirit is endowed with formal expression. The subtly woven words, with all their sky colours, seem to grow out of the thought or emotion, as the flower from its stalk, or the flame from its feeding oil. The music of his verse, too, especially of what he has written in rhyme, is as sweet and as characteristic as anything in the language, placing him for that rare excellence in the same small band with Shakespeare, and Beaumont and Fletcher (in their lyrics), and Milton, and Collins, and Shelley, and Tennyson. It was probably only quantity that was wanting to make Coleridge the greatest poet of his day. Certainly, at least, some things that he has written have not been surpassed, if they have been matched, by any of his contemporaries. And (as indeed has been the case with almost all great poets) he continued to write better and better the longer he wrote; some of his happiest verses were the produce of his latest years. To quote part of what we have said in a paper published immediately after Coleridge's death:—"Not only, as we proceed from his earlier to his later compositions, does the execution become much more artistic and perfect, but the informing spirit is refined and purified—the tenderness grows more delicate and deep, the fire brighter and keener, the sense of beauty more subtle and exquisite. Yet from the first there was in all he wrote the divine breath which essentially makes poetry what it is. There was 'the shaping spirit of imagination,' evidently of soaring pinion and full of strength, though as yet sometimes unskilfully directed, and encumbered in its flight by an affluence of power which it seemed hardly to know how to manage: hence an unselecting impetuosity in these early compositions, never indicating anything like poverty of thought, but producing occasionally considerable awkwardness and turgidity of style, and a declamatory air, from which no poetry was ever more free than that of Coleridge in its maturer form. Yet even among these juvenile productions are many passages, and some whole pieces, of perfect gracefulness, and radiant with the purest sunlight of poetry. There is, for example, the most beautiful delicacy of sentiment, as well as sweetness of versification and expression, in the following lines, simple as they are:—

> Maid of my love, sweet Genevieve!
> In beauty's light you glide along;
> Your eye is like the star of eve,
> And sweet your voice as Seraph's song.
> Yet not your heavenly beauty gives
> This heart with passion soft to glow;
> Within your soul a voice there lives!
> It bids you hear the tale of woe.
> When, sinking low, the sufferer wan
> Beholds no hand outstretched to save,
> Fair, as the bosom of the swan
> That rises graceful o'er the wave,
> I've seen your breast with pity heave;
> And therefore love I you, sweet Genevieve!

And the following little picture, entitled Time, Real and Imaginary, is a gem worthy of the poet in the most thoughtful and philosophic strength of his faculties:—

> On the wide level of a mountain's head
> (I knew not where, but 'twas some fairy place),
> Their pinions, ostrich-like, for sails outspread,
> Two lovely children ran an endless race;
>   A sister and a brother!
> That far outstripped the other;
> Yet ever runs she with reverted face,
> And looks and listens for the boy behind:
>   For he, alas! is blind!
> O'er rough and smooth with even step he passed,
> And knows not whether he be first or last.

In a different manner, and more resembling that of these early poems in general, are many passages of great power in the Monody on the Death of Chatterton, and in the Religious Musings, the latter written in 1794, when the author was only in his twenty-third year. And, among other remarkable pieces of a date not much later, might be mentioned the ode entitled France, written in 1797, which Shelley regarded as the finest ode in the language; his Fire, Famine, and Slaughter, written, we believe, about the same time; his ode entitled Dejection; his blank verse lines entitled The Nightingale; his Rime of the Ancient Mariner, and his exquisite verses entitled Love, to which last for their union of passion with delicacy, and of both with the sweetest, richest music, it would be difficult to find a match in our own or any language.

"Of Coleridge's poetry, in its most matured form and in its best specimens, the most distinguishing characteristics are vividness of imagination and subtlety of thought, combined with unrivalled beauty and expressiveness of diction, and the most exquisite melody of verse. With the exception of a vein of melancholy and meditative tenderness, flowing rather from a contemplative survey of the mystery —the strangely mingled good and evil—of all things human, than connected with any individual interests, there is not in general much of passion in his compositions, and he is not well fitted, therefore, to become a very popular poet, or a favourite with the multitude. His love itself, warm and tender as it is, is still Platonic and spiritual in its tenderness, rather than a thing of flesh and blood. There is nothing in his poetry of the pulse of fire that throbs in that of Burns; neither has he much of the homely every-day truth, the proverbial and universally applicable wisdom, of Wordsworth. Coleridge was, far more than either of these poets, 'of imagination *all* compact.' The fault of his poetry is the same that belongs to that of Spenser; it is too purely or unalloyedly poetical. But rarely, on the other hand, has there existed an imagination in which so much originality and daring were associated and harmonized with so gentle and tremblingly delicate a sense of beauty. Some of his minor poems especially, for the richness of their colouring combined with the most perfect finish, can be compared only to the flowers which spring up into loveliness at the touch of 'great creating nature.' The words, the rhyme, the whole flow of the music seem to be not so much the mere expression or sign of the thought as its blossoming or irradiation—of the bright essence the equally bright though sensible effluence."*

In most of Coleridge's latest poetry, however, along with this perfection of execution, in which he was unmatched, we have more body and warmth—more of the inspiration of the heart mingling with that of the fancy. The following lines are entitled Work without Hope, and are stated to have been composed 21st February, 1827:—

> All nature seems at work. Slugs leave their lair—
> The bees are stirring—birds are on the wing—
> And winter, slumbering in the open air,
> Wears on his smiling face a dream of spring!
> And I, the while, the sole unbusy thing,
> Nor honey make, nor pair, nor build, nor sing.
>
> Yet well I ken the banks where amaranths blow,
> Have traced the fount whence streams of nectar flow.

* Printing Machine, No. 12, for 16th August, 1834.

Bloom, O ye amaranths! bloom for whom ye may,
For me ye bloom not! Glide, rich streams, away!
With lips unbrightened, wreathless brow, I stroll;
And would you learn the spells that drowse my soul?
Work without hope draws nectar in a sieve,
And hope without an object cannot live.

To about the same date belongs the following, entitled Youth and Age:—

Verse, a breeze mid blossoms straying,
Where Hope clung feeding, like a bee—
Both were mine! Life went a maying
With Nature, Hope, and Poesy,
  When I was young!
When I was young?—Ah, woeful when!
Ah! for the change 'twixt now and then!
This breathing house not built with hands,
This body that does me grievous wrong,
O'er airy cliffs and glittering sands
How lightly then it flashed along:—
Like those trim skiffs, unknown of yore,
On winding lakes and rivers wide,
That ask no aid of sail or oar,
That fear no spite of wind or tide!
Nought cared this body for wind or weather
When youth and I lived in't together.

Flowers are lovely; love is flower-like;
Friendship is a sheltering tree;
O! the joys that came down shower-like,
Of Friendship, Love, and Liberty,
  Ere I was old!
Ere I was old?—Ah, woeful ere,
Which tells me, Youth's no longer here!
O Youth! for years so many and sweet
'Tis known that thou and I were one;
I'll think it but a fond conceit—
It cannot be, that thou art gone!
Thy vesper-bell hath not yet tolled;—
And thou wert aye a masker bold!
What strange disguise hast now put on,
To make believe that thou art gone?
I see these locks in silvery slips,
This drooping gait, this altered size;
But springtide blossoms on thy lips,
And tears take sunshine from thine eyes!
Life is but thought; so think I will
That Youth and I are house-mates still.

Dew-drops are the gems of morning,
But the tears of mournful eve!
Where no hope is, life's a warning
That only serves to make us grieve,
  When we are old;

> That only serves to make us grieve,
> With oft and tedious taking leave;
> Like some poor nigh-related guest,
> That may not rudely be dismist,
> Yet hath outstayed his welcome while,
> And tells the jest without the smile.

The following may have been written a few years later. It winds up a prose dialogue between two girls and their elderly male friend the Poet, or Improvisatore, as he is more familiarly styled, who, after a most eloquent description of that rare mutual love, the possession of which he declares would be more than an adequate reward for the rarest virtue, to the remark, "Surely, he who has described it so well must have possessed it?" replies, "If he were worthy to have possessed it, and had believingly anticipated and not found it, how bitter the disappointment!" and then, after a pause, breaks out into verse thus:—

> Yes, yes! that boon, life's richest treat,
> He had, or fancied that he had;
> Say, 'twas but in his own conceit—
> The fancy made him glad!
> Crown of his cup, and garnish of his dish,
> The boon prefigured in his earliest wish
> The fair fulfilment of his poesy,
> When his young heart first yearned for sympathy!
>
> But e'en the meteor offspring of the brain
> Unnourished wane;
> Faith asks her daily bread,
> And fancy must be fed.
> Now so it chanced—from wet or dry,
> It boots not how—I know not why—
> She missed her wonted food; and quickly
> Poor fancy staggered and grew sickly,
> Then came a restless state, 'twixt yea and nay,
> His faith was fixed, his heart all ebb and flow;
> Or like a bark, in some half-sheltered bay,
> Above its anchor driving to and fro.
>
> That boon, which but to have possest
> In a belief gave life a zest—
> Uncertain both what it had been,
> And if by error lost, or luck;
> And what it was:—an evergreen
> Which some insidious blight had struck,
> Or annual flower, which, past its blow,
> No vernal spell shall e'er revive!
> Uncertain, and afraid to know,

Doubts tossed him to and fro:
Hope keeping Love, Love Hope, alive,
Like babes bewildered in the snow,
That cling and huddle from the cold
In hollow tree or ruined fold.

Those sparkling colours, once his boast,
    Fading, one by one away,
Thin and hueless as a ghost,
    Poor fancy on her sick-bed lay;
Ill at a distance, worse when near,
Telling her dreams to jealous fear!
Where was it then, the sociable sprite
That crowned the poet's cup and decked his dish
Poor shadow cast from an unsteady wish,
Itself a substance by no other right
But that it intercepted reason's light;
It dimmed his eye, it darkened on his brow:
A peevish mood, a tedious time, I trow!
    Thank heaven! 'tis not so now.

O bliss of blissful hours!
The boon of heaven's decreeing,
While yet in Eden's bowers
Dwelt the first husband and his sinless mate!
The one sweet plant, which, piteous heaven agreeing,
They bore with them through Eden's closing gate!
Of life's gay summer tide the sovran rose!
Late autumn's amaranth, that more fragrant blows
When passion's flowers all fall or fade;
If this were ever his in outward being,
Or but his own true love's projected shade,
Now that at length by certain proof he knows
That, whether real or a magic show,
Whate'er it was, it is no longer so;
Though heart be lonesome, hope laid low,
Yet, lady, deem him not unblest:
The certainty that struck hope dead
Hath left contentment in her stead:
    And that is next to best!

And still more perfect and altogether exquisite, we think, than anything we have yet given, is the following, entitled Love, Hope and Patience, in Education:—

O'er wayward childhood would'st thou hold firm rule,
And sun thee in the light of happy faces;
Love, Hope, and Patience, these must be thy graces,
And in thine own heart let them first keep school.
For, as old Atlas on his broad neck places
Heaven's starry globe, and there sustains it,—so
Do these upbear the little world below
Of Education,—Patience, Love, and Hope.

> Methinks, I see them grouped in seemly show,
> The straitened arms upraised, the palms aslope,
> And robes that touching, as adown they flow,
> Distinctly blend, like snow embossed in snow.
>
> O part them never! If Hope prostrate lie,
> Love too will sink and die.
> But Love is subtle, and doth proof derive
> From her own life that Hope is yet alive;
> And, bending o'er with soul-transfusing eyes,
> And the soft murmurs of the mother dove,
> Woos back the fleeting spirit, and half supplies:—
> Thus Love repays to Hope what Hope first gave to Love.
>
> Yet haply there will come a weary day,
> When overtasked at length
> Both Love and Hope beneath the load give way.
> Then, with a statue's smile, a statue's strength,
> Stands the mute sister, Patience, nothing loth,
> And both supporting does the work of both.

Southey.

Coleridge died in 1834; his friend Southey, born three years later, survived to 1843. If Coleridge wrote too little poetry, Southey may be said to have written too much and too rapidly. Southey, as well as Coleridge, has been popularly reckoned one of the Lake poets; but it is difficult to assign any meaning to that name which should entitle it to comprehend either the one or the other. Southey, indeed, was, in the commencement of his career, the associate of Wordsworth and Coleridge; a portion of his first poem, his Joan of Arc, published in 1796, was written by Coleridge: and he afterwards took up his residence, as well as Wordsworth, among the lakes of Westmoreland. But, although in his first volume of minor poems, published in 1797, there was something of the same simplicity or plainness of style, and choice of subjects from humble life, by which Wordsworth sought to distinguish himself about the same time, the manner of the one writer bore only a very superficial resemblance to that of the other; whatever it was, whether something quite original, or only, in the main, an inspiration caught from the Germans, that gave its peculiar character to Wordsworth's poetry, it was wanting in Southey's; he was evidently, with all his ingenuity and fertility, and notwithstanding an ambition of originality which led him to be continually seeking after strange models, from Arabian and Hindoo mythologies to Latin hexameters, of a genius radically imitative, and not qualified to put forth its strength except while moving in a beaten track and under the guidance of long-established rules. Southey was by nature a conservative in literature as well as in politics, and the eccentricity of his Thalabas and Kehamas was as merely spasmodic as the Jacobinism of his Wat Tyler. But even Thalaba and Kehama, whatever they may be, are surely not poems of the Lake school. And in most of his other poems, especially in his latest epic, Roderick, the Last of the Goths, Southey is in verse what he always was in prose, one of the most thoroughly and unaffectedly English of our modern writers. The verse, however, is too like prose to be poetry of a very high order; it is flowing and eloquent, but has little of the distinctive life or lustre of poetical composition. There is much splendour and beauty, however, in the Curse of Kehama, the most elaborate of his long poems.

Scott.

Walter Scott, again, was never accounted one of the Lake poets; yet he, as well as Wordsworth and Coleridge, was early a drinker at the fountain of German poetry; his commencing publication was a translation of Bürger's Lenore (1796), and the spirit and manner of his original compositions were, from the first, evidently and powerfully influenced by what had thus awakened his poetical faculty. His robust and manly character of mind, however, and his strong nationalism, with the innate disposition of his imagination to live in the past rather than in the future, saved him from being seduced into either the puerilities or the extravagances to which other imitators of the German writers among us were thought to have, more or less, given way; and, having soon found in the popular ballad-poetry of his own country all the qualities which had most attracted him in his foreign favourites, with others which had an equal or still greater charm for his heart and fancy, he henceforth gave himself up almost exclusively to the more congenial inspiration of that native minstrelsy. His poems are all lays and romances of chivalry, but infinitely finer than any that had ever before been written. With all their irregularity and carelessness (qualities which in some sort are characteristic of and essential to this kind of poetry), that element of life in all writing, which comes of the excited feeling and earnest belief of the writer, is never wanting; this animation, fervour, enthusiasm,—call it by what name we will,—exists in greater strength in no poetry than in that of Scott, redeeming a thousand defects, and triumphing over all the reclamations of criticism. It was this, no doubt, more than anything else, which at once took the public admiration by storm. All cultivated and perfect enjoyment of poetry, or of any other of the fine arts, is partly emotional, partly critical; the enjoyment and appreciation are only perfect when these two qualities are blended; but most of the poetry that had been produced among us in modern times had aimed at affording chiefly, if not exclusively, a critical gratification. The Lay of the Last Minstrel (1805) surprised readers of all degrees with a long and elaborate poem, which carried them onward with an excitement of heart as well as of head which many of them had never experienced before in the perusal of poetry. The narrative form of the poem no doubt did much to produce this effect, giving to it, even without the poetry, the interest and enticement of a novel; but all readers, even the least tinctured with a literary taste, felt also, in a greater or less degree, the charm of the verse, and the poetic glow with which the work was all alive. Marmion (1808) carried the same feelings to a much higher pitch; it is undoubtedly Scott's greatest poem, or the one at any rate in which the noblest passages are found; though the more domestic attractions of the Lady of the Lake (1810) made it the most popular on its first appearance. Meanwhile, his success, the example he had set, and the tastes which he had awakened in the public mind, had affected our literature to an extent in various directions which has scarcely been sufficiently appreciated. Notwithstanding the previous appearance of Wordsworth, Coleridge, Southey, and some other writers, it was Scott who first in his day made poetry the rage, and with him properly commences the busy poetical production of the period we are now reviewing; those who had been in the field before him put on a new activity, and gave to the world their principal works, after his appearance; and it was not till then that the writer who of all the poets of this age attained the widest blaze of reputation, eclipsing Scott himself, commenced his career. But what is still more worthy of note is, that Scott's poetry impressed its own character upon all the poetry that was produced among us for many years after: it put an end to long works in verse of a didactic or merely reflective character, and directed the current of all writing of that kind into the form of narrative. Even Wordsworth's Excursion (1814) is for the most part a collection of tales. If Scott's own genius, indeed, were to be described by any single epithet, it would be called a narrative genius. Hence, when he left off writing verse, he betook himself to the production of fictions in prose, which were really substantially the same thing with his poems, and in that freer form of composition succeeded in achieving a second reputation still more brilliant than his first.

We cannot make room for the whole of the battle in Marmion and the following extracts, which describe the fighting, lose part of their effect by being separated from the picture of Marmion's death-scene, with the pathos and touching solemnity of which they are in the original canvas so finely intermingled and relieved; but, even deprived of the advantages of this contrast, most readers will probably agree with a late eloquent critic, that, "of all the poetical battles which have been fought from the days of Homer, there is none comparable for interest and animation — for breadth of drawing and magnificence of effect — with this:" * —

> Blount and Fitz-Eustace rested still
> With Lady Clare upon the hill;
> On which (for far the day was spent)
> The western sun-beams now were bent.
> The cry they heard, its meaning knew,
> Could plain their distant comrades view:
> Sadly to Blount did Eustace say,
> "Unworthy office here to stay !
> No hope of gilded spurs to-day.—
> But see ! look up—on Flodden bent,
> The Scottish foe has fired his tent."
>   And sudden, as he spoke,
> From the sharp ridges of the hill,
> All downward to the banks of Till
>   Was wreathed in sable smoke.
> Volumed and fast, and rolling far,
> The cloud enveloped Scotland's war,
>   As down the hill they broke:
> Nor martial shout, nor minstrel tone,
> Announced their march; their tread alone,
> At times one warning trumpet blown,
>   At times a stifled hum,
> Told England, from his mountain throne
>   King James did rushing come.—
> Scarce could they hear, or see, their foes
> Until at weapon point they close.
> They close, in clouds of smoke and dust,
> With sword-sway, and with lance's thrust;
>   And such a yell was there
> Of sudden and portentous birth,
> As if men fought upon the earth
>   And fiends in upper air;
> O life and death were in the shout,
> Recoil and rally, charge and rout,
>   And triumph and despair.
> Long looked the anxious squires; their eye
> Could in the darkness nought descry.
> At length the freshening western blast
> Aside the shroud of battle cast.
> And, first, the ridge of mingled spears
> Above the brightening cloud appears;
> And in the smoke the pennons flew,
> As in the storm the white sea-mew.
> Then marked they, dashing broad and far,
> The broken billows of the war,
> And plumed crests of chieftains brave,
> Floating like foam upon the wave;

    * Jeffrey, in Edinburgh Review.

But nought distinct they see:
Wide raged the battle on the plain;
Spears shook and falchions flashed amain;
Fell England's arrow-flight like rain;
Crests rose, and stooped, and rose again,
  Wild and disorderly.
Amid the scene of tumult, high
They saw Lord Marmion's falcon fly:
And stainless Tunstall's banner white,
And Edmund Howard's lion bright,
Still bear them bravely in the fight;
  Although against them come
Of gallant Gordons many a one,
And many a stubborn Badenoch man,
And many a rugged border clan,
  With Huntley, and with Home.

Far on the left, unseen the while,
Stanley broke Lennox and Argyle;
Though there the western mountaineer
Rushed with bare bosom on the spear,
And flung the feeble targe aside,
And with both hands the broadsword plied.
'Twas vain:—but Fortune, on the right,
With fickle smile cheered Scotland's fight.
Then fell that spotless banner white,
  The Howard's lion fell;
Yet still Lord Marmion's falcon flew
With wavering flight, while fiercer grew
  Around the battle-yell,
The Border slogan rent the sky!
A Home! a Gordon! was the cry:
  Loud were the clanging blows;
Advanced,—forced back,—now low, now high
  The pennon sunk and rose;
As bends the bark's mast in the gale,
When rent are rigging, shrouds, and sail,
  It wavered 'mid the foes.
No longer Blount the view could bear:
"By Heaven, and all its saints! I swear
  I will not see it lost!
Fitz-Eustace, you with Lady Clare
May bid your beads, and patter prayer,—
  I gallop to the host."
And to the fray he rode amain,
Followed by all the archer train.
The fiery youth, with desperate charge,
Made, for a space, an opening large,—
  The rescued banner rose;—
But darkly closed the war around;
Like pine-tree, rooted from the ground,
  It sunk among the foes.
Then Eustace mounted too, yet staid,
As loth to leave the helpless maid,

When, fast as shaft can fly,
Bloodshot his eyes, his nostrils spread,
The loose rein dangling from his head,
  Housing and saddle bloody red,
  Lord Marmion's steed rushed by;
And Eustace, maddening at the sight,
A look and sign to Clara cast,
To mark he would return in haste,
  Then plunged into the fight.

. . . . .

The war, that for a space did fail,
Now trebly thundering swelled the gale,
  And Stanley! was the cry:—
A light on Marmion's visage spread,
  And fired his glazing eye;
With dying hand, above his head,
He shook the fragment of his blade,
  And shouted "Victory!"—
"Charge, Chester, charge! On, Stanley, on!"
Were the last words of Marmion.

By this, though deep the evening fell,
Still rose the battle's deadly swell;
For still the Scots, around their king,
Unbroken, fought in desperate ring.
Where's now their victor vaward wing?
Where Huntley, and where Home?
O, for a blast of that dread horn,
On Fontarabian echoes borne,
  That to King Charles did come,
When Roland brave, and Olivier,
And every paladin and peer,
  On Roncesvalles died!

Such blast might warn them, not in vain,
To quit the plunder of the slain,
And turn the doubtful day again,
  While yet on Flodden side,
Afar, the Royal standard flies,
And round it toils, and bleeds, and dies
  Our Caledonian pride!
In vain the wish—for far away,
While spoil and havoc mark their way,
Near Sybil's Cross the plunderers stray.—
"O lady," cried the Monk, "away!"
  And placed her on her steed,
And led her to the chapel fair
  Of Tilmouth upon Tweed.

. . . . .

But, as they left the darkening heath,
More desperate grew the strife of death.
The English shafts in volleys hailed;
In headlong charge their horse assailed;
Front, flank, and rear the squadrons sweep
To break the Scottish circle deep,

That fought around their king:
But yet, though thick the shafts as snow,
Though charging knights like whirlwinds go,
Though billmen ply the ghastly blow,
  Unbroken was the ring;
The stubborn spearmen still made good
Their dark impenetrable wood,
Each stepping where his comrade stood
  The instant that he fell.
No thought was there of dastard flight;
Linked in the serried phalanx tight,
Groom fought like noble, squire like knight,
  As fearlessly and well;
Till utter darkness closed her wing
O'er their thin host and wounded king.
Then skilful Surrey's sage commands
Led back from strife his shattered bands;
  And from the charge they drew,
As mountain waves from wasted lands;
  Sweep back to ocean blue.
Then did their loss his foemen know;
Their king, their lords, their mightiest low,
They melted from the field as snow,
When streams are swollen and south winds blow,
  Dissolves in silent dew.

Tweed's echoes heard the ceaseless plash,
  While many a broken band,
Disordered, through her currents dash,
  To gain the Scotish land;
To town and tower, to down and dale,
To tell red Flodden's dismal tale,
And raise the universal wail.
Tradition, legend, tune, and song
Shall many an age that wail prolong:
Still from the sire the son shall hear
Of the stern strife, and carnage drear,
  Of Flodden's fatal field,
Where shivered was fair Scotland's spear,
  And broken was her shield!

Scott, born in 1771, died in 1832.

CRABBE; CAMPBELL; MOORE.

Crabbe, Campbell, and Moore, were all known as poetical writers previous to the breaking forth of Scott's bright day: Crabbe had published his first poem, The Library, so far back as in 1781, The Village in 1783, and The Newspaper in 1785; Campbell, his Pleasures of Hope in 1799; Moore, his

Anacreon in 1800. But Campbell alone had before that epoch attracted any considerable share of the public attention; and even he, after following up his first long poem with his Hohenlinden, his Battle of the Baltic, his Mariners of England, and a few other short pieces, had laid aside his lyre for some five or six years. Neither Crabbe nor Moore had as yet produced anything that gave promise of the high station they were to attain in our poetical literature, or had even acquired any general notoriety as writers of verse. No one of the three, however, can be said to have caught any part of his manner from Scott. Campbell's first poem, juvenile as its execution in some respects was, evinced in its glowing impetuosity and imposing splendour of declamation the genius of a true and original poet, and the same general character that distinguishes his poetry in its maturest form, which may be described as a combination of fire and elegance; and his early lyrics, at least in their general effect, are not excelled by anything he subsequently wrote, although the tendency of his style towards greater purity and simplicity was very marked in all his later compositions. It was with a narrative poem — his Pennsylvanian Tale of Gertrude of Wyoming — that Campbell (in 1809) returned to woo the public favour, after Scott had made poetry, and that particular form of it, so popular; and, continuing to obey the direction which had been given to the public taste, he afterwards produced his exquisite O'Connor's Child and his Theodric; the former the most passionate, the latter the purest, of all his longer poems. Crabbe, in like manner, when he at last, in 1807, broke his silence of twenty years, came forth with a volume, all that was new in which consisted of narrative poetry, and he never afterwards attempted any other style. Narrative, indeed, had formed the happiest and most characteristic portions of Crabbe's former compositions; and he was probably led now to resume his pen mainly by the turn which the taste and fashion of the time had taken in favour of the kind of poetry to which his genius most strongly carried him. His narrative manner, however, it is scarcely necessary to observe, has no resemblance either to that of Scott or to that of Campbell. Crabbe's poetry, indeed, both in its form and in its spirit, is of quite a peculiar and original character. It might be called the poetry of matter-of-fact, for it is as true as any prose, and, except the rhyme, has often little about it of the ordinary dress of poetry; but the effect of poetry, nevertheless, is always there in great force, its power both of stirring the affections and presenting vivid pictures to the fancy. Other poets may be said to exalt the truth to a heat naturally foreign to it in the crucible of their imagination; he, by a subtler chemistry, draws forth from it its latent heat, making even things that look the coldest and deadest sparkle and flash with passion. It is remarkable, however, in how great a degree, with all its originality, the poetical genius of Crabbe was acted upon and changed by the growth of new tastes and a new spirit in the times through which he lived,—how his poetry took a warmer temperament, a richer colour, as the age became more poetical. As he lived, indeed, in two eras, so he wrote in two styles: the first, a sort of imitation, as we have already observed, of the rude vigour of Churchill, though marked from the beginning by a very distinguishing quaintness and raciness of its own, but comparatively cautious and commonplace, and dealing rather with the surface than with the heart of things; the last, with all the old peculiarities retained, and perhaps exaggerated, but greatly more copious, daring, and impetuous, and infinitely improved in penetration and general effectiveness. And his poetical power, nourished by an observant spirit and a thoughtful tenderness of nature, continued to grow in strength to the end of his life; so that the last poetry he published, his Tales of the Hall, is the finest he ever wrote, the deepest and most passionate in feeling as well as the happiest in execution. In Crabbe's sunniest passages, however, the glow is still that of a melancholy sunshine: compared to what we find in Moore's poetry, it is like the departing flush from the west, contrasted with the radiance of morning poured out plentifully over earth and sky, and making all things laugh in light. Rarely has there been seen so gay, nimble, airy a wonder-worker in verse as Moore; rarely such a conjuror with words, which he makes to serve rather as wings for his thoughts than as the gross attire or embodiment with which they must be encumbered to render them palpable or visible. His wit is not only the sharpest and brightest to be almost anywhere found, but is produced apparently with more of natural facility, and shapes itself into expression more spontaneously, than that of any other poet. But there is almost as much humour as wit in Moore's gaiety; nor are his wit and humour together more than a small part of his poetry, which, preserving in all its forms the same matchless brilliancy, finish, and apparent ease and fluency, breathes in its tenderer strains the very soul of sweetness and pathos. Moore, after having risen to the ascendant in his proper region of the poetical firmament, at last followed the rest into the walk of narrative poetry, and produced his Lalla Rookh (1817): it is a poem, with all its defects, abounding in passages of great beauty and splendour; but his Songs are, after all, probably, the compositions for which he will be best remembered.

No poetry of this time is probably so deeply and universally written upon the popular heart and memory as Campbell's great lyrics; these, therefore, it is needless to give here; some things that he has written in another style will have a greater chance of being less familiar to the reader. With all his classic taste and careful finish, Campbell's writing, especially in his earlier poetry, is rarely altogether free for any considerable number of lines from something hollow and false in expression, into which he was seduced by the conventional habits of the preceding bad school of verse-making in which he had been partly trained, and from which he emerged, or by the gratification of his ear lulling his other faculties asleep for the moment; even in his Battle of the Baltic, for instance, what can be worse than the two lines—

> But the might of England flushed
> To anticipate the scene?

And a similar use of fine words with little or no meaning, or with a meaning which can only be forced out of them by torture, is occasional in all his early compositions. In the Pleasures of Hope, especially, swell of sound without any proportionate quantity of sense, is of such frequent occurrence as to be almost a characteristic of the poem. All his later poetry, however, is of much purer execution; and some of it is of exquisite delicacy and grace of form. A little incident was never, for example, more perfectly told than in the following verses:—

> The ordeal's fatal trumpet sounded,
>   And sad pale Adelgitha came,
> When forth a valiant champion bounded,
>   And slew the slanderer of her fame.
>
> She wept, delivered from her danger;
>   But, when he knelt to claim her glove—
> "Seek not," she cried, "oh! gallant stranger,
>   For hapless Adelgitha's love.
>
> "For he is in a foreign far land
>   Whose arm should now have set me free;
> And I must wear the willow garland
>   For him that's dead or false to me."
>
> "Nay! say not that his faith is tainted!"
>   He raised his vizor—at the sight
> She fell into his arms and fainted:
>   It was indeed her own true knight.

Equally perfect, in a higher, more earnest style, is the letter to her absent husband, dictated and signed by Constance in her last moments, which closes the tale of Theodric:—

> "Theodric, this is destiny above
>   Our power to baffle; bear it then, my love!
>   Rave not to learn the usage I have borne,
>   For one true sister left me not forlorn;
>   And, though you're absent in another land,
>   Sent from me by my own well-meant command,
>   Your soul, I know, as firm is knit to mine
>   As these clasped hands in blessing you now join!

> Shape not imagined horrors in my fate—
> Even now my sufferings are not very great;
> And, when your grief's first transports shall subside,
> I call upon your strength of soul and pride
> To pay my memory, if 'tis worth the debt,
> Love's glorying tribute—not forlorn regret:
> I charge my name with power to conjure up
> Reflection's balmy, not its bitter, cup.
> My pardoning angel, at the gates of heaven,
> Shall look not more regard than you have given
> To me: and our life's union has been clad
> In smiles of bliss as sweet as life e'er had.
> Shall gloom be from such bright remembrance cast?
> Shall bitterness outflow from sweetness past?
> No! imaged in the sanctuary of your breast,
> There let me smile, amidst high thoughts at rest;
> And let contentment on your spirit shine,
> As if its peace were still a part of mine:
> For, if you war not proudly with your pain,
> For you I shall have worse than lived in vain.
> But I conjure your manliness to bear
> My loss with noble spirit—not despair;
> I ask you by our love to promise this,
> And kiss these words, where I have left a kiss,—
> The latest from my living lips for yours."
> Words that will solace him while life endures!
> For, though his spirit from affliction's surge
> Could ne'er to life, as life had been, emerge,
> Yet still that mind, whose harmony elate
> Rang sweetness even beneath the crush of fate,—
> That mind in whose regard all things were placed
> In views that softened them, or light that graced,—
> That soul's example could not but dispense
> A portion of its own blest influence;
> Invoking him to peace and that self-sway
> Which fortune cannot give, nor take away;
> And, though he mourned her long, 'twas with such woe
> As if her spirit watched him still below.

It is difficult to find a single passage, not too long for quotation, which will convey any tolerable notion of the power and beauty of Crabbe's poetry, where so much of the effect lies in the conduct of the narrative—in the minute and prolonged but wonderfully skilful as well as truthful pursuit and exposition of the course and vicissitude of passions and circumstances; but we will give so much of the story of the Elder Brother, in the Tales of the Hall, as will at least make the catastrophe intelligible. We select this tale, among other reasons, for its containing one of those pre-eminently beautiful lyric bursts which seem to contrast so strangely with the general spirit and manner of Crabbe's poetry. After many years, the narrator, pursuing another inquiry, accidentally discovers the lost object of his heart's passionate but pure idolatry living in infamy:—

> Will you not ask, how I beheld that face,
> Or read that mind, and read it in that place?
> I have tried, Richard, ofttimes, and in vain,
> To trace my thoughts, and to review their train—
> If train there were—that meadow, grove, and stile,
> The fright, the escape, her sweetness, and her smile;
> Years since elapsed, and hope, from year to year,
> To find her free—and then to find her here!
> But is it she?—O! yes; the rose is dead,
> All beauty, fragrance, freshness, glory, fled;
> But yet 'tis she--the same and not the same—
> Who to my bower a heavenly being came:
> Who waked my soul's first thought of real bliss,
> Whom long I sought, and now I find her—this.
> I cannot paint her—something I had seen
> So pale and slim, and tawdry and unclean;
> With haggard looks, of vice and woe the prey,
> Laughing in languor, miserably gay:
> Her face, where face appeared, was amply spread,
> By art's warm pencil, with ill-chosen red,
> The flower's fictitious bloom, the blushing of the dead;
> But still the features were the same, and strange
> My view of both—the sameness and the change,
> That fixed me gazing, and my eye enchained,
> Although so little of herself remained;
> It is the creature whom I loved, and yet
> Is far unlike her—would I could forget
> The angel or her fall; the once adored
> Or now despised! the worshipped or deplored!
> "O! Rosabella!" I prepared to say,
> "Whom I have loved;" but Prudence whispered, Nay,
> And Folly grew ashamed—Discretion had her day.
> She gave her hand; which, as I lightly pressed,
> The cold but ardent grasp my soul oppressed;
> The ruined girl disturbed me, and my eyes
> Looked, I conceive, both sorrow and surprise.
> . . . .
> If words had failed, a look explained their style;
> She could not blush assent, but she could smile:
> Good heaven! I thought, have I rejected fame,
> Credit, and wealth, for one who smiles at shame?
> She saw me thoughtful—saw it, as I guessed,
> With some concern, though nothing she expressed.
> "Come, my dear friend, discard that look of care," &c.
> . . . .
> Thus spoke the siren in voluptuous style,
> While I stood gazing and perplexed the while,
> Chained by that voice, confounded by that smile.

And then she sang, and changed from grave to gay,
Till all reproach and anger died away.

"My Damon was the first to wake
  The gentle flame that cannot die;
My Damon is the last to take
  The faithful bosom's softest sigh:
The life between is nothing worth,
  O I cast it from thy thoughts away;
Think of the day that gave it birth,
  And this its sweet returning day.

"Buried be all that has been done,
  Or say that nought is done amiss;
For who the dangerous path can shun
  In such bewildering world as this?
But love can every fault forgive,
  Or with a tender look reprove;
And now let nought in memory live,
  But that we meet, and that we love."

And then she moved my pity; for she wept,
And told her miseries, till resentment slept:
For, when she saw she could not reason blind,
She poured her heart's whole sorrows on my mind
With features graven on my soul, with sighs
Seen, but not heard, with soft imploring eyes,
And voice that needed not, but had, the aid
Of powerful words to soften and persuade.
  "O! I repent me of the past;" &c.

Softened, I said, "Be mine the hand and heart,
If with your world you will consent to part."
She would—she tried.—Alas! she did not know
How deeply-rooted evil habits grow:
She felt the truth upon her spirits press,
But wanted ease, indulgence, show, excess,
Voluptuous banquets, pleasures—not refined,
But such as soothe to sleep the opposing mind—
She looked for idle vice, the time to kill,
And subtle, strong apologies for ill.
And thus her yielding, unresisting soul
Sank, and let sin confuse her and control:
Pleasures that brought disgust yet brought relief,
And minds she hated helped to war with grief.

I had long lost her; but I sought in vain
To banish pity;—still she gave me pain.

  . . . .
  ———— There came at length request
That I would see a wretch with grief oppressed;
By guilt affrighted—and I went to trace

Once more the vice-worn features of that face,
That sin-wrecked being! and I saw her laid
Where never worldly joy a visit paid:
That world receding fast! the world to come
Concealed in terror, ignorance, and gloom;
Sin, sorrow, and neglect; with not a spark
Of vital hope,—all horrible and dark.—
It frightened me!—I thought, and shall not I
Thus feel?—thus fear?—this danger can I fly?
Do I so wisely live that I can calmly die?

Still as I went came other change—the frame
And features wasted, and yet slowly came
The end; and so inaudible the breath,
And still the breathing, we exclaimed—'Tis death!
But death it was not: when indeed she died
I sat and his last gentle stroke espied:
When—as it came—or did my fancy trace
That lively, lovely flushing o'er the face?
Bringing back all that my young heart impressed!
It came—and went!—She sighed, and was at rest!

From Moore, whose works are more, probably, than those of any of his contemporaries in the hands of all readers of poetry, we will make only one short extract. Here is the exquisitely beautiful description in the Fire Worshippers, the finest of the four tales composing Lalla Rookh, of the calm after a storm, in which the heroine, the gentle Hinda, awakens in the war-bark of her lover Hafed, the noble Gheber chief, into which she had been transferred from her own galley while she had swooned with terror from the tempest and the fight:—

How calm, how beautiful comes on
The stilly hour when storms are gone!
When warring winds have died away,
And clouds, beneath the dancing ray,
Melt off, and leave the land and sea
Sleeping in bright tranquillity—
Fresh as if day again were born,
Again upon the lap of morn!
When the light blossoms, rudely torn
And scattered at the whirlwind's will,
Hang floating in the pure air still,
Filling it all with precious balm,
In gratitude for this sweet calm:—
And every drop the thunder-showers
Have left upon the grass and flowers

Sparkles, as 'twere that lightning gem
Whose liquid flame is born of them!
  When, 'stead of one unchanging breeze,
There blow a thousand gentle airs,
And each a different perfume bears,—
  As if the loveliest plants and trees
Had vassal breezes of their own,
To watch and wait on them alone,
And waft no other breath than theirs!
When the blue waters rise and fall,
In sleepy sunshine mantling all;
And even that swell the tempest leaves
Is like the full and silent heaves
Of lovers' hearts when newly blest—
Too newly to be quite at rest!
Such was the golden hour that broke
Upon the world, when Hinda woke
From her long trance, and heard around
No motion but the water's sound
Rippling against the vessel's side,
As slow it mounted o'er the tide.—
But where is she?—her eyes are dark,
Are wildered still—is this the bark,
The same that from Harmozia's bay
Bore her at morn—whose bloody way
The sea-dog tracks?—No! strange and new
Is all that meets her wondering view
Upon a galliot's deck she lies,
  Beneath no rich pavilion's shade,
No plumes to fan her sleeping eyes,
  Nor jasmin on her pillow laid.
But the rude litter, roughly spread
With war-cloaks, is her homely bed,
And shawl and sash, on javelins hung,
For awning o'er her head are flung
Shuddering she looked around—there lay
  A group of warriors in the sun
Resting their limbs, as for that day
Their ministry of death were done;
Some gazing on the drowsy sea,
Lost in unconscious reverie;
And some, who seemed but ill to brook
That sluggish calm, with many a look
To the slack sail impatient cast,
As loose it flagged before the mast.

Crabbe, born in 1754, lived till 1832; Campbell, born in 1777, died in 1844; Moore, born in 1780, died in 1851.

Byron.

Byron was the writer whose blaze of popularity it mainly was that threw Scott's name into the shade, and induced him to abandon verse. Yet the productions which had this effect—the Giaour, the Bride of Abydos, the Corsair, &c., published in 1813 and 1814 (for the new idolatry was scarcely kindled by the two respectable, but somewhat tame, cantos of Childe Harold, in quite another style, which appeared shortly before these effusions), were, in reality, only poems written in what may be called a variation of Scott's own manner—Oriental lays and romances, Turkish Marmions and Ladies of the Lake. The novelty of scene and subject, the exaggerated tone of passion in the outlandish tales, and a certain trickery in the writing (for it will hardly now be called anything else) materially aided by the mysterious interest attaching to the personal history of the noble bard, who, whether he sung of Giaours, or Corsairs, or Laras, was always popularly believed to be "himself the great sublime he drew," wonderfully excited and intoxicated the public mind at first, and for a time made all other poetry seem spiritless and wearisome; but, if Byron had adhered to the style by which his fame was thus originally made, it probably would have proved transient enough. Few will now be found to assert that there is anything in these earlier poems of his comparable to the great passages in those of Scott—to the battle in Marmion, for instance, or the raising of the clansmen by the fiery cross in the Lady of the Lake, or many others that might be mentioned. But Byron's vigorous and elastic genius, although it had already tried various styles of poetry, was, in truth, as yet only preluding to its proper display. First, there had been the very small note of the Hours of Idleness; then, the sharper, but not more original or much more promising, strain of the English Bards and Scotch Reviewers (a satirical attempt in all respects inferior to Gifford's Baviad and Mæviad, of which it was a slavish imitation); next, the certainly far higher and more matured, but still quiet and commonplace, manner of the first two cantos of Childe Harold; after that, suddenly the false glare and preternatural vehemence of these Oriental rhapsodies which yet, however, with all their hollowness and extravagance, evinced infinitely more power than anything he had previously done, or rather were the only poetry he had yet produced that gave proof of any remarkable poetic genius. The Prisoner of Chillon and Parisina, The Siege of Corinth and Mazzeppa, followed, all in a spirit of far more truth, and depth, and beauty than the other tales that had preceded them; but the highest forms of Byron's poetry must be sought for in the two concluding cantos of Childe Harold, and in what else he wrote in the last seven or eight years of his short life.

Shelley.

Yet the greatest poetical genius of this time, if it was not that of Coleridge, was, probably, that of Shelley. Byron died in 1824, at the age of thirty-six; Shelley in 1822, at that of twenty-nine. What Shelley produced during the brief term allotted to him on earth, much of it passed in sickness and sorrow, is remarkable for its quantity, but much more wonderful for the quality of the greater part of it. His Queen Mab, written when he was eighteen, crude and defective as it is, and unworthy to be classed with what he wrote in his maturer years, was probably the richest promise that was ever given at so early an age of poetic power, the fullest assurance that the writer was born a poet. From the date of his Alastor, or The Spirit of Solitude, the earliest written of the poems published by himself, to his death, was not quite seven years. The Revolt of Islam, in twelve cantos, or books, the dramas of Prometheus Unbound, The Cenci, and Hellas, the tale of Rosalind and Helen, The Masque of Anarchy, The Sensitive Plant, Julian and Maddalo, The Witch of Atlas, Epipsychidion, Adonais, The Triumph of Life, the translations of Homer's Hymn to Mercury, of the Cyclops of Euripides, and of the scenes from Calderon and from Goethe's Faust, besides many short poems, were the additional produce of this springtime of a life destined to know no summer. So much poetry, so rich in various beauty, was probably never poured forth with so rapid a flow from any other mind. Nor can much of it be charged with either immaturity or carelessness: Shelley, with all his abundance and facility, was a fastidious writer, scrupulously attentive to the effect of words and syllables, and accustomed to elaborate whatever he wrote to the utmost; and, although it is not to be doubted that if he had lived longer he would have developed new powers and a still more masterly command over the several resources of his art, anything that can properly be called unripeness in his composition had, if not before, ceased with his Revolt of Islam, the first of his poems which he gave to the world, as if the exposure to the public eye had burned it out. Some haziness of thought and uncertainty of expression may be found in some of his later, or even latest, works; but that is not to be confounded with rawness; it is the dreamy ecstasy, too high for speech, in which his poetical nature, most subtle, sensitive, and voluptuous, delighted to dissolve and lose itself. Yet it is marvellous how far he had succeeded in reconciling even this mood of thought with the necessities of distinct expression: witness his Epipsychidion (written in the last year of his life), which may be regarded as his crowning triumph in that kind of writing, and as, indeed, for its wealth and fusion of all the highest things—of imagination, of expression, of music,—one of the greatest miracles ever wrought in poetry. In other styles, again, all widely diverse, are the Cenci, the Masque of Anarchy, the Hymn to Mercury (formally a translation, but essentially almost as much an original composition as any of the others). It is hard to conjecture what would have been impossible to him by whom all this had been done.

It will suffice to give one of the most brilliant and characteristic of Shelley's shorter poems—his Ode, or Hymn, as it may be called, To a Skylark, written in 1820:—

> Hail to thee, blithe spirit,
> Bird thou never wert,
> That from heaven, or near it,
> Pourest thy full heart
> In profuse strains of unpremeditated art.
>
> Higher still and higher
> From the earth thou springest;
> Like a cloud of fire
> The blue deep thou wingest,
> And singing still dost soar, and soaring ever singest.
>
> In the golden lightning
> Of the sunken sun,
> O'er which clouds are brightening,
> Thou dost float and run;
> Like an embodied Joy whose race is just begun.
>
> The pale purple even
> Melts around thy flight;
> Like a star of heaven
> In the broad daylight,
> Thou art unseen, but yet I hear thy shrill delight,
>
> Keen as are the arrows
> Of that silver sphere,
> Whose intense lamp narrows
> In the white dawn clear,
> Until we hardly see, we feel that it is there.
>
> All the earth and air
> With thy voice is loud,
> As, when night is bare,
> From one lonely cloud
> The moon rains out her beams, and heaven is overflowed.
>
> What thou art we know not:
> What is most like thee!
> From rainbow clouds there flow not
> Drops so bright to see
> As from thy presence showers a rain of melody.
>
> Like a poet hidden
> In the light of thought,
> Singing hymns unbidden,
> Till the world is wrought
> To sympathy with hopes and fears it heeded not:
>
> Like a highborn maiden
> In a palace tower,
> Soothing her love-laden
> Soul in secret hour
> With music sweet as love, which overflows her bower:

Like a glow-worm golden
   In a dell of dew,
Scattering unbeholden
   Its aërial hue
Among the flowers and grass, which screen it from the view:

Like a rose embowered
   In its own green leaves,
By warm winds deflowered,
   Till the scent it gives
Makes faint with too much sweet these heavy-winged thieves:

Sound of vernal showers
   On the twinkling grass,
Rain-awakened flowers,
   All that ever was
Joyous and clear and fresh, thy music doth surpass.

Teach us, sprite or bird,
   What sweet thoughts are thine:
I have never heard
   Praise of love or wine
That panted forth a flood of rapture so divine.

Chorus hymeneal,
   Or triumphal chant,
Matched with thine would be all
   But an empty vaunt—
A thing wherein we feel there is some hidden want.

What objects are the fountains
   Of thy happy strain?
What fields, or waves, or mountains?
   What shapes of sky or plain?
What love of thine own kind? what ignorance of pain?

With thy clear keen joyance
   Languor cannot be:
Shadow of annoyance
   Never came near thee:
Thou lovest; but ne'er knew love's sad satiety.

Waking or asleep,
   Thou of death must deem
Things more true and deep
   Than we mortals dream,
Or how could thy notes flow in such a crystal stream?

We look before and after,
   And pine for what is not:
Our sincerest laughter
   With some pain is fraught;
Our sweetest songs are those that tell of saddest thought.

Yet if we could scorn
   Hate, and pride, and fear;
If we were things born
   Not to shed a tear,
I know not how thy joy we ever should come near.

> Better than all measures
> Of delightful sound,
> Better than all treasures
> That in books are found,
> Thy skill to poet were, thou scorner of the ground!
>
> Teach me half the gladness
> That thy brain must know,
> Such harmonious madness
> From my lips would flow,
> The world should listen then, as I am listening now.

KEATS.

Keats, born in 1796, died the year before Shelley, and, of course, at a still earlier age. But his poetry is younger than Shelley's in a degree far beyond the difference of their years. He was richly endowed by nature with the poetical faculty, and all that he has written is stamped with originality and power; it is probable, too, that he would soon have supplied, as far as was necessary or important, the defects of his education, as indeed he had actually done to a considerable extent, for he was full of ambition as well as genius; but he can scarcely be said to have given full assurance by anything he has left that he would in time have produced a great poetical work. The character of his mental constitution, explosive and volcanic, was adverse to every kind of restraint and cultivation; and his poetry is a tangled forest, beautiful indeed and glorious with many a majestic oak and sunny glade, but still with the unpruned, untrained savagery everywhere, constituting, apparently, so much of its essential character as to be inseparable from it, and indestructible without the ruin at the same time of everything else. There is not only the absence of art, but a spirit antagonistic to that of art. Yet this wildness and turbulence may, after all, have been only an affluence of true power too great to be soon or easily brought under regulation,—the rankness of a tropic vegetation, coming of too rich a soil and too much light and heat. Certainly to no one of his contemporaries had been given more of passionate intensity of conception (the life of poetry) than to Keats. Whatever he thought or felt came to him in vision, and wrapped and thrilled him. Whatever he wrote burns and blazes. And his most wanton extravagances had for the most part a soul of good in them. His very affectations were mostly prompted by excess of love and reverence. In his admiration and worship of our Elizabethan poetry he was not satisfied without mimicking the obsolete syllabication of the language which he found there enshrined, and, as he conceived, consecrated. Even the most remarkable of all the peculiarities of his manner—the extent, altogether, we should think, without a parallel in our literature, to which he surrenders himself in writing to the guidance of the mere wave of sound upon which he happens to have got afloat, often, one would almost say, making ostentation of his acquiescence and passiveness—is a fault only in its excess, and such a fault, moreover, as only a true poet could run into. Sound is of the very essence of song; and the music must always in so far guide the movement of the verse, as truly as it does that of the dance. It only is not the all in all. If the musical form be the mother of the verse, the sense to be expressed is the father. Yet Keats, by what he has thus produced in blind obedience to the tune that had taken possession of him—allowing the course of the composition to be directed simply by the rhyme sometimes for whole pages—has shown the same sensibility to the musical element in poetry, and even something of the same power of moulding language to his will, which we find in all our greatest poets—in Spenser especially, whose poetry is ever as rich with the charm of music as with that of picture, and who makes us feel in so many a victorious stanza that there is nothing his wonder-working mastery over words cannot make them do for him. Keats's Endymion was published in 1817; his Lamia, * Isabella, Eve of St. Agnes, and the re-

* " If any one," Leigh Hunt has said , " could unite the vigour of Dryden with the ready and easy variety of pause in the works of the late Mr. Crabbe and the lovely poetic consciousness in the *Lamia* of Keats, in which the lines

markable fragment, Hyperion, together in 1820, a few months before his death. The latter volume also contained several shorter pieces, one of which, of great beauty, the Ode to a Nightingale, may serve as a companion to Shelley's Skylark:—

> My heart aches, and a drowsy numbness pains
> My sense, as though of hemlock I had drunk,
> Or emptied some dull opiate to the drains
> One minute past, and Lethe-ward had sunk:
> 'Tis not through envy of thy happy lot,
> But being too happy in thine happiness,—
> That thou, light-winged Dryad of the trees,
> In some melodious plot
> Of beechen green, and shadows numberless,
> Singest of summer in full-throated ease.
>
> O for a draught of vintage that hath been
> Cooled a long age in the deep-delved earth,
> Tasting of Flora and the country green,
> Dance, and Provençal song, and sun-burnt mirth!
> O for a beaker full of the warm South,
> Full of the true, the blissful Hippocrene,
> With beaded bubbles winking at the brim,
> And purple-stained mouth;
> That I might drink, and leave the world unseen,
> And with thee fade away into the forest dim:
>
> Fade far away, dissolve, and quite forget
> What thou among the leaves hast never known,
> The weariness, the fever, and the fret
> Here, where men sit and hear each other groan;
> Where palsy shakes a few, sad, last grey hairs;
> Where youth grows pale, and spectre-thin, and dies;
> Where but to think is to be full of sorrow
> And leaden-eyed despairs;
> Where beauty cannot keep her lustrous eyes,
> Or new love pine at them beyond to-morrow.
>
> Away! away! for I will fly to thee,
> Not charioted by Bacchus and his pards,
> But on the viewless wings of Poesy,
> Though the dull brain perplexes and retards!
> Already with thee! Tender is the night,
> And haply the Queen-moon is on her throne,
> Clustered around by all her starry fays;
> But here there is no light
> Save what from heaven is with the breezes blown
> Through verdurous glooms and winding mossy ways.

seem to take pleasure in the progress of their own beauty, like sea-nymphs luxuriating through the water, he would be a perfect master of rhyming heroic verse."

I cannot see what flowers are at my feet,
  Nor what soft incense hangs upon the boughs,
But in embalmed darkness guess each sweet
  Wherewith the seasonable month endows
The grass, the thicket, and the fruit-tree wild;
  White hawthorn, and the pastoral eglantine;
  Fast-fading violets, covered up in leaves;
    And mid-day's eldest child,
  The coming musk-rose, full of dewy wine,
  The murmurous haunt of flies on summer eves.

Darkling I listen, and, for many a time,
  I have been half in love with easeful Death,[1]
Called him soft names in many a mused rhyme,
  To take into the air my quiet breath;
Now more than ever seems it rich to die,
  To cease upon the midnight with no pain,
  While thou art pouring forth thy soul abroad
    In such an ecstasy!
  Still would'st thou sing, and I have ears in vain—
  To thy high requiem become a sod.

Thou wast not born for death, immortal Bird!
  No hungry generations tread thee down;
The voice I hear this passing night was heard
  In ancient days by emperor and clown;
Perhaps the self-same song hath found a path
  Through the sad heart of Ruth, when, sick for home
  She stood in tears amid the alien corn;
    The same that oft-times hath
  Charmed magic casements, opening on the foam
  Of perilous seas, in faery lands forlorn.

Forlorn! the very word is like a bell
  To toll me back from thee to my soul's self!
Adieu! the fancy cannot cheat so well
  As she is famed to do, deceiving elf.
Adieu! adieu! thy plaintive anthem fades
  Past the near meadows, over the still stream,
  Up the hill-side; and now 'tis buried deep
    In the next valley-glades:
  Was it a vision, or a waking dream?
  Fled is that music:—do I wake or sleep?

---

[1] Shelley had probably this line in his ear, when in the Preface to his Adonais, which is an elegy on Keats, he wrote—describing "the romantic and lonely cemetery of the Protestants" at Rome, where his friend was buried— "The cemetery is an open space among the ruins, covered in winter with violets and daisies. It might make one in love with death, to think that one should be buried in so sweet a place."

HUNT.

These last names can hardly be mentioned without suggesting another—that of one who has only the other day been taken from us. Leigh Hunt, the friend of Shelley and Keats, had attracted the attention of the world by much that he had done, both in verse and prose, long before the appearance of either. His Story of Rimini, published in 1816, being, as it was, indisputably the finest inspiration of Italian song that had yet been heard in our modern English literature, had given him a place of his own as distinct as that of any other poetical writer of the day. Whatever may be thought of some peculiarities in his manner of writing, nobody will now be found to dispute either the originality of his genius, or his claim to the title of a true poet. Into whatever he has written he has put a living soul; and much of what he has produced is brilliant either with wit and humour, or with tenderness and beauty. In some of the best of his pieces too there is scarcely to be found a trace of anything illegitimate or doubtful in the matter of diction or versification. Where, for example, can we have more unexceptionable English than in the following noble version of the Eastern Tale?—

> There came a man, making his hasty moan,
> Before the Sultan Mahmoud on his throne,
> And crying out—"My sorrow is my right,
> And I *will* see the Sultan, and to-night."
> "Sorrow," said Mahmoud, "is a reverend thing:
> I recognise its right, as king with king;
> Speak on." "A fiend has got into my house,"
> Exclaimed the staring man, "and tortures us;
> One of thine officers—he comes, the abhorred,
> And takes possession of my house, my hoard,
> My bed:—I have two daughters and a wife,
> And the wild villain comes, and makes me mad with life."
> "Is he there now?" said Mahmoud:—"No; he left
> The house when I did, of my wits bereft:
> And laughed me down the street, because I vowed
> I'd bring the prince himself to lay him in his shroud.
> I'm mad with want—I'm mad with misery,
> And, oh thou Sultan Mahmoud, God cries out for thee!"

The Sultan comforted the man, and said,
"Go home, and I will send thee wine and bread"
(For he was poor), "and other comforts. Go:
And, should the wretch return, let Sultan Mahmoud know."

In three days' time, with haggard eyes and beard,
And shaken voice, the suitor re-appeared,
And said, "He's come."—Mahmoud said not a word,
But rose and took four slaves, each with a sword,
And went with the vexed man. They reach the place,
And hear a voice, and see a female face,
That to the window fluttered in affright:
"Go in," said Mahmoud, "and put out the light;
But tell the females first to leave the room;
And, when the drunkard follows them, we come."

The man went in. There was a cry, and hark:
A table falls, the window is struck dark:
Forth rush the breathless women; and behind
With curses comes the fiend in desperate mind.
In vain: the sabres soon cut short the strife,
And chop the shrieking wretch, and drink his bloody life.

"Now *light* the light," the Sultan cried aloud.
'Twas done; he took it in his hand, and bowed
Over the corpse, and looked upon the face;
Then turned and knelt beside it in the place,
And said a prayer, and from his lips there crept
Some gentle words of pleasure, and he wept.

In reverent silence the spectators wait,
Then bring him at his call both wine and meat;
And when he had refreshed his noble heart,
He bade his host be blest, and rose up to depart.

The man amazed, all mildness now, and tears,
Fell at the Sultan's feet, with many prayers,
And begged him to vouchsafe to tell his slave
The reason, first, of that command he gave
About the light; then, when he saw the face,
Why he knelt down; and lastly, how it was
That fare so poor as his detained him in the place.

The Sultan said, with much humanity,
"Since first I saw thee come, and heard thy cry,
I could not rid me of a dread, that one
By whom such daring villanies were done
Must be some lord of mine, perhaps a lawless son.
Whoe'er he was, I knew my task, but feared
A father's heart, in case the worst appeared;
For this I had the light put out; but when
I saw the face, and found a stranger slain,
I knelt, and thanked the sovereign arbiter,
Whose work I had performed through pain and fear;
And then I rose, and was refreshed with food,
The first time since thou cam'st, and marr'dst my solitude."

Other short pieces in the same style are nearly as good —such as those entitled The Jaffar and The Inevitable. Then there are the admirable modernizations of Chaucer— of whom and of Spenser, whom he has also imitated with wonderful cleverness, no one of all his contemporaries probably had so true and deep a feeling as Hunt. But, passing over likewise his two greatest works, The Story of Rimini and The Legend of Florence (published in 1840), we will give one other short effusion, which attests, we think, as powerfully as anything he ever produced, the master's triumphant hand, in a style which he has made his own, and in which, with however many imitators, he has no rival:—

THE FANCY CONCERT.

They talked of their concerts, their singers, and scores,
And pitied the fever that kept me in doors;
And I smiled in my thought, and said, "O ye sweet fancies,
And animal spirits, that still in your dances
Come bringing me visions to comfort my care,
Now fetch me a concert,—imparadise air."

Then a wind, like a storm out of Eden, came pouring
Fierce into my room, and made tremble the flooring,
And filled, with a sudden impetuous trample
Of heaven, its corners; and swelled it to ample
Dimensions to breathe in, and space for all power;
Which falling as suddenly, lo! the sweet flower
Of an exquisite fairy-voice opened its blessing;
And ever and aye, to its constant addressing,
There came, falling in with it, each in the last,
Flageolets one by one, and flutes blowing more fast,
And hautboys and clarinets, acrid of reed,
And the violin, smoothlier sustaining the speed
As the rich tempest gathered, and buz-ringing moons
Of tambours, and huge basses, and giant bassoons;
And the golden trombone, that darteth its tongue
Like a bee of the gods; nor was absent the gong,
Like a sudden fate-bringing oracular sound
Of earth's iron genius, burst up from the ground,
A terrible slave come to wait on his masters
The gods, with evultings that clanged like disasters;
And then spoke the organs, the very gods they,
Like thunders that roll on a wind-blowing day;
And, taking the rule of the roar in their hands,
Lo! the Genii of Music came out of all lands;
And one of them said, "Will my lord tell his slave
What concert 'twould please his Firesideship to have?"

Then I said, in a tone of immense will and pleasure,
" Let orchestras rise to some exquisite measure;
And let there be lights and be odours; and let
The lovers of music serenely be set;
And then, with their singers in lily-white stoles,
And themselves clad in rose-colour, fetch me the souls
Of all the composers accounted divinest,
And, with their own hands, let them play me their finest."

Then, lo! was performed my immense will and pleasure,
And orchestras rose to an exquisite measure:
And lights were about me and odours; and set
Were the lovers of music, all wondrously met;
And then, with their singers in lily-white stoles,
And themselves clad in rose-colour, in came the souls
Of all the composers accounted divinest,
And, with their own hands, did they play me their finest.

Oh! truly was Italy heard then, and Germany,
Melody's heart, and the rich brain of harmony;
Pure Paisiello, whose airs are as new
Though we know them by heart, as May-blossoms and dew;
And nature's twin son, Pergolesi: and Bach,
Old father of fugues, with his endless fine talk:
And Gluck, who saw gods; and the learned sweet feeling
Of Haydn; and Winter, whose sorrows are healing;
And gentlest Corelli, whose bowing seems made
For a hand with a jewel; and Handel, arrayed
In Olympian thunders, vast lord of the spheres,
Yet pious himself, with his blindness in tears,
A lover withal, and a conqueror, whose marches
Bring demi-gods under victorious arches;
Then Arne, sweet and tricksome; and masterly Purcell,
Lay-clerical soul; and Mozart universal,
But chiefly with exquisite gallantries found,
With a grove in the distance of holier sound;
Nor forgot was thy dulcitude, loving Sacchini;
Nor love, young and dying, in shape of Bellini;
Nor Weber, nor Himmel, nor Mirth's sweetest name,
Cimarosa; much less the great organ-voiced fame
Of Marcello, that hushed the Venetian sea;
And strange was the shout, when it wept, hearing thee,
Thou soul full of grace as of grief, my heart-cloven,
My poor, my most rich, my all-feeling Beethoven.
O'er all, like a passion, great Pasta was heard,
As high as her heart, that truth-uttering bird;
And Banti was there; and Grassini, that goddess!
Dark, deep-toned, large, lovely, with glorious boddice;
And Mara; and Malibran, stung to the tips
Of her fingers with pleasure: and rich Fodor's lips
And, manly in face as in tone, Angrisani:
And Naldi, thy whim; and thy grace, Tramezzani;
And was it a voice?—or what was it?—say—
That, like a fallen angel beginning to pray,
Was the soul of all tears and celestial despair!
Paganini it was, 'twixt his dark-flowing hair,

> So now we had instrument, now we had song—
> Now chorus, a thousand-voiced one-hearted throng:
> Now pauses that pampered resumption, and now—
> But who shall describe what was played us, or how?
> 'Twas wonder, 'twas transport, humility, pride;
> 'Twas the heart of the mistress that sat by one's side;
> 'Twas the graces invisible, moulding the air
> Into all that is shapely, and lovely, and fair,
> And running our fancies their tenderest rounds
> Of endearments and luxuries, turned into sounds;
> 'Twas argument even, the logic of tones;
> 'Twas memory, 'twas wishes, 'twas laughters, 'twas moans;
> 'Twas pity and love, in pure impulse obeyed;
> 'Twas the breath of the stuff of which passion is made,
>
> And these are the concerts I have at my will;
> Then dismiss them, and patiently think of your "bill."—
> (*Aside*) Yet Lablache, after all, makes me long to go, still.

Leigh Hunt died, at the age of seventy-five, in 1859,— the last survivor, although the earliest born, of the four poets, with the other three of whom he had been so intimately associated, and the living memory of whom he thus carried far into another time, indeed across an entire succeeding generation.* To the last, even in outward form, he forcibly recalled Shelley's fine picture of him in his Elegy on Keats, written nearly forty years before:—

> "What softer voice is hushed over the dead?
> Athwart what brow is that dark mantle thrown?
> What form leans sadly o'er the white death-bed,
> In mockery of monumental stone,
> The heavy heart heaving without a moan?
> If it be he, who, gentlest of the wise,
> Taught, soothed, loved, honoured the departed one,
> Let me not vex, with inharmonious sighs,
> The silence of that heart's accepted sacrifice."

OTHER POETICAL WRITERS OF THE EARLIER PART OF THE NINETEENTH CENTURY.

The names that have been mentioned are the chief of those belonging, wholly or principally, to the earlier part of the present century, or to that remarkable literary era which may be regarded as having expired with the reign of the

---

* Hunt—Byron—Shelley—Keats, born in that order (in 1784, 1788, 1793, and 1796), died in exactly the reverse, and also at ages running in a series contrary throughout to that of their births; Keats, at 25, in 1821,—Shelley, at 29, in 1822,—Byron, at 36, in 1824, Hunt, at 75, in 1859.

last of the Georges. Many others, however, also brighten this age of our poetical literature, which cannot be here noticed.

On the whole, this space of somewhat less than half a century, dating from the first appearance of Cowper and Burns, must be pronounced to be the most memorable period in the history of our poetical literature after the age of Spenser and Shakespeare. And if, in comparing the produce of the two great revivals, the one happening at the transition from the sixteenth century into the seventeenth, the other at that from the eighteenth into the nineteenth, we find something more of freshness, freedom, raciness, and true vigour, warmth, and nature, in our earlier than in our recent poetry, it is not to be denied, on the other hand, that in some respects the latter may claim a preference over the former. It is much less debased by the intermixture of dross or alloy with its fine gold—much less disfigured by occasional pedantry and affectation—much more correct and free from flaws and incongruities of all kinds. In whatever regards form, indeed, our more modern poetry must be admitted, taken in its general character, to be the more perfect; and that notwithstanding many passages to be found in the greatest of our elder poets which in mere writing have perhaps never since been equalled, nor are likely ever to be excelled; and notwithstanding also something of greater boldness with which their position enabled them to handle the language; thereby attaining sometimes a force and expressiveness not so much within the reach of their successors in our own day. The literary cultivation of the language throughout two additional centuries, and the stricter discipline under which it has been reduced, may have brought loss or inconvenience in one direction, as well as gain in another; but the gain certainly preponderates. Even in the matter of versification, the lessons of Milton, of Dryden, and of Pope have no doubt been upon the whole instructive and beneficial; whatever of misdirection any of them may have given for a time to the form of our poetry passed away with his contemporaries and immediate followers, and now little or nothing but the good remains— the example of the superior care and uniform finish, and also something of sweetest and deepest music, as well as much of spirit and brilliancy, that were unknown to our earlier poets. In variety and freedom, as well as in beauty, majesty, and richness of versification, some of our latest writers have hardly been excelled by any of their predecessors; and the versification of the generality of our modern poets is greatly superior to that of the common run of those of the age of Elizabeth and James.

Prose Literature.

Among the most distinguished ornaments of the prose literature of this recent era were some of the chief poetical writers of the time. Southey and Scott were two of the most voluminous prose writers of their day, or of any day; Coleridge also wrote much more prose than verse; both Campbell and Moore are considerable authors in prose; there are several prose pieces among the published works of Byron, of Shelley, and of Wordsworth; both Leigh Hunt and Wilson perhaps acquired more of their fame, and have given more wide-spread delight, as prose writers than as poets; Charles Lamb's prose writings, his golden Essays of Elia, and various critical papers, abounding in original views and the deepest truth and beauty, have made his verse be nearly forgotten. Among the other most conspicuous prose writers of the period we have been reviewing may be mentioned, in general literature and speculation, Sidney Smith, Hazlitt, Jeffrey, Playfair, Stewart, Alison, Thomas Brown; in political disquisition, Erskine, Cobbett, Mackintosh, Bentham, Brougham; in theological eloquence, Horsley, Wilberforce, Foster, Hall, Irving, Chalmers; in history, Fox, Mitford, Lingard, James Mill, Hallam, Turner; in fictitious narrative, Miss Edgeworth, Mrs. Opie, Miss Owenson (Lady Morgan), Mrs. Brunton, Miss Austen, Madame d'Arblay (Miss

Burney), Godwin, Maturin. The most remarkable prose works that were produced were Scott's novels, the first of which, Waverley, appeared in 1814.* A powerful influence upon literature was also exerted from the first by the Edinburgh Review, begun in 1802; the Quarterly Review, begun in 1809; and Blackwood's Magazine, established in 1817.

PROGRESS OF SCIENCE.

A few of the most memorable facts connected with the progress of scientific discovery in England, during this period, may be very briefly noted. In astronomy Herschel continued to pursue his observations, commenced a short time before 1781, in which year he discovered the planet Uranus; in 1802, appeared in the Philosophical Transactions his catalogue of 500 new nebulæ and nebulous stars; in 1803 his announcement of the motions of double stars around each other; and a long succession of other important papers, illustrative of the construction of the heavens, followed down to within a few years of his death, at the age of eighty-four, in 1822. In chemistry, Davy, who had published his account of the effects produced by the respiration of nitrous oxide (the laughing gas) in 1800, in 1807 extracted metallic bases from the fixed alkalis, in 1808 demonstrated the similar decomposability of the alkaline earths, in 1811 detected the true nature of chloride (oxymuriatic acid), and in 1815 invented his safety lamp; in 1804 Leslie published his Experimental Enquiry into the Nature and Properties of Heat; in 1808 the Atomic Theory was announced by Dalton; and in 1814 its development and illustration were completed by Wollaston, to whom both chemical science and optics are also indebted for various other valuable services.

* With the second title of 'Tis Sixty Years Since, the work professing (in the Introductory Chapter) to have been written, as it really was in part, nine years before

LITERATURE OF THE PRESENT DAY.

WHAT is properly the History of our Literature closes with the age or generation preceding the present; for history takes cognizance only of that which is past. What of literary production has taken place within the last thirty years, much or most of it by writers who are still alive, is hardly yet ripe for impartial appreciation. We may call this period the Victorian era. If we compare its poetical literature with that of the immediately preceding period of the same length, which will take us back to the beginning of the century, and may be called the last age of the Georges, confining ourselves to writers of established reputation, or whose names are universally more or less familiar, we shall find about the same number, between forty and fifty, in each; but differently distributed in the two cases in respect of their degrees of eminence. While of those of the Georgian thirty years we may reckon about ten as belonging to the first rank, and about as many more as belonging to the second, leaving only twenty-five for the third, of the equal number belonging to the subsequent portion of the century we cannot account more than three, or at most four, as being of the first rank, leaving, with again ten or eleven of the second, about thirty who must be assigned to the third or lowest. The difference, then, between the two periods will be, that in the poetical literature of the first we have ten writers of the highest and only twenty-five who must be held to belong to the lowest of the three ranks, and that in that of the second we have only three or four of the highest with about thirty of the lowest. This enumeration takes account of the leading poetical writers who have arisen in the American division of the English race, two or three of whom may be reckoned as of the second rank, though certainly not one as of the first.

In the prose literature of the two periods, however, we should probably find the above proportions more than reversed. The literary greatness of the Victorian age has hitherto manifested itself mostly in the works of our writers in prose. It is as if the one age were distinguished for its production of gold, the other for its production of silver. Probably in no other period, moreover, has there been seen so much activity of female genius and talent as we have had in the present, displaying itself principally, indeed, in fictitious narrative, but yet ranging, too, in several instances, above or beyond that. Of the writers in verse, however, who have attained any considerable eminence in the two periods, while about ten are women in the first, there are only five or six in the second.

Yet it is a memorable distinction of the present age, and one which belongs to no other in any literature (unless, indeed, we are to except that in which Sappho flourished), that one of its greatest writers in verse is a woman. And, if we put aside the possible case of Sappho, of whom so little remains that, exquisite as that little is held to be by all who are best able to judge, we are left to estimate her in the main merely from her fame among her countrymen—which, however, resounds through all the after ages of Greece—probably Elizabeth Barrett (Mrs. Browning) is entitled to be regarded as the greatest woman poet that has yet appeared in any language. With whatever her poetry may be chargeable whether of defect or of excess—whatever it either wants which it should have, or has which it should not have—there are two vital elements, and they are the chief ingredients of the poetical, in which it is never wanting;—subtlety of imagination and force of conception and feeling. In not much modern verse shall we find more of Greek intensity than in the following lines, entitled "A Child's

Grave at Florence (A. A. E. C.; born July, 1848; died November, 1849)":—

> Of English blood, of Tuscan birth,
> What country should we give her?
> Instead of any on the earth,
> The civic Heavens receive her.
>
> And here, among the English tombs,
> In Tuscan ground we lay her,
> While the blue Tuscan sky endomes
> Our English words of prayer.
>
> A little child!—how long she lived
> By months, not years, is reckoned;
> Born in one July, she survived
> Alone to see a second;
>
> Bright-featured, as the July sun
> Her little face still played in,
> And splendours, with her birth begun,
> Had had no time for fading.
>
> So, LILY, from those July hours,
> No wonder we should call her;
> She looked such kinship to the flowers,
> Was but a little taller.
>
> A Tuscan lily,—only white,
> As Dante, in abhorrence
> Of red corruption, wished aright
> The lilies of his Florence.[1]
>
> We could not wish her whiter,—her
> Who perfumed with pure blossom
> The house!—a lovely thing to wear
> Upon a mother's bosom!
>
> This July creature thought perhaps
> Our speech not worth assuming;
> She sat upon her parents' laps,
> And mimicked the gnats humming;
>
> Said "father," "mother,"—then left off,
> For tongues celestial fitter,
> Her hair had grown just long enough
> To catch heaven's jasper-glitter.
>
> Babes! Love could always hear and see[2]
> Behind the cloud that hid them.
> "Let little children come to me,
> And do not thou forbid them."

[1] The emphasis on the *his;* and in the next line on the *we* and the *her*.
[2] The *always* emphasised.

So, unforbidding, have we met,
  And gently here have laid her,
Though winter is no time to get
  The flowers that should o'erspread her.

We should bring pansies quick with spring,
  Rose, violet, daffodilly,
And also, above everything,
  White lilies for our Lily.

Nay, more than flowers this grave exacts,—
  Glad, graceful attestations
Of her sweet eyes and pretty acts,
  With calm renunciations.

Her very mother with light feet
  Should leave the place too earthy,
Saying, "The angels have thee, Sweet,
  Because we are not worthy."

But winter kills the orange buds,
  The gardens in the frost are,
And all the heart dissolves in floods,
  Remembering we have lost her!

Poor earth, poor heart,—too weak, too weak,
  To miss the July shining!
Poor heart!—what bitter words we speak [1]
  When God speaks of resigning!

Sustain this heart in us that faints,
  Thou God, the self-existent!
We catch up wild at parting saints,
  And feel thy heaven too distant.

The wind that swept them out of sin
  Has ruffled all our vesture;
On the shut door that let them in
  We beat with frantic gesture,—

To us—us also—open straight!
  The outer life is chilly—
Are we too, like the earth, to wait
  Till next year for our Lily?

—Oh, my own baby on my knees,
  My leaping, dimpled treasure,
At every word I write like these
  Clasped close, with stronger pressure!

Too well my own heart understands,—
  At every word beats fuller—
My little feet, my little hands, [2]
  And hair of Lily's colour!

[1] The *we* emphatic.
[2] The *my* strongly emphasised, both times, of course.

—But God gives patience, Love learns strength,
And Faith remembers promise,
And Hope itself can smile at length
On other hopes gone from us.

Love, strong as Death, shall conquer Death,
Through struggle made more glorious.
This mother stills her sobbing breath,
Renouncing, yet victorious.

Arms, empty of her child, she lifts,
With spirit unbereaven,—
"God will not all take back his gifts:
My Lily's mine in heaven!

"Still mine! maternal rights serene
Not given to another!
The crystal bars shine faint between
The souls of child and mother.

"Meanwhile," the mother cries, "content!
Our love was well divided.
Its sweetness following where she went,
Its anguish stayed where I did.

"Well done of God, to halve the lot,
And give her all the sweetness;
To us, the empty room and cot,—
To her, the Heaven's completeness.

"To us, this grave—to her, the rows
The mystic palm-trees spring in;
To us, the silence in the house,—
To her, the choral singing.

"For her, to gladden in God's view,—
For us, to hope and bear on!—
Grow, Lily, in thy garden new,
Beside the rose of Sharon.

"Grow fast in heaven, sweet Lily clipped,
In love more calm than this is,—
And may the angels dewy-lipped
Remind thee of our kisses!¹

"While none shall tell thee of our tears,
These human tears now falling,
Till, after a few patient years,
One home shall take us all in.

"Child, father, mother,—who left out?
Not mother, and not father!—
And when, our dying couch about,
The natural mists shall gather,

¹ The *our* emphatic.

> "Some smiling angel close shall stand,
> In old Correggio's fashion,
> And bear a LILY in his hand,
> For death's ANNUNCIATION."

Mrs. Browning's Aurora Leigh has some serious and pervading faults, both in manner and in spirit,—too much evidence of effort and ambition, both in the thought and the language, exploding occasionally in mere tricks of style, oftener putting us off with wit instead of poetry, and generally over-charging and over-straining the expression, together with a constantly recurring tone of dictation and sarcasm, which is the more unpleasant inasmuch as it does not seem natural to the writer, and, what is perhaps worst of all, a visibly uneasy consciousness, or at least apprehension, never long absent, that her task is after all beyond her strength; but, with all its faults, it may fairly claim to be, so far as is known, the greatest poetical work ever produced by a woman. Yet it is still all over and all through, in form and in substance, as evidently a product of the female mind as any other long poem by a woman that we possess. It is, indeed, we should say, pre-eminently feminine in character. It would be almost as impossible to take it for the work of a man as to take the Iliad for the work of a woman.

Born in Tuscany, the child of an English father and an Italian mother, who died when she was four years old, Aurora thus vividly describes what she felt when, left an orphan by her father having been also taken away, and sent for by his relations, she first looked upon her new country with her native one fresh in her memory:—

> The train swept us on.
> Was this my father's England? the great isle?
> The ground seemed cut up from the fellowship
> Of verdure, field from field, as man from man;
> The skies themselves looked low and positive,
> As almost you could touch them with a hand,
> And dared to do it they were so far off
> From God's celestial crystals; all things blurred,
> And dull and vague. Did Shakspeare and his mates

> Absorb the light here?—not a hill or stone
> With heart to strike a radiant colour up
> Or active outline on the indifferent air.

Gradually, however, she comes to appreciate something of the tamer landscape:—

> Not a grand nature. Not my chestnut-woods
> Of Vallombrosa, cleaving by the spurs
> To the precipices. Not my headlong leaps
> Of waters, that cry out for joy or fear
> In leaping through the palpitating pines,
> Like a white soul tossed out to eternity
> With thrills of time upon it. Not indeed
> My multitudinous mountains, sitting in
> The magic circle, with the mutual touch
> Electric, panting from their full deep hearts
> Beneath the influent heavens, and waiting for
> Communion and commission. Italy
> Is one thing, England one.
>   On English ground,
> You understand the letter—ere the fall
> How Adam lived in a garden. All the fields
> Are tied up fast with hedges, nosegay-like:
> The hills are crumpled plains, the plains parterres,
> The trees, round, woolly, ready to be clipped,
> And if you seek for any wilderness
> You find, at best, a park. A nature tamed
> And grown domestic like a barn-door fowl,
> Which does not awe you with its claws and beak
> Nor tempt you to an eyrie too high up,
> But which, in cackling, sets you thinking of
> Your eggs to-morrow at breakfast, in the pause
> Of finer meditation.
>   Rather say,
> A sweet familiar nature, stealing in
> As a dog might, or child, to touch your hand
> Or pluck your gown, and humbly mind you so
> Of presence and affection, excellent
> For inner uses, from the things without.

Ere long her heart opens to it all:—

> Whoever lives true life will love true love.
> I learnt to love that England. Very oft,
> Before the day was born, or otherwise
> Through secret windings of the afternoons,
> I threw my hunters off and plunged myself
> Among the deep hills, as a hunted stag
> Will take the waters, shivering with the fear
> And passion of the course. And when at last

> Escaped, so many a green slope built on slope
> Betwixt me and the enemy's house behind,
> I dared to rest, or wander, in a rest
> Made sweeter for the step upon the grass,
> And view the ground's most gentle dimplement,
> (As if God's finger touched but did not press
> In making England) such an up and down
> Of verdure,—nothing too much up or down,
> A ripple of land; such little hills, the sky
> Can stoop to tenderly and the wheatfields climb;
> Such nooks of valleys lined with orchises,
> Fed full of noises by invisible streams;
> And open pastures where you scarcely tell
> White daisies from white dew,—at intervals
> The mythic oaks and elm-trees standing out
> Self-poised upon their prodigy of shade,—
> I thought my father's land was worthy too
> Of being my Shakspeare's.

Equally brilliant and cordial with this picture of English nature is this other of the artificial in France (whatever may be exactly the meaning of some parts of it). We give the passage as rewritten, and very considerably altered from its original form, for the fourth edition of the poem:—

> I mused
> Up and down, up and down, the terraced streets,
> The glittering boulevards, the white colonnades
> Of fair fantastic Paris, who wears trees
> Like plumes, as if man made them, spire and tower
> As if they had grown by nature, tossing up
> Her fountains in the sunshine of the squares,
> As if in beauty's game she tossed the dice,
> Or blew the silver down-balls of her dreams
> To sow futurity with seeds of thought
> And count the passage of her festive hours.
> The city swims in verdure, beautiful
> As Venice on the waters, the sea-swan;
> What bosky gardens, dropped in close-walled courts
> As plums in ladies' laps who start and laugh:
> What miles of streets that run on after trees,
> Still carrying all the necessary shops,
> Those open caskets with the jewels seen!
> And trade is art, and art's philosophy,
> In Paris. There's a silk for instance, there,
> As worth an artist's study for the folds
> As that bronze opposite! nay, the bronze has faults,
> Art's here too artful,—conscious as a maid
> Who leans to mark her shadow on the wall
> Until she lose a 'vantage in her step.
> Yet Art walks forward, and knows where to walk;
> The artists also are idealists,
> Too absolute for nature, logical

> To austerity in the application of
> The special theory—not a soul content
> To paint a crooked pollard and an ass,
> As the English will because they find it so
> And like it somehow.—There the old Tuileries
> Is pulling its high cap down on its eyes,
> Confounded, conscience-stricken, and amazed
> By the apparition of a new fair face
> In those devouring mirrors. Through the grate
> Within the gardens, what a heap of babes,
> Swept up like leaves beneath the chestnut-trees
> From every street and alley of the town,
> By the ghosts perhaps that blow too bleak this way
> A-looking for their heads! dear pretty babes,
> I wish them luck to have their ball-play out
> Before the next change. Here the air is thronged
> With statues, poised upon their columns fine
> As if to stand a moment were a feat,
> Against that blue! What squares, what breathing-room
> For a nation that runs fast,—ay, runs against
> The dentist's teeth at the corner in pale rows,
> Which grin at progress in an epigram.

We add one passage more, wonderful for the imaginative subtlety with which it is conceived and worked out,— Aurora's account of her mother's picture, which hung upon the wall of the silent house, "among the mountains above Pelago," to which her father had retired after losing her, with his child and their faithful old Assunta:—

> The painter drew it after she was dead,
> And when the face was finished, throat and hands,
> Her cameriera carried him, in haste
> Of the English-fashioned shroud, the last brocade
> She dressed in at the Pitti; "he should paint
> No sadder thing than that," she swore, "to wrong
> Her poor signora." Therefore very strange
> The effect was. I, a little child, would crouch
> For hours upon the floor with knees drawn up,
> And gaze across them, half in terror, half
> In adoration, at the picture there,—
> That swan-like supernatural white life
> Just sailing upward from the red stiff silk
> Which seemed to have no part in it, nor power
> To keep it from quite breaking out of bounds.
> For hours I sat and stared. Assunta's awe
> And my poor father's melancholy eyes
> Still pointed that way. That way went my thoughts
> When wandering beyond sight. And as I grew
> In years, I mixed, confused, unconsciously,
> Whatever I last read or heard or dreamed,
> Abhorrent, admirable, beautiful,

> Pathetical, or ghastly, or grotesque,
> With still that face ... which did not therefore change,
> But kept the mystic level of all forms.
> Hates, fears, and admirations was by turns
> Ghost, fiend, and angel, fairy, witch, and sprite,
> A dauntless Muse who eyes a dreadful Fate,
> A loving Psyche who loses sight of Love,
> A still Medusa with mild milky brows
> All curdled and all clothed upon with snakes
> Whose slime falls fast as sweat will; or anon
> Our Lady of the Passion, stabbed with swords
> Where the Babe sucked; or Lamia in her first
> Moonlighted pallor, ere she shrunk and blinked
> And shuddering wriggled down to the unclean;
> Or my own mother, leaving her last smile
> In her last kiss upon the baby-mouth
> My father pushed down on the bed for that,—
> Or my dead mother, without smile or kiss,
> Buried at Florence.

There are only two other names in the poetical literature of the present age that can be held to stand incontestably in the first rank;—Tennyson and Robert Browning. Diverse in much, they have nevertheless also much in common. They are both of them profound and subtle thinkers as well as richly endowed with the divine faculty of poetry in special; thinkers, and also workers; and so each has made himself a consummate artist in addition to whatever he might otherwise have been of a great poet. Tennyson, our present English King of Song, crowned as such not more by official nomination than by the general voice, has won to himself the personal attachment of his countrymen in a degree that has been rarely equalled in the history of literature. Among ourselves, Scott is the only other great writer who ever was held during his lifetime in anything like the same universal love and honour. The poetry of Tennyson has charmed all hearts by something more than its artistic qualities. It is as full of nobleness as of beauty. The laurel when he resigns it to another will again be acknowledged by all to be "greener from the brows of him that uttered nothing base." Everywhere his verse, whether tender or lofty, whether light-hearted or sad, breathes the kindest and manliest nature. Not only the chief of his shorter poems, but his In

Memoriam and his Idylls of the King, are familiar to all readers. The following is in his simplest and quietest manner, but it is very perfect:—

> In her ear he whispers gaily,
> "If my heart by signs can tell,
> Maiden, I have watched thee daily,
> And I think thou lov'st me well."
> She replies, in accents fainter,
> "There is none I love like thee."
> He is but a landscape-painter,
> And a village maiden she.
> He to lips that fondly falter
> Presses his without reproof;
> Leads her to the village altar,
> And they leave her father's roof.
> "I can make no marriage present:
> Little can I give my wife.
> Love will make our cottage pleasant,
> And I love thee more than life."
> They by parks and lodges going,
> See the lordly castles stand:
> Summer woods, about them blowing,
> Made a murmur in the land.
> From deep thought himself he rouses,
> Says to her that loves him well,
> "Let us see these handsome houses
> Where the wealthy nobles dwell."
> So she goes by him attended,
> Hears him lovingly converse,
> Sees whatever fair and splendid
> Lay betwixt his home and hers;
> Parks with oak and chestnut shady,
> Parks and ordered gardens great,
> Ancient homes of lord and lady,
> Built for pleasure and for state.
> All he shows her makes him dearer;
> Evermore she seems to gaze
> On that cottage growing nearer,
> Where they twain will spend their days.
> O but she will love him truly!
> He shall have a cheerful home;
> She will order all things duly,
> When beneath his roof they come.
> Thus her heart rejoices greatly,
> Till a gateway she discerns
> With armorial bearings stately,
> And beneath the gate she turns;
> Sees a mansion more majestic
> Than all those she saw before:
> Many a gallant gay domestic,
> Bows before him at the door.
> And they speak in gentle murmur,
> When they answer to his call,

While he treads with footstep firmer,
 Leading on from hall to hall.
And, while now she wonders blindly,
 Nor the meaning can divine,
Proudly turns he round and kindly,
 "All of this is mine and thine."
Here he lives in state and bounty,
 Lord of Burleigh, fair and free,
Not a lord in all the county
 Is so great a lord as he.
All at once the colour flushes
 Her sweet face from brow to chin:
As it were with shame she blushes,
 And her spirit changed within.
Then her countenance all over
 Pale again as death did prove:
But he clasped her like a lover,
 And he cheered her soul with love.
So she strove against her weakness,
 Though at times her spirits sank:
Shaped her heart with woman's meekness
 To all duties of her rank:
And a gentle consort made he,
 And her gentle mind was such
That she grew a noble lady,
 And the people loved her much.
But a trouble weighed upon her,
 And perplexed her, night and morn.
With the burden of an honour
 Unto which she was not born.
Faint she grew, and ever fainter,
 As she murmured, "Oh, that he
Were once more that landscape-painter
 Which did win my heart from me!"
So she drooped and drooped before him,
 Fading slowly from his side:
Three fair children first she bore him,
 Then before her time she died.
Weeping, weeping, late and early,
 Walking up and pacing down,
Deeply mourned the Lord of Burleigh,
 Burleigh House, by Stamford Town.
And he came to look upon her,
 And he looked at her and said,
"Bring the dress and put it on her,
 That she wore when she was wed."
Then her people, softly treading,
 Bore to earth her body, drest
In the dress that she was wed in,
 That her spirit might have rest.

By way of contrast to this true English ballad, and to exemplify Tennyson's extent of range, we will give now a few lines from the Ode on the Death of the Duke of Wellington, which make one of the great passages in the poetry of the world:—

> —This is England's greatest son,
> He that gained a hundred fights,
> Nor ever lost an English gun;
> This is he that far away
> Against the myriads of Assaye
> Clashed with his fiery few and won;
> And underneath another sun,
> Warring on a later day,
> Round affrighted Lisbon drew
> The treble work, the vast designs
> Of his laboured rampart-lines,
> Where he greatly stood at bay,
> Whence he issued forth anew,
> And ever great and greater grew,
> Beating from the wasted vines
> Back to France her banded swarms,
> Back to France with countless blows,
> Till o'er the hills her eagles flew
> Past the Pyrenean pines,
> Followed up in valley and glen
> With blare of bugle, clamour of men,
> Roll of cannon and clash of arms,
> And England pouring on her foes.
> Such a war had such a close.
> Again their ravening eagle rose
> In anger, wheeled on Europe-shadowing wings,
> And barking for the thrones of kings;
> Till one that sought but Duty's iron crown
> On that loud sabbath shook the spoiler down;
> A day of onsets of despair!
> Dashed on every rocky square
> Their surging charges foamed themselves away;
> Last, the Prussian trumpet blew;
> Through the long tormented air
> Heaven flashed a sudden jubilant ray,
> And down we swept and charged and overthrew.[1]
> So great a soldier taught us there
> What long-enduring hearts could do,
> In that world's earthquake, Waterloo!

Pope is singular among our modern poets as having written nothing in blank verse; we do not remember that Tennyson has published so much as a sentence of prose. Not even, we believe, the shortest preface, dedication, or foot-note. In this as in other ways he has treated the public

[1] The emphasis on *we*, as perhaps also on *their* four lines above.

with almost ceremonious respect. Being by nature and vocation a poet, he declines to show himself without his singing robes about him. He will not make himself common, as he will do nothing carelessly or in haste. Nor has Browning either ever attempted to palm off careless work upon his readers. His Paracelsus, published when he was only three-and-twenty, marvellous as it was for the depth and completeness of the conception, was perhaps still more remarkable for the delicacy and perfection of the execution, peculiar as the manner was in some respects. And everything that he has produced since, even when departing farthest from established models, has been elaborated and finished with the same masterly skill. But, although he too has now made himself a great name, he has never attained, and is not likely ever to attain, the universal popularity of Tennyson, the general admiration at once of the few and of the many. There is scarcely anything in his poetry that is specially English. What of it is not distinctly of another country is either cosmopolitan or not of the earth at all. He has no special sympathies with the people whose language he writes, or with anything belonging to them—either their literature, their history, their political institutions, or any feeling that makes the national heart beat highest. It is irksome to most people to read English poetry, however fine artistically regarded, with so little in it of an English heart. Yet much of Browning's poetry, considered simply as poetry, is certainly, both in the soul of passionate vision that animates it and in grace and expressiveness of form, as exquisite as anything that has been produced in our day. He is often complained of as difficult to understand; and no doubt the train of thought is sometimes remote and subtle, and the language wrought to a corresponding degree of compression and fineness of edge, doing its work like the lancet or like the lightning. But this is equally true of much of Tennyson's poetry. Neither is to be read running. Browning, however, is so great a master of words that there is nothing he cannot make them do for him, no manner of using them in which he is not at home. Here is a portion (we must not be so unconscionable as to appropriate the whole) of one poem of his which is as simple and easy in style as it is airy and brilliant, and is in every way fitted to charm both old and young,—"The Pied Piper of Hamelin; A Child's Story," as it is entitled, "(written for, and inscribed to, W. M. the younger.)":—

> Hamelin town 's in Brunswick,
> By famous Hanover city;
> The river Weser, deep and wide,
> Washes its walls on the southern side;
> A pleasanter spot you never spied;
> But when begins my ditty,
> Almost five hundred years ago,
> To see the townsfolk suffer so
> From vermin, was a pity.
>
> Rats!
> They fought the dogs, and killed the cats,
> And bit the babies in the cradles,
> And ate the cheeses out of the vats,
> And licked the soup from the cooks' own ladles,
> Split open the kegs of salted sprats,
> Made nests inside men's Sunday hats,
> And even spoiled the women's chats,
> By drowning their speaking
> With shrieking and squeaking
> In fifty different sharps and flats.
>
> At last the people in a body
> To the Town Hall came flocking:
> "'Tis clear," cried they, "our Mayor's a noddy;
> "And as for our Corporation—shocking
> "To think we buy gowns lined with ermine
> " For dolts who can't or won't determine
> "What's best to rid us of our vermin!
> " You hope, because you're old and obese
> "To find in the furry civic robe ease?
> "Rouse up, Sirs! Give your brains a racking
> "To find the remedy we're lacking,
> "Or, sure as fate, we'll send you packing!"
> At this the Mayor and Corporation
> Quaked with a mighty consternation.
>
> An hour they sat in council;
> At length the Mayor broke silence:
> " For a guilder I'd my ermine gown sell;
> " I wish I were a mile hence!

"It's easy to bid one rack one's brain—
"I'm sure my poor head aches again,
"I've scratched it so, and all in vain.
"Oh, for a trap, a trap, a trap!"
Just as he said this, what should hap
At the chamber door but a gentle tap?
"Bless us," cried the Mayor, "what's that?
(With the Corporation as he sat,
Looking little, though wondrous fat;
Nor brighter was his eye, nor moister
Than a too-long-opened oyster,
Save when at noon his paunch grew mutinous
For a plate of turtle green and glutinous)
"Only a scraping of shoes on the mat?
"Anything like the sound of a rat
"Makes my heart go pit-a-pat!"

"Come in!" the Mayor cried, looking bigger:
And in did come the strangest figure!
His queer long coat from heel to head
Was half of yellow and half of red;
And he himself was tall and thin,
With sharp blue eyes, each like a pin,
And light loose hair, yet swarthy skin,
No tuft on cheek nor beard on chin,
But lips where smiles went out and in—
There was no guessing his kith and kin!
And nobody could enough admire
The tall man and his quaint attire:
Quoth one: "It's as my great-grandsire,
"Starting up at the trump of Doom's tone,
"Had walked this way from his painted tombstone."

He advanced to the council-table:
And, "Please your honours," said he, "I'm able,
"By means of a secret charm, to draw
"All creatures living beneath the sun,
"That creep, or swim, or fly, or run,
"After me so as you never saw!
"And I chiefly use my charm
"On creatures that do people harm,
"The mole, and toad, and newt, and viper;
"And people call me the Pied Piper."
(And here they noticed round his neck
A scarf of red and yellow stripe,
To match with his coat of the selfsame cheque;
And at the scarf's end hung a pipe;
And his fingers, they noticed, were ever straying
As if impatient to be playing
Upon this pipe, as low it dangled
Over his vesture so old-fangled).
"Yet," said he, "poor piper as I am,
"In Tartary I freed the Cham,
"Last June, from his huge swarms of gnats;

"I eased in Asia the Nizam
"Of a monstrous brood of vampire-bats:
"And, as for what your brain bewilders,
"If I can rid your town of rats
"Will you give me a thousand guilders?"
"One? fifty thousand!" was the exclamation
Of the astonished Mayor and Corporation.

Into the street the Piper stept,
  Smiling first a little smile,
As if he knew what magic slept
  In his quiet pipe the while;
Then, like a musical adept,
To blow the pipe his lips he wrinkled,
And green and blue his sharp eyes twinkled
Like a candle-flame where salt is sprinkled;
And ere three shrill notes the pipe uttered,
You heard as if an army muttered;
And the muttering grew to a grumbling;
And the grumbling grew to a mighty rumbling:
And out of the houses the rats came tumbling.
Great rats, small rats, lean rats, brawny rats,
Brown rats, black rats, grey rats, tawny rats,
Grave old plodders, gay young friskers
  Fathers, mothers, uncles, cousins,
Cocking tails and pricking whiskers,
  Families by tens and dozens,
Brothers, sisters, husbands, wives—
Followed the piper for their lives.
From street to street he piped advancing,
And step for step they followed dancing,
Until they came to the river Weser,
Wherein all plunged and perished—
Save one, who, stout as Julius Cæsar,
Swam across and lived to carry
(As he the manuscript he cherished)
To Rat-land home his commentary,
Which was, "At the first shrill notes of the pipe,
"I heard a sound as of scraping tripe.
"And putting apples, wondrous ripe,
"Into a cider-press's gripe:
"And a moving away of pickle-tub hoards,
"And a leaving ajar of conserve-cupboards,
"And a drawing the corks of train-oil-flasks,
"And a breaking the hoops of butter-casks:
"And it seemed as if a voice
"(Sweeter far than by harp or by psaltery
"Is breathed) called out, Oh rats, rejoice!
"The world is grown to one vast drysaltery!
"So munch on, crunch on, take your nuncheon,
"Breakfast, supper, dinner, luncheon!
"And just as a bulky sugar-puncheon,
"All ready staved, like a great sun shone
"Glorious scarce an inch before me,
"Just as methought it said, Come, bore me!
"—I found the Weser rolling o'er me."

You should have heard the Hamelin people
Ringing the bells till they rocked the steeple;
"Go," cried the Mayor, "and get long poles!
"Poke out the nests and block up the holes!
"Consult with carpenters and builders,
"And leave in our town not even a trace
"Of the rats!"—when suddenly up the face
Of the Piper perked in the market-place,
With a "First, if you please, my thousand guilders!"

But for the manner in which this fair demand was received by the rulers of the delivered town, and all that thence ensued, the reader must be left to resort to the poet's own pages. We give as a specimen of another kind the concluding lines of Paracelsus's long and eloquent dying declamation:—

        Love's undoing
Taught me the worth of love in man's estate,
And what proportion love should hold with power
In his right constitution: love preceding
Power, and with much power always much more love;
Love still too straitened in its present means,
And earnest for new power to set it free.
I learned this, and supposed the whole was learned;
And thus, when men received with stupid wonder
My first revealings, would have worshipped me,
And I despised and loathed their proffered praise—
When, with awakened eyes, they took revenge
For past credulity in casting shame
On my real knowledge, and I hated them—
It was not strange I saw no good in man,
To overbalance all the wear and waste
Of faculties, displayed in vain, but born
To prosper in some better sphere: and why?
In my own heart love had not been made wise
To trace love's faint beginnings in mankind,
To know even hate is but a mask of love's,
To see a good in evil, and a hope
In ill-success; to sympathize, be proud
Of their half-reasons, faint aspirings, dim
Struggles for truth, their poorest fallacies,
Their prejudice, and fears, and cares, and doubts;
Which all touch upon nobleness, despite
Their error, all tend upwardly though weak,
Like plants in mines which never saw the sun,
But dream of him, and guess where he may be,
And do their best to climb and get to him.
All this I knew not, and I failed. Let men
Regard me, and the poet dead long ago

> Who once loved rashly; and shape forth a third,
> And better-tempered spirit, warned by both:
> As from the over-radiant star too mad
> To drink the light-springs, beamless thence itself—
> And the dark orb which borders the abyss,
> Ingulfed in icy night,—might have its course
> A temperate and equi-distant world.
> Meanwhile, I have done well, though not all well.
> As yet men cannot do without contempt—
> 'Tis for their good, and therefore fit awhile
> That they reject the weak, and scorn the false,
> Rather than praise the strong and true, in me.
> But, after, they will know me! If I stoop
> Into a dark tremendous sea of cloud,
> It is but for a time; I press God's lamp
> Close to my breast—its splendour, soon or late,
> Will pierce the gloom: I shall emerge one day!

And thus the finished music of the poem returns to the same note from which it had sprung up on its grand parabolic sweep, and the self-willed and daring but always noble as well as brilliant visionary to the words with which he had broken away long ago from his two friends Festus and Michal:—

> I go to prove my soul!
> I see my way as birds their trackless way—
> I shall arrive! what time, what circuit first,
> I ask not: but, unless God send his hail
> Or blinding fire-balls, sleet, or stifling snow,
> In some time—his good time—I shall arrive:
> He guides me and the bird. In his good time!

If there be a fourth name belonging to this period, the middle portion of the present century, which after-times will recognize as that of a poet of the first class, it is that of the late Thomas Hood. No one of his contemporaries has surpassed him either in perfection of workmanship or in originality of conception. Upon whatever he has written he has stamped the impress of himself, and as with a diamond signet. Nor, although his most distinctive manner is comic, is he at all inferior to himself when he adopts a different style, as he has done in several of his best-known poems. As in other instances, indeed,—for example, in Horace and in Burns—what gives their peculiar character and charm to his most pathetic touches is essentially the same thing which makes the brilliancy of his comic manner. All that is most characteristic of him in expression and thought is to be discerned in the curious felicity of the following exquisitely beautiful and tender lines:—

> We watched her breathing through the night,
> Her breathing soft and low,
> As in her breast the wave of life
> Kept heaving to and fro.
>
> So silently we seemed to speak,
> So slowly moved about,
> As we had lent her half our powers
> To eke her living out.
>
> Our very hopes belied our fears,
> Our fears our hopes belied—
> We thought her dying when she slept,
> And sleeping when she died.
>
> For when the morn came dim and sad,
> And chill with early showers,
> Her quiet eyelids closed—she had
> Another morn than ours.

INDEX

A.

Accentual verse, i. 153, 166
Addison, Joseph, ii. 105
Akenside, Dr. Mark, ii. 132
Alchemists, i. 102
Aldred, Archbishop, Curse of, i. 122, 123
Alfred the Great, i. 28
Alliterative verse, i. 150
Ancren Riwle, i. 137
Andrews, Bishop, i. 345
Anglo-Saxon, or Saxon, i. 37
Anne, age of, ii. 285-287
Anselm, i. 53, 56, 64
Arabic learning, i. 49
Arabic numerals, i. 101
Arbuthnot, Dr. John, ii. 111
Armstrong, Dr. John, ii. 132
Ascham, Roger, i. 238
Atterbury, Bishop, ii. 113

B.

Bacon, Francis, i. 347
Bacon, Roger, i. 100, 105
Baker, Sir Richard, ii. 46
Bale's Kynge Johan, i. 262
Barbour, John, i. 202
Barklay, Alexander, i. 249
Barrow, Dr. Isaac, ii. 80
Baxter, Richard, ii. 79
Beattie, James, ii. 151

Beaumont, Francis, i. 335, ii. 11, 72
Ben Jonson, i. 340
Bible, Translation of the, i. 344
Blackmore, Sir Richard, ii. 115
Blank verse, i. 266
Bolingbroke, Lord, ii. 114
Browne, Sir Thomas, ii. 40
Browne, William, ii. 29
Browning, Mrs. ii. 287
Browning, Robert, ii. 299
Brunne, Robert de, i. 145
Buckhurst, Lord, vide Sackville, T.
Bunyan, John, ii. 18
Burke, Edmund, ii. 170
Burnet, Bishop, ii. 89
Burnet, Thomas, ii. 91
Burns, Robert. ii. 207
Burton, Robert, i. 350
Butler, Samuel, ii. 61
Byron, Lord, ii. 260

C.

Campbell, Thomas, ii. 252
Carew, Thomas, ii. 18
Cartwright, William, ii. 15
Celtic Languages and Literatures, i. 21
Chapman, George, i. 316
Charles I., ii. 30
Chatterton, Thomas, i. 153
Chaucer, Geoffrey, i. 161
Chaucer's prose, i. 212
Chillingworth, William, ii. 35

INDEX.   307

Chroniclers, i. 216
Churchill, Charles, ii. 150
Cibber, Colley, ii. 121
Clarendon, Lord, ii. 74
Classical learning, i. 65
Cleveland, John, ii. 21
Coleridge, S. T., ii. 244
Collins, William, ii. 129
Commonwealth Literature, ii. 46
Compound English, i. 161
Congreve, William, ii. 120
Conquest, the Norman, i. 43
Corbet, Bishop, ii. 16
Cowley, Abraham, ii. 60
Cowper, William, ii. 192
Crabbe, George, ii. 192, 259, 264
Cranmer, Archbishop, i. 236
Cudworth, Dr. Ralph, ii. 79

D.

Daniel, Samuel, i. 305, 352
Darwin, Erasmus, ii. 204
Davies, Sir John, i. 319
Defoe, Daniel, ii. 116
Denham, Sir John, ii. 20
Donne, Dr. John, i. 320, 346
Dorset, Earl of, vide Sackville, T.
Douglas, Gawin, i. 247
Drama, end of the old, ii. 10
Drama, the regular, i. 254
Dramatists of Eighteenth Century, ii. 119, 154
Dramatists of Seventeenth Century, ii. 72
Drayton, Michael, i. 310
Drummond, Sir William, i. 318
Dryden, John, ii. 68
Dunbar, William, i. 248
Dyer, John, ii. 122

E.

Edwards, Richard, i. 267
Eighteenth Century, latter part of, ii. 192
Elizabethan Literature, i. 251
Elizabethan Poetry, i. 299
Elizabethan Prose Writers, i. 277, 343

Elyot, Sir Thomas, i. 235
English as a literary tongue, i. 117
English after the Conquest, i. 84
English Language, i. 33, 48
English, Original (Saxon or Anglo-Saxon), i. 37
English, Revolutions of, i. 119
Essayists, Periodical, ii. 137
Euphuism, i. 277
Europe, Languages of Modern, i. 13

F.

Fairfax, Edward, i. 317
Falconer, William, ii. 151
Fanshawe, Sir Richard, i. 318
Farquhar, George, ii. 120
Female Writers, ii. 255
Ferrex and Porrex, i. 263
Fielding, Henry, ii. 137
Fletcher, Giles, ii. 12
Fletcher, John, i. 335, ii. 11, 72
Fletcher, Phineas, ii. 12
Ford, John, i. 343
Fortescue, Sir John, i. 218
French Language in England, i. 74, 113
French School of Poetry, ii. 17
Fuller, Thos., ii. 37

G.

Gammer Gurton's Needle, i. 259
Garth, Sir Samuel, ii. 115
Gay, John, ii. 111
Georges, last Age of the, ii. 228
Gibbon, Edward, ii. 188
Gloucester, Robert of, i. 143
Glover, Richard, ii. 133
Goldsmith, Oliver, ii. 144
Gorboduc, Tragedy of, i. 263
Gower, John, i. 199
Gray, Thomas, ii. 129
Greene, Robert, i. 270, 280

20*

INDEX.

H.

Hales, John, II. 35
Hall, Bishop, I. 346
Hall, Joseph, I. 313
Harington, Sir John, I. 317
Harrington, Sir James, II. 43
Hawes, Stephen, I. 242
Henry the Minstrel, I. 228
Henryson, Robert, I. 228
Herbert, George, II. 14
Herrick, Robert, II. 14
Heywood, John, I. 246, 256
Historical Writers, I. 350
Hobbes, Thomas, II. 75
Hood, Thomas, II. 304
Hooker, Richard, I. 347
Hume, David, II. 186
Hunt, Leigh, II. 278

J.

James I. of Scotland, I. 226
Johnson, Samuel, II. 164
Junius, II. 162

K.

Keats, John, II. 274
Knolles, Richard, I. 351
Kyd, Thomas, I. 273

L.

Langue d'Oc and Langue d'Oyl, I. 80
Latimer, Bishop, I. 236
Latin after the Conquest, I. 70
Latin Chroniclers, I. 72

Latin Literature of Britain, early, I. 15
Layamon, I. 125
Learned tongues, the, I. 108
Leighton, Archbishop, II. 79
Locke, John, II. 93
Lodge, Thomas, I. 274
Lovelace, Richard, II. 19
Lydgate, John, I. 223
Lyly, John, I. 272, 277, 280
Lyndsay, Sir David, I. 248

M.

Malory, Sir Thomas, I. 220
Mandevil, Sir John, I. 210
Mandeville, Bernard de, II. 108
Mannyng, Robert, I. 145
Marlow, Christopher, I. 270
Marvel, Andrew, II. 65
Mason, William, II. 152
Massinger, Philip, I. 342
Mathematical Studies, I. 100
Metaphysical Writers, II. 184
Milton, John, Poetry of, II. 48
Milton, John, Prose of, II. 32
Minor Poets of Eighteenth Century, II. 122
Minot, Lawrence, I. 146
Miracle Plays, I. 254
Mirror for Magistrates, I. 251
Misogonus, I. 261
Mixed English, I. 161
Moore, Thomas, II. 261, 267
Moral Plays, I. 255
More, Dr. Henry, II. 79
More, Sir Thomas, I. 234

N.

Nash, Thomas, I. 282
Nevile, Henry, II. 78
Newspapers, II. 44
Nineteenth Century, II. 225
Nineteenth Century, early part of, II. 282

O.

Occleve, Thomas, i. 222
Oriental Learning, i. 110
Ormulum, the, i. 132
Ossian, Macpherson's, ii. 154

P.

Parnell, Dr. Thomas, ii. 113
Pecock, Bishop, i. 217
Peele, George, i. 269
Percy's Reliques, ii. 153
Piers Ploughman, i. 150
Political Economy, ii. 190
Pope, Alexander, ii. 100
Present day, Literature of, ii. 286
Printing in England, i. 214
Prior, Matthew, ii. 112
Prose, English, i. 210, 232

Q.

Quarles, Francis, ii. 13

R.

Raleigh, Sir Walter, i. 350
Ralph Roister Doister, i. 257
Randolph, Thomas, ii. 15
Religious Poets, ii. 13
Revolution, Effects of, ii. 84
Revolution, Survivors of, ii. 85
Richardson, Samuel, ii. 137
Ridley, Bishop, i. 236
Robertson, William, ii. 198
Roman de la Rose, i. 181
Romance, Metrical, i. 140
Roy, William, i. 246

S.

Sackville, Thomas, i. 252, 263
Saxon, or Anglo-Saxon, i. 37
Scholarship, English, Earliest, i. 27
Scholastic Philosophy, i. 62, 97
Scott, Sir Walter, ii. 253
Scottish Poetry, ii. 133
Scottish Poets, i. 224, 247
Scottish Prose Writers, i. 241
Second English, i. 121
Sedley, Sir Charles, ii. 66
Semi-Saxon, i. 121
Shaftesbury, Earl of, ii. 107
Shakespeare's Dramatic Contemporaries, i. 334
Shakespeare, William, i. 323, 324
Shelley, P. R., ii. 270
Shenstone, William, ii. 129
Shirley, James, ii. 10
Sidney, Sir Philip, i. 278
Skelton, John, i. 244
Smollett, Tobias, ii. 140
South, Dr. Robert, ii. 92
Southey, Robert, ii. 257
Spenser, Edmund, i. 283
Steele, Sir Richard, ii. 105
Sterne, Laurence, ii. 143
Suckling, Sir John, ii. 19
Surrey, Earl of, i. 249
Swift, Jonathan, ii. 94
Sylvester, Joshua, i. 314

T.

Taylor, Jeremy, ii. 36
Tennyson, Alfred, ii. 295
Theological Elizabethan Writers, i. 345
Third English, i. 161
Thomson, James, ii. 131
Tillotson, Archbishop, ii. 91

U.

Udall, Nicholas, i. 257
Universities and Schools, i. 56, 105

V.

Vanbrugh, Sir John, ii. 120

W.

Waller, Edmund, ii. 62
Warner, William, i. 100
Warton, Thomas and Joseph, ii. 152
Wiclif, John de, i. 212
Wilkes, John, ii. 161
Wilkie, William, ii. 132
Wilson, Thomas, i. 240
Wither, George, ii. 22
Wordsworth, William, ii. 228
Wyatt, Sir Thomas, i. 249
Wynton, Andrew of, i. 224

Y.

Young, Dr. Edward, ii. 110

THE END.

www.ingramcontent.com/pod-product-compliance
Lightning Source LLC
Chambersburg PA
CBHW022056230426
43672CB00008B/1186